Lee Iacola
(Thank you
Ron)

Placing the Academy

Placing the Academy
Essays on Landscape, Work, and Identity

Edited by
Jennifer Sinor and Rona Kaufman

Utah State University Press
Logan, Utah

Copyright © 2007 Utah State University Press
All rights reserved

Utah State University Press
Logan, UT 84322-7800

ISBN-13: 978-0-87421-657-8
ISBN-10: 0-87421-657-5

Manufactured in the United States of America
Printed on acid-free, recycled paper

Library of Congress Cataloging-in-Publication Data

Placing the academy : essays on landscape, work, and identity / edited by Jennifer Sinor and Rona Kaufman.
    p. cm.
  ISBN-13: 978-0-87421-657-8 (cloth : alk. paper)
  1. College teaching--Philosophy. 2. College teachers--United States. 3. Identity (Psychology) 4. Place (Philosophy) 5. Creative writing. I. Sinor, Jennifer, 1969- II. Kaufman, Rona, 1970-
  LB2331.P57 2007
  378.1'2--dc22
                              2006038145

For Michael,
my bedrock
J. S.

For Tim,
who keeps me rooted
R. K.

Table of Contents

I. Introduction — 1

1. Writing Place
   Jennifer Sinor — 3

II. Here — 25

2. Six Kinds of Rain: Searching for a Place in the Academy
   Kathleen Dean Moore and Erin E. Moore — 27
3. The Work the Landscape Calls Us To
   Michael Sowder — 39
4. Valley Language
   Diana Garcia — 52
5. What I Learned from the Campus Plumber
   Charles Bergman — 65
6. M-I-Crooked Letter-Crooked Letter
   Katherine Fischer — 83
7. On Frogs, Poems, and Teaching at a Rural Community College
   Seán W. Henne — 98

III. There — 107

8. Levittown Breeds Anarchists! Film at 11
   Kathryn T. Flannery — 109
9. Living in a Transformed Desert
   Mitsuye Yamada — 125
10. A More Fortunate Destiny
    Jayne Brim Box — 139

11. Imagined Vietnams
    Charles Waugh   152

IV. Everywhere   166

12. Teaching on Stolen Ground
    Deborah A. Miranda   169
13. The Blind Teaching the Blind: The Academic as Naturalist, or Not
    Robert Michael Pyle   188
14. Where Are You From?
    Lee Torda   202

V. In Between   215

15. Going Away to Think
    Scott Slovic   217
16. Fronteriza Consciousness: The Site and Language of the Academy and of Life
    Norma Elia Cantú   233
17. Bones of Summer
    Mary Clearman Blew   243
18. Singing, Speaking, and Seeing a World
    Janice M. Gould   254
19. Making Places Work: Felt Sense, Identity, and Teaching
    Jeffrey M. Buchanan   269

VI. Coda   285

20. Running in Place: The Personal at Work, in Motion, on Campus, and in the Neighborhood
    Rona Kaufman   287

    Contributors   303

I
Introduction

1
Writing Place

Jennifer Sinor

My way of finding a place in this world is to write one.

Barbara Kingsolver

When I was nine, my family moved from Seattle where we had lived less than a year. It rained almost daily those nine months, causing mildew to grow on the bathroom tiles and in shoes that were not worn every day. The morning we left, the car was packed tightly, the last-minute pile of possessions having grown immeasurably overnight. While my parents worried about where my brothers and I were going to sit for the long drive, my babysitter stood with me in the driveway saying good-bye. I cannot see her face and no longer know her name, but she gave me a terrarium to remember her by, a miniature ecosystem housed in a Sanka jar. Requiring neither water, nor air, nor fertilizer, it was complete, like an egg. Even though I was moving, I thought, a tiny part of the earth would be coming with me.

Though I cared for my piece of the planet as if my livelihood depended on what it produced, the plants died. Two weeks in a hot car were too much for their tiny green limbs.

Writing about the experience now, I find myself wondering if I am not confused in my memories. After all, we were moving to Hawaii, so why would we be driving? A plane seems much more likely. Perhaps it was my babysitter in Virginia who gave me the terrarium and I was seven. Perhaps it was in Seattle, but maybe it was a birthday present. Perhaps I only dreamed the terrarium. Casting, casting, casting back, I work to remember the car we owned, how many siblings I had, the way my mother wore her hair, any detail that will help me to attach this memory to a particular place, in hopes my past travels better than the plants. In the end, there is only the image of a short-lived terrarium sweating in a jar with an orange lid.

For me, the loss of those tiny plants has become metaphorical for the tenuous connection I have to the land. I remain envious of those I know who have lived their entire lives in one place, who can hail neighbors by name, and who recall the feel of the air when the goldfinches return. I know so little about the places I have lived; so many of my memories are unplaced, as if the box of family photos were upturned and pictures scattered underneath the table and the bed.

I cannot even tell you for sure where I was standing when I lost the earth.

When Scott Russell Sanders suggests in *Writing from the Center* that "we need a richer vocabulary of place," he does not explicitly name the need for ways to talk about how the work being done in the academy is shaped by where we, as academics, live (18). Instead he is asking for a "literature of . . . inhabitation," a broad call for writing that examines who we are by detailing where we are (50). Having recently moved to new landscapes and new jobs, Rona and I realize that literature would be incomplete if it did not explore how place shapes our professional identities. We know intimately that who we are as teachers, writers, and scholars is intricately connected to where we live and have lived.

Part of our awareness of the shaping force of place comes from moving west, to landscapes that with their extremities of weather and geology demand conversation. We have begun to understand how our teaching and our writing have changed in response. Even though Rona knows that Mount Rainier is always there, on those clear bright mornings when it dominates the Tacoma skyline, she is reminded that this volcanic landscape is unfamiliar, and she relies on that sense of displacement to understand the distances her students must travel as they learn the discourse of the university. In similar ways, I drive along the floor of Cache Valley to work every morning, descending into the bed of Lake Bonneville, an ancient sea that beat its retreat fifty thousand years ago. Its absence and the literal loss of land it carved out inform the way I think about the possibilities found in writing to revise the traumatic into a narrative that heals. Encountering new places brought into sharp relief how the two of us teach, how we write, and how we continue to learn the channeled ways of academic life. In paying attention to the new places we find ourselves—both as new professors in academic departments and new residents of western states—we find it important to develop not just any vocabulary of place, but one capacious enough to place the academy.

This collection begins such a conversation. It fills a gap in the fields of place writing and academic memoir. While place writers have learned to talk about the connections between landscape and self, they are rarely concerned with occupation and more rarely with the academy. Academic memoirists like Alice Kaplan, Jane Tompkins, Eva Hoffman, and Marianna Torgovnick, in turn, reflect on their professional lives but rarely on the landscapes that surround them as they move between classes, ideas, or meetings. *Who* we are is dependent on *where* we are, and the influence of landscape does not end with our habits or customs as residents and citizens but extends to how we read, write, think, learn, and teach.

Because, as Wayne Franklin writes, "it is in our stories that we locate place most powerfully," this is a collection of personal essays (xi). In their efforts to make legible the land that lies within, here teachers and scholars tell stories of growing up and growing older, of moving and remaining, of working and playing, and of being placed. We learn what the campus plumber can teach us about the classroom, how one might continue to work on fragile ecosystems knowing that you are responsible for killing the last of an endangered species, what the Mississippi has to say to the teaching of writing, as well as the difficulty of imagining places like Vietnam for your students. Their diverse answers to how geography shapes their academic identities mirror the diversity of the authors' backgrounds. Some essayists have been in the academy for decades, while others are just starting out. Contributors with national reputations adjoin those who are relatively unknown. Here are writers from the East, the West, the South, the Midwest, writers from English to biology, and those occupying the center as well as the borderlands. In common, they believe in writing as a way of making meaning. Through their words, a new vocabulary of place is meted out, one that makes visible the connections between being placed and creating knowledge, being placed and teaching others, being placed and writing.

Conscripted at birth and raised in the military, I have never lived in any one place longer than five years. Some places I have known only for the length of the school year, not even long enough to experience all the seasons. To this day I wonder what the sun feels like in Seattle in July. Now, as an adult with no connections to the military and still no long-term commitment to any particular landscape, I have begun to wonder if transience is a pathology, if change is the only stability I know.

Military children pride themselves in their ability to recover from loss. They wear their relocations like badges, or scars maybe. I remember, once, talking with a fifteen-year-old girl named Brianna about her experiences as a military dependent. We sat in her living room underneath a sign on the wall that proclaimed, "Home is Wherever the Air Force Sends You." The central location of the plaque made me wonder if it served less as a decoration and more as a reminder to the family of the portability of home. As I did as a child, Brianna saw moving as the single defining characteristic of being a military dependent, what made military brats different from others in their classes, the reason they ate lunch alone. At fifteen, she had already lived in nine places and on two continents. Toward the end of our conversation, her mother and sister safely upstairs and out of hearing range, she confessed to me that she "longed for a home." Home, like a secret, lying on the couch between us.

In his book *Mapping the Invisible Landscape*, Kent Ryden suggests that "a sense of place results gradually and unconsciously from inhabiting a landscape over time, becoming familiar with its physical properties, accruing a history within its confines" (38). Given that, I am the last person in the world who should be co-editing a collection examining the relationship between locale and work. When I look inside for the land that moors me, I find nothing, only a series of not homes. No landscape converses with me; no rivers run through my body. I know how to move, less how to remain. Which is, maybe, why I am attracted to writing that attempts to make visible the invisible landscape, the unseen layers of usage and memory that turn space into place and house into home. I want to know how land becomes story; I want to acquire a vocabulary of place. At times my desire borders on the desperate. After all, Scott Russell Sanders suggests in *Staying Put* that "if you are not yourself *placed*, then you wander the world like a sightseer, a collector of sensations, with no gauge for measuring what you see" (114). Without a home, knowing no one place more intimately than another, pressed to name the particulars of any landscape, I have become a tourist in my own life.

And yet, how can I fail to be placed? Even if that place has shifted and changed, even if my experience of place has long been casual and cursory. I cannot live and write and speak from nowhere. I am somewhere. Which makes me wonder about how place writing has been defined as a genre. If who we are is shaped in part by where we live, then are we not all placed, regardless of the length of time we have lived somewhere, our intimacy with the land, our ability to articulate that relationship? To say one person is "placed" more than another seems akin to saying one person is more of a woman than another, or more Asian than another, or more working class than another. If place works like ethnicity and gender in shaping us, then how can any of us be left to "wander"? We are all rooted, even when we have no home.

Part of the answer to my questions, no doubt, is in the awareness we bring to the places we inhabit. While we all may be placed, few of us are able to articulate our placedness. And place writers have developed a language for talking about the connections between self and land. From their ability to identify and reflect upon the "place-creating elements" in the world, we learn better how to name the landscapes that lie within each of us.[1] But fair, too, I think is the concern that place writing often, and I would argue unfairly, honors a certain kind of connection to the land—one based largely on length of time and ecological savvy—that leaves many of us "with no gauge for measuring what [we] see." So while I come to place writing with a desire to understand how landscape becomes story, I also come ready to broaden what it means to be placed and what it looks like to write the land.

Place writing is an act of healing, meant to mend the divisions that threaten to undo us. While these divisions include human/nature, artificial/natural, sacred/ordinary, public/private, mind/body, and civilization/wilderness, place writers tend to see the most damaging division as the one the separates nature from experience. Only when we view ourselves as existing apart from the earth, its creatures, and its future are poverty, environmental destruction, degradation, war, and genocide possible. To heal this breach, place writers work to make visible the ties that bind each of us to this quietly spinning planet with an urgency that suggests continued ignorance will mean our extinction. Story, they hope, will save us.

What caused the division between self and land is both complicated and arguable. Kent Ryden points to the eighteenth century and new methods of surveying that perceived land as an "abstract entity" meant only for division. Prior to the eighteenth century, cartographers made maps reflecting their experience of the world. The maps they drew, autobiographies of sorts, told viewers how to feel about a place, its spirit. In other words, these maps revealed more about the mind than the earth. In the eighteenth century, Ryden argues, when land became something to measure rather than experience, maps also changed. The world became "a matrix of objective geographical facts distilled from the messiness of real life" (37). Centuries later, tutored by maps that would have us believe that something as shifting and subjective as the natural world can be reduced to a two-dimensional object that fits in the glove box, we remain disconnected from the world around us.

Kathleen Dean Moore, herself a philosopher, points further back in history to the beginnings of western philosophy. In *The Pine Island Paradox*, she returns us to the temples of ancient Greece and the words of Democritus and Leucippus, who taught that "all of reality can be reduced to hard little particles, mechanical substances that humans can measure, understand, manipulate, and ultimately control" (5). Moore tells us that Descartes appeared hundreds of years later to detail the separation of mind and body, followed closely by Bacon, Kant, Hobbes, and Locke, all of whom did their part to ensure that humans are separate from, and superior to, the natural world around them.

Others find different reasons for the division. They point at city walls that created a literal (and later figurative) separation from the woods and hills, industrialization that took us from the fields and into the factories, the invention of streetlamps that removed us from the diurnal rhythm, or late twentieth-century capitalism that takes the measure of the world in terms of monetary rather than humanistic value. Clearly, the separation of land and experience did not happen overnight, nor did it happen easily. But it did happen. As we move from parking structures to office buildings and then home to the garage, it is quite possible to go through an entire day without ever literally putting foot to earth. Nature and its movements have become something you capture on film while on vacation, not a force that we recognize as shaping who we are.

Place writers recognize that separation allows for destruction. We are more willing to do harm to something we can objectify and impersonalize. And they are at pains in their work, therefore, to place themselves, to embed their experience in the land around them. To fail to do so means that we will suffer as the land suffers.

Place writing becomes, then, an ethical act. To belong to a place and to write about that connection mean that one more place might escape damage either because you become invested in saving that place or because you convince others to save it. Through the essays in this collection, for example, we learn about the Suwannee River, the box elder bugs in Utah, the fragility of the Mojave Desert, places where these writers live, work, and teach. Their work parallels the efforts of writers like Rick Bass, Terry Tempest Williams, and Bruce Chatwin, who bring national attention to potential losses. Writing about a place can equate to saving it.

On a local level, place writers contend that once they become rooted in a place, even if that place is their own backyard, or the stream near their house, or a path that runs through campus, they attend to its survival. In telling stories of place, people remain connected to the land, they love it, and they will not leave it or abuse it. And if each of us were to save only the land nearest to us, think of the global effect.

Even when the land is not literally saved—for example, when Scott Russell Sanders remembers his childhood home in Indiana before it was flooded—it is saved in story and passed down. Rockwell Gray honors the connection between autobiographical memory and place when he describes autobiography's function as "an antidote to anonymity, disconnection and uprootedness" (57). When literal places pass away—falling prey to new construction, environmental ruin, or natural decline—they are still preserved in story. To write of these places keeps them alive, keeps our hearts and minds connected to them. As we learn from Bruce Chatwin's work, *Songlines*, the land of the Australian aboriginal people is literally sustained through telling stories and singing songs—every rock, every tree, every river being sung into continual existence. Place writers are conservationists then, even when the places they write about are preserved only in memory. In fact, Gray suggests, the remembered place can become more meaningful than the land that has been lost.

It is the turning of land into a story that creates places in our lives. "Places do not exist," Ryden says, "until they are verbalized" (241). Without narrative, a place is merely space, a geographical entity without any emotional resonance. In many ways, stories of place work like sculpture, defining a way for us to see and experience what was formerly invisible and formless. Story transforms space into place first in memory. We carry with us the memories of all the places we have experienced in the past—comparing each new place to our "primal landscapes."[2] These memories of place help us understand who we are, help make us whole. So in telling the story of who we are, we tell the story of where we have stood. While place is important, it is narrative that makes place possible, bringing "place" and "writing" into a symbiotic relationship. We understand ourselves, in part, through the landscapes that surround us, but the landscapes that surround us do not become significant until we turn them into narrative.

Ryden takes the connection between landscape and narrative even further by suggesting that narrative is an unstated component of any landscape. Your autobiography is written on the land—in the way you see it and feel it and in the way that each new place becomes enmeshed with all the other places you have experienced. We literally "write place into being," and in that sense I wonder, then, if we can ever truly be without a home.[3]

Not surprisingly, place writers turn to the natural world for metaphors that explain the relationship between identity and place. Linda Hogan, in her collection of essays, *Dwellings*, writes about caves, bats, wolves, and feathers to describe how "the land merges with us." In her essay "All My Relations," her body and the land become one, where the "stones come to dwell inside the person" and there is "no real aloneness" (41). In a similar vein, Terry Tempest Williams imagines the desert as her lover in *Desert Quartet*, and Sanders ponders what we can learn from rivers in *Staying Put*. For me, one of the strongest metaphors is that of the island, one which Kathleen Dean Moore explores in *The Pine Island Paradox*. Standing at the edge of the shore, she tells us, it is impossible to know where land ends and water begins. The line shifts with the tide. It is the same, she suggests, as the line that separates the human from the natural, the present from the future, the sacred from the mundane—which is to say there is no line. For too long we have relied upon metaphors of the natural world that make the land strange and that place us in positions of superiority. But islands are different. "Not even an island is an island," Moore reminds us. It is all part of the same "continuous skin of the planet, the small part we can see of the hidden substance that connects everything on earth" (4).

I like Moore's use of the island as a figurative vehicle for moving beyond the land/experience division. Maybe because I know the elusiveness of the coastline, her metaphor resonates with me. Having been stationed on Oahu three different times growing up, I claim that island as the closest thing I have to home. I have stood on the shore of the Pacific as waves wrapped around my ankles and buried my feet deeper and deeper in the cool sand. As a child, I often wondered what would happen if I were to stand, unmoved, on the shore for hours, days even. Would the sand eventually bury me, pulling me deep into the belly of the earth? Would I become part of the land?

Place writers stand in this surf line, insisting that we are intimately connected with the landscapes around us. Sanders describes the relationship in marital terms while Linda Hogan prefers the spiritual; Williams defines her relationship with the desert as sexual; Pattiann Rogers in *Song of the Marsh Wren* feels her connection to the southern landscape as a bodily one; and for Kathleen Dean Moore the relationship between self and land is familial. Regardless of how these writers describe the connection, wholeness and healing are what they write toward. "There is no division," Sanders says in *Staying Put*, "between where we live and what we are" (51).

What happens, though, if I do not experience land in any of these terms? What if I have not lived anywhere long enough or with enough awareness to know how that land enters my body? Does it mean that landscapes have not shaped me? Does it mean that I have no way of gauging my experience? In general, place writers privilege time over every other factor in determining the authenticity of one's connection to land. Staying put, Sanders tells us, is how we learn to love a place. But I find myself wondering if migration is not also a way of knowing. Because remaining in one place for a great length of time is a privilege that not all of us have. There must be ways that I have been shaped by the lands that I have passed through. In the stillness of the early morning hours, when I am awake and staring at the ceiling, it is the surf I feel moving the length of my body, quieting me, shushing me to sleep. And it is the ocean in all its terrifying force that enters my nightmares, pounding my body, pulling me under. I smell Virginia in the fall when I rake leaves, hear Nebraska corn rustle through the spruce trees outside my window, know variety in flatness, color in the desert, wealth in tones of brown. That I have spent my life passing through rather than remaining makes me question if placedness comes less from staying put and more from paying attention, less from the ability to name the land in all its particulars and more from honoring the particulars that you can name.

When I returned to Hawaii several years ago, having been away from the islands for a longer period than I had ever lived there at one time, I was hoping to find home. What that was and how I would know it were not clear to me. Having been interested in place writing for several years at that point, I assumed home would register in my body. After all, everything I had read suggested, to paraphrase Mary Clearman Blew, that place, like landscape, was bone deep.

What I found when I arrived was that I needed a map to get around the island, that I could not name the mountains or the birds, and that I was little better off than the tourists. Here was the tiny bit of land that I had long clung to as home, and I found I could not even discern its shape from the airplane. It was a rude awakening.

Is it that as a child I did not learn the names of things? Did my parents tell me that we would eat lunch under the kukui trees at Waimea Bay and I just not listen? Did they explain to me that the plumeria tree whose flowers we picked to make leis was originally used to ring graveyards and traditionally the flowers were thought to bring bad luck? Did they name the peaks and the beaches for me? Maybe I have learned the importance of naming—of honoring—the natural world only in later life. Maybe I have come to realize only recently how the particulars of things are the birthplace of both story and memory.

While I think this is partially true, my deeper sense is that although I have forgotten much, I was also never told. Not because my parents were preoccupied or selfish, but because as a military family we bore a complicated relationship to the land and in particular to naming. In the broadest sense, naming means knowing and knowing brings with it the possibility of grief. And a military family must reduce the number of losses incurred with every move, the number of grieved things. Since you cannot grieve what you do not know that you have lost, it is safest not to name that which you don't have to. To operate at a level of generality becomes a defense mechanism. Trees, after all, are everywhere, whereas the kukui is confined to the tropics.

For two years after my youngest brother, Bryan, was born, my father called him George. In a startling example of how the refusal to name can appear to protect a person from the deep pain of loss, my father chose to call my brother George because, for the first few months of his life, Bryan struggled to remain alive. Seriously burned over his entire body when a grossly negligent nurse immersed him in scalding water right after his birth, Bryan spent the first part of his life in continual and what can only be imagined as excruciating pain. He lost most of the flesh on the lower half of his body. There was an enormous chance that he would die. Even when it appeared that Bryan would be okay, my dad continued to call him George. As if "George's" loss could be tolerated in ways that the loss of "Bryan" could not. It was only when Bryan, at the age of two, told my dad that his name was not George that my father began calling his son by name.

Landscapes, however, do not talk back. They do not insist that you honor them by calling them by name. They do not even require that you know them or pay attention to them at the level of the particular. As the United States' own colonial past attests, you can appear to control the land by renaming it, by making it fit your own system. If the autonomy and individuality of an object, a place, or a person are maintained, in part, through naming, then renaming or misnaming denies a thing its own history, its "beingness" apart from you. You supercede, in this case, the land. It exists only when you call it into existence, and it fails to exist—as you have named it—once you leave.

I think as a child I was not given the names of things—or more often given the wrong names of things—because it allowed us, as a family, to remain in charge of the degree of intimacy we had with the land and ultimately with a home. We would make up names for everything—for the beaches, for stores, for campsites, for people, even for our own pets—and in making up we would not have to really "know." We would not have to fit into a history or a geography that we would only be leaving. We would not have to acknowledge that this landscape was any different from any other.

What my experience with land tells me is that being placed has little to do with the length of time you remain and much more to do with the willingness to open yourself up to the possibility of loss. Land becomes an intimate when you are willing to grieve it, and you do not need to have spent a long time in one place to feel loss. In fact, you could be passing through.

The tennis court tree in Maloelap.

The way the sky and sea meet seamlessly on the Puget Sound ferry.

The rattle of palm fronds against the house.

Gnats in your eyes and your nose.

Fireflies skittering over prairie grass.

And always the ocean.

Perhaps place writing is less about the specific relationship between the writer and the land and more about a particular stance a writer takes toward the land. Like memory itself, place resides in the details. It is not so much *that* you remember but *how* you remember. In the same essay in which Rockwell Gray suggests that memory of places can become more significant than the actual places, he also cautions against what he calls the practice of "guerrilla autobiography," where place becomes reduced to snippets of information that read like a résumé (58). These narratives lack "a deep sense of place" and trade in clichés, becoming a part of the growing number of anonymous and interchangeable landscapes that exist in modern society (58). For autobiographical memory to serve as an antidote to dislocation and disconnection, it must be drawn with patience, he tells us, and with particulars.

In thinking about the place writing that has moved me, the particulars are what I recall. Scott Russell Sanders standing in his backyard in the early morning hours, his arms wrapped around a tree. Terry Tempest Williams rearranging the limbs of a dead swan as she will later care for her mother's body. Annie Dillard paying attention to clouds. These are moments that these writers have chosen to translate their experience of landscape for their readers. Small, specific, and personal moments with the land.

In the end, it seems to me, the acts of writing and of being placed are the same. To be placed and to write place both require the distillation of experience into certain, specific details. When we write, we reduce the complexity of the world around us into ordered lines of prose. It is little different when we place ourselves. Through the selection and honoring of certain details, we turn spaces into places. Much is left out of the sentence, and much is left out of the landscapes we carry with us, but what remains tells the story of who we are. Harold Simonson is right when he suggests that "real placement requires effort," that it is not a birthright (174). But the effort required is not one of staying put or even one of extended study. It is the effort that begins with the knowledge that what you see is fleeting, partial, and never whole and that, at the same time, it is all that you have.

I began this introduction with the words of Barbara Kingsolver, who tells us that we find our place in the world by writing one. For a former military brat without a home, I find her words very comforting. Placedness can be most certainly found in staying put, but it can also be found in migration. It can develop from close study, but it can also develop by simply opening yourself up to the possibility that what you see might be lost. We write place into being. It is the act of writing that brings us home, the crafting of story that gives us the guide to measure the rest of the world.

As I wrote at the beginning of this essay, the goal Rona and I have for this collection is to establish a vocabulary of place that includes our relationship between our work—specifically our academic work—and where we live. The title of our book, *Placing the Academy*, is in some ways more shifting than it might syntactically sound. As our contributors indicate, the academy and our work in the academy are anything but fixed or determined. Rather, our understanding of the academy as a place must be as broad and as fluid as the work that we do. We do not stop being teachers or writers or researchers the moment we leave campus, as if our scholarly selves were coats that could be checked at the door. Instead, we bring our sense of ourselves as academics into our beds at night when we read, into the mountains when we hike, to the table when we eat. Plato's foundational idea that an academy must be less about a physical location and more about a way of exchange, a kind of conversation, a path for seeking knowledge plays out within and among the essays in this collection.

That said, our contributors understand that the academy is always local and, in fact, can only be local, even as we consider common work that academies do or common foundations that academies rest upon. Each person experiences place differently, and no one understanding of place can fit an entire department, campus, field, discipline, or profession. The place of the academy shifts between people and even within a person. While some of the writers do indeed write about their literal campuses or offices, most conceptualize academic work and the academic landscapes in alternative terms. In exploring the connections between landscape and academic identity, we have divided the collection into four sections that honor the shifting nature of place and the reach of the academy. The movement between the four sections is meant to mirror the argument made in the introduction, namely, that place must be fluid and shifting even as it requires attention to particulars and that potentially the most exhilarating work being done on place is that which is not literally rooted but which ranges, straddles, and roams.

The six writers in the first section, "Here," ask us to pay attention to the place we find ourselves the most, the place many of us call our homes. All of these essays are strongly rooted in the present—in the here and now. For some of these writers, this means calling attention to the literal place in which we write, read, and work—the campus—a place mostly ignored and devalued in comparison to intellectual endeavors, or, worse yet, threatened with toxins, concrete, and overuse. They wonder, explicitly and implicitly, just where the university is—in the classrooms, on the quad, in our minds, in the buildings? Others who move off campus ask us to consider ways of seeing and hearing our most immediate surroundings that can also enable us to see and hear—to reimagine—our work as teachers and scholars. "Here" for these writers is always ecological, always interconnected, always interanimating.

Through long conversations with her daughter Erin E. Moore, an architect, Kathleen Dean Moore, a philosopher and nature writer, begins this section by exploring her own uneasy place in an academy where she long existed "in two worlds: the world of Ideas, which thrilled [her] and paid [her] bills, and the world of rain and wind, which [she] loved." In a critique of the university's strategic plans to globalize, Moore refuses separation between land and work. She explores how much is lost when the personal and place-based is "banished . . . from the philosophically meaningful world."

Michael Sowder's sojourns in eleven different geographies and four different professions have helped teach him the gift of paying attention. Sowder is guided by the "question of seeing—for landscape can inform our identity only to the extent that, day by day, moment by moment, throughout our ordinary lives, we truly see it." Seeing, however, is simple "but not easy," as we can be easily distracted by the busy-ness of everyday life or feel the discomfort of worry and memory. Relying on his practice in Zen meditation as a metaphor for thinking about how we learn to be at home, Sowder writes that he is "learning that finding a right livelihood and a place to be may finally end in what we have to give."

In contrast to Sowder's peripatetic past, Diana Garcia's rootedness in California's San Joaquin Valley shapes her commitment to writing and teaching. Her childhood landscape taught her "a focused gaze and close attention to detail," and the public school system rewarded her intelligence and good studentship by busing her to an almost-all-white class of gifted children on the other side of town. There she speaks English, "the language of parity"; there she goes by Karen, "a name centered somewhere north of Scandinavia; not Diana, redolent of sage cracking through dirt in August." Now teaching in the creative writing and social action program at California State University, Monterey Bay, Garcia is dedicated to teaching students like herself and students who remind her of kids with whom she grew up, kids who disappeared in the fog.

Charles Bergman insists that we understand our environment—particularly our campus—as a powerful teacher. Drawing on his training as an English Renaissance scholar and his experiences with his Pacific northwestern university's sustainability committee, Bergman argues that academics tend to look past the literal place of the academy in favor of the pastoral ideal, "as a place set apart from the real world, a refuge and a retreat into contemplation." Yet "we can learn not only *at* a college campus," Bergman writes, "but *from* a college campus." He helps us read "the silent syllabus" of the university, the material reality of boilers, showers, and sewers that sustains the intellectual life we typically (and incorrectly) identify as the "landscape of the mind." Bergman argues that placing the campus any place other than *here* proves damaging, even deadly: English ivy, the symbol of the academy, is an invasive species that chokes to death native Douglas fir and western hemlock, and water, the symbol of the region in its waterways and rain, is at its limits in terms of use.

Katherine Fischer also finds a teacher in water. Overflowing its banks, changing forms with the seasons, the Mississippi River of Fischer's adulthood in the floodplain encourages "[f]antasy and metaphor, adventure and [her] own yearning heart." The Mississippi also makes her rethink her pedagogy. As a new teacher, Fischer believed that teaching and learning were as precise, as controllable, as she once imagined the river to be: "Schooled in education departments of the early 1970s," she writes, "I believed that if I poured flowing streams of lessons and sage advice into student heads, their knowledge would flow downstream like a contained river—kept neatly to its shores." Yet paying attention to the rhythms, the fecundity of the Mississippi allows her to revise her metaphor and value the wildness and unpredictability of the classroom, as well as the pleasure of movement and surfaces.

Seán W. Henne concludes this section by writing of his return home. A Michigan teacher from a long line of Michigan teachers, Henne inherits his family's love of stories, teaching, and place, and he understands storytelling, teaching, and farming as interdependent acts. At the community college on Lake Michigan at which he works, Henne's workload is as heavy as the one his students bear living in a district with high unemployment rates and rural isolation. As Henne develops a curriculum to help students lift themselves out of the poverty of the place, he listens to frogsongs. Amphibians, he tells us, are indicator species: "Hearing them in such abundance is, in part, a signal that the natural world I inhabit is functioning richly." And hearing frogsongs reminds him that his "curricula need to be aware of the realities brought into [his] room by the other inhabitants that share [his] space."

In the second section, "There," we look at academics who argue that their professional identities are most shaped by another place, one not necessarily where they work or live but one equally powerful in its shaping influence. For these writers, who they are now is largely dependent on where they have stood before.

Kathryn T. Flannery begins this conversation with an essay that attends to the cultural geography of her childhood spent in Levittown, the largest planned community in the United States. Through a series of reflections that meander through floor plans and racial covenants, Flannery comes to understand how strongly this "There" of her childhood informs her chosen field of study, the literacy practices of those "from below." Having once been under the gaze of those who wanted to document, she has dedicated her career to studying what happens when the subject speaks back. Unwilling to allow Levittown to remain neither uniformly tidy nor uniformly bleak, Flannery relies on personal experience to argue that place is never singular. In her desire to explore the dissonance created when "personal and public stories are in tension," Flannery refuses any easy alliances between place and the academy or landscape and knowledge.

Mitsuye Yamada turns the focus from research to the classroom and her work with students. She devotes her time to reconsidering a place that was once barren to her, once a place of pain. Imprisoned as a child with 120,000 other Japanese nationals and

Japanese Americans in a concentration camp in the Idaho desert during World War II, Yamada associated the desert with barbed wire and watchtowers, with sameness, sterility, and nonproductivity. Yet coteaching a class with a biologist for writing and biology students alike "transforms" the desert for Yamada and fuels her work as a teacher, poet, and activist. Ultimately, Yamada identifies with the desert and its ability to "emerg[e] out of obscurity," thereby taking solace and strength in a place that once threatened to destroy her.

For Jayne Brim Box, the stakes are equally high with her work on the Suwannee River. A conservation biologist, Brim Box has spent her career focused on the life cycle of freshwater mussels, in particular the Suwannee moccasinshell, a species that is now extinct. What complicates Brim Box's work is the fact that she found what may well be the last specimen of the Suwannee moccasinshell and then killed it. Caught in a "twisted biological Greek tragedy," Brim Box works to save what she may have helped kill, putting her own body at risk by swimming in the same polluted waters. It is only when the other biologists around her begin getting sick that Brim Box considers how she partakes in the trauma experienced by the mussels and the river they inhabit. The antithesis to Yamada, Brim Box must learn to balance a once calming riverscape with the toxic zone it has become.

Both a fiction writer and a postcolonial scholar, Charles Waugh has also spent time negotiating different cultural geographies. His work in Vietnam grounds both his novels and his scholarship, and in "Imagining Vietnam" he explores how Vietnam became, for him, "a place in its own right" rather than a set of received stereotypes. Through his writing he tries to "demonstrate how this place in which we live is irrevocably bound to that one, tied together by our choice to go there and do what we did, forever linked by common experience and responsibilities." For Waugh, the far away becomes understood when one attends to the near and thus provides a fitting conclusion to a section that argues collectively that who we are as writers and teachers may be most shaped by places we have already passed through.

The third section, "Everywhere," includes writers for whom literal places become either interchangeable or cumulative in their efforts to focus on a kind of meta-landscape that speaks most powerfully to them. In this section, one specific place is not enough to describe their relationship to their environment and their work. They make the argument that being no place and every place at the same time raises the stakes in the conversation about landscape and academic identity.

Deborah A. Miranda, an indigenous teacher, writer, and scholar, begins this section by reminding us that no matter where we teach, we are teaching "on stolen ground." She explores the tensions that exist among her body, place, and the academy as she educates her students and her colleagues about what it means to teach in occupied territory. She uses her felt connection to the land to suggest that "[t]here is a knowing that cannot be held in words alone," complicating just what it means for a profession that trades in words and texts to be placed. In describing her efforts to repatriate the academy, she forcefully shows just how intertwined land, self, and work are. Only when we pay attention to where we stand literally every day, Miranda concludes, can that land teach us our "place in this world."

Independent scholar Robert Michael Pyle reflects on the "disconnection many people feel with regard to their nonhuman neighbors" and the inability of most academics to see the "distinct, physical, inhabited place" of the campus. In chronicling his observations and discoveries on "dozens of campuses" in his career, he makes an impassioned argument to pay attention to the land that surrounds us, to become "naturalist[s], day by day, regardless of [our] academic discipline." Only by dissolving the divisions between the human and the natural, the arts and the sciences, the mind and the land can we bear the burden of responsibility we have to the places in which we work, places that are threatened by our continued ignorance. He invites academics to open their eyes to the "vast reservoir of inspiration, grounding, instruction, authority, tranquillity, consolation, physical and intellectual stimulation, spiritual succor, fun, and sometimes ecstasy, but above all, interest in the real world."

Lee Torda widens the scope of this section even further by considering the at-times competing impulses of looking for a job and securing tenure. "[I]f you choose to live an academic life," she writes, "you are subject to a fickle job market and, thus, to a certain amount of moving around." Those fortunate to secure a job somewhere must then work very hard to gain that "coveted measure of academic security: tenure." Tenure is understood as a means of securing academic freedom; it is also, for better or for worse, a way of securing a literal and intellectual home. Yet getting tenure at a place does not guarantee a desire to stay there. What's more, often the work (heavy teaching and service) that helps secure tenure at one institution is precisely the work that would make it difficult to find a job elsewhere. Casting a wide geographical net, Torda traces her journey from an immigrant neighborhood outside Cleveland to her university outside Boston, where she now holds tenure, and contemplates the emotional complexity involved in answering the oft-asked question, "Where are you from?"

The fourth section, "In Between," is shaped by contributors who feel caught between two competing landscapes that claim equal attention on their professional lives. They refuse to name a single defining landscape as most important and never feel completely at home, especially in their work.

Scott Slovic begins this section far from home in another country, surrounded by water rather than mountains. His work, he suggests, draws its energy from "the tension between going away and coming home." Only in traveling, in being in a new place that requires him to pay attention, does he find a "renewed openness" to, or awareness of, home. At the same time, he recognizes that home creates "a kind of ballast or core of meaning that helps [him] to appreciate and understand the implications of [his] travels." We move from surf, to airplane, to the American Southwest, as Slovic considers how much more we can know of ourselves and our work when we leave the familiar behind.

Norma Elia Cantú takes us to the borderlands. For Cantú, it is the borderland between Texas and Mexico that shapes her "*fronteriza* consciousness," a borderland that often comes in conflict "with what the academic world expect[s]." While she writes that "[g]eography is destiny," she acknowledges the work she has had to do to translate her experience for her colleagues and her institutions. The borderland appears again and again in her research, teaching, and service, ultimately giving her the strength needed to speak back to a culture that would have her remain on the edge.

Mary Clearman Blew faced similar obstacles as a young PhD in the 1960s with little support and little understanding of how the academy works. Through a third-person narrative, Blew tries to find the distance needed from her young self to describe the literal impact landscape has on our work and our lives. Caught between the Montana of her childhood and the Montana she occupies as a professional, she describes how her focus on Ben Jonson in graduate school, work that "grew from her fear of suffocation, of being buried alive under [the] blinding sun" of her Montana childhood, fails her when she returns to northern Montana to teach. Instead she follows the barren landscape of the Highline and begins to write stories that "bare the bones of her people and the bones of the people they displaced," occupying both the present and the past in order to understand the future.

Like Blew, Janice M. Gould also works to reclaim the past, straddling eras, languages, and heritages in order to understand her current place. A Konkow Maidu poet, Janice Gould writes that she became a scholar to answer questions that her mother couldn't answer about her heritage; she become a poet to "start talking about [her] life—[her] experience as a lesbian, a mixed-blood, a woman with an inner landscape of mountains and stars, sunrises and setting moons, pastures in fog and rain, bright noontides." As a professor of creative writing, Gould uses photographs, poetry, fiction, and United Statesian propaganda—as well as the presence of Chemawa Indian Boarding School a few miles away from the university—to teach her students about the kinship between Native people and land and how to "question what the 'other side' of the story of this nation . . . could be."

Jeffrey M. Buchanan rounds out this section by defining his obligations to particular populations of students, namely working-class students in urban areas, places "scarred and storied," places marked by "uncertainty, failure, [and] loss." Buchanan speaks to the importance of "making places work," of actively shaping spaces to become places. Drawing on his father's labor as a tree trimmer in Detroit and his place as his father's assistant, Buchanan describes teaching as work that requires a similar kind of felt sense, and he endeavors to teach his students to read the landscapes of their lives, to read the selves they present in those places, and to change, adapt, and rearrange. Buchanan reminds us of the work that goes into making a place in the academy, work that is replicated by his students who feel equally at sea, and how we might never feel at home in our professional lives but rather remain dislocated.

Rona Kaufman concludes the collection with a coda meditating on the relationships among bodies, texts, and land, bringing the themes explored in the four sections together and arguing for an expansive definition of what it means to place the academy. Relying on her experience as a runner whose body type does not resemble that of the "typical" runner, Kaufman considers how easily bodies—like texts and landscapes—are misread because of readers' tendencies to "reduce all surfaces to signs." She argues that all texts, like all landscapes, are embodied and that "[e]ventually, we have to deal with [that] body." More importantly, the body can be a "site of learning," a place, not unlike landscape, where knowledge is made. Too often scholars "use place as a metaphor, as a point of social location—place stands in for ethnicity, or class, or religion—rather than speak to the particularities of landscapes themselves as a shaping force." When that happens, "[p]lace collapses into *placeholder*, a stand-in for something else, to be chronically displaced and replaced and displaced more." Kaufman concludes by reminding us that "places and texts are bodies first." In doing so, she extends the reach of landscape to include the one we inhabit every day, the landscape we inscribe on our bodies.

Notes

Parts of this introduction originally appeared in "Through the Particular," *Ecotone* (Winter 2005).

1. Kent Ryden uses the term "place-creating elements" (225).
2. In *Staying Put*, Scott Sanders uses the phrase "primal landscape" to define the "place by which [one] measure[s] every other place" (4).
3. Kent Ryden argues that essayists, in particular, have the function or even responsibility to "write place into being" (241).

Bibliography

Blew, Mary Clearman. *Bone Deep in Landscape: Reading, Writing, and Place*. Norman: U of Oklahoma P, 1999.

Chatwin, Bruce. *Songlines*. New York: Penguin, 1988.

Franklin, Wayne. Foreword. *Mapping the Invisible Landscape: Folklore, Writing, and the Sense of Place*. By Kent Ryden. Iowa City: U of Iowa P, 1993.

Gray, Rockwell. "Autobiographical Memory and Sense of Place." *Essays on the Essay: Redefining the Genre*. Ed. Alexander J. Butrym. Athens: U of Georgia P, 1990. 53–70.

Hogan, Linda. *Dwellings: A Spiritual History of the Living World*. New York: Touchstone, 1996.

Kingsolver, Barbara. *Small Wonder: Essays*. New York: Harper, 2002.

Moore, Kathleen Dean. *The Pine Island Paradox*. Minneapolis: Milkweed, 2004.

Rogers, Pattiann. *Dream of the Marsh Wren: Writing as Reciprocal Creation*. Minneapolis: Milkwood, 1999.

Ryden, Kent. *Mapping the Invisible Landscape: Folklore, Writing, and the Sense of Place*. Iowa City: U of Iowa P, 1993.

Sanders, Scott Russell. *Staying Put: Making a Home in a Restless World.* Boston: Beacon, 1993.

———. *Writing from the Center.* Bloomington: Indiana UP, 1995.

Simonson, Harold. *Beyond the Frontier: Writers, Western Regionalism, and a Sense of Place.* Fort Worth: Texas Christian UP, 1984.

Williams, Terry Tempest. *Desert Quartet: An Erotic Landscape.* New York: Pantheon, 1995.

II
Here

2

Six Kinds of Rain
Searching for a Place in the Academy

Kathleen Dean Moore and Erin E. Moore

1. Silver Thaw

On January 10, my college town wakes up to a silver thaw. All through the day, oak limbs thunder to earth in a flurry of ice and robins. Ice coats every laurel leaf, every branch of every oak and bundle of mistletoe, every stop sign and sidewalk. The whole world shines. "Warm rain is falling through cold air," the radio announces, and the university is closed. It's too dangerous to drive, even if people *could* open their car doors through a half inch of ice. I pull on a parka and skid out to see. Rain continues to fall, building ice-knobs on the buds of dogwood trees, outlining azaleas with light, transforming rose thorns into glass swords. Even as I watch, the weight of the ice becomes too much for an old Douglas fir in the next block. With a great crackling, a limb falls through the lower branches and smashes into the street, taking down an electric wire in a cloud of sparks and smoke. Still the rain falls. By the time this silver thaw is over, the neighborhoods and campus will be a tangle of split limbs and littered branches.

> *place n : SPACE <all are strangers,*
> *rootless in place or time>*[1]

When I look at a mosaic of Plato gathered with his students under the branches of an olive tree, I can almost smell the rosemary and feel the sun on my shoulders, feel the energy of argument and hear the shouts of the marketplace beyond the garden walls. Because the hero Academos was buried there, the garden was called the Academy. My discipline, philosophy, began in this sacred grove, a garden of olive trees and myrtle on the outskirts of Athens.

So I have always paid close attention to what Plato is telling his students as they sit on warm stones. Plato has traveled to Italy and studied with Pythagoras, and what he tells his students is that true knowledge aspires to the abstraction and perfection of mathematics. The blue of the rosemary flowers, the blue of the bank swallow or the late afternoon sky are changing and particular—and so imperfect. They only participate fleetingly in the Idea of Blue, the unchanging, perfect color. According to Plato, we should aspire to true knowledge—not knowledge of the particulars (the distractions of a particular place), but knowledge of the perfect (the universal and unchanging Everyplace) (Bks. VI, VII).

Of course, as Plato knew, humans can't ever achieve this kind of knowledge. We see only the dancing shadows of Ideas, as if they were projected by firelight on the back wall of a cave (Bk. VII, 514a–517a). But at least we know the extent of our ignorance, which is a kind of wisdom, and we know the nature of the knowledge we should seek.

If truth is universal, then everything that is not universal falls off the academic agenda. Philosophers will study Beauty, but not black crows in a green field or a father's cheek against his child's. Philosophers will study Justice, but not a friend's broken promise or her remorse. Attention to place? If truth is universal, philosophers will firmly turn their backs on their own olive groves and rosemary patches—it makes no difference where they are.

2. Pineapple Express

There is no mercy in this rain. It falls hard, it falls loud, it falls for three days and nights unceasing. Low, dusky clouds weigh on the students' shoulders and rest heavily on their souls. Classroom windows steam, increasing the gloom, and water drains across the classroom floor, fed by streams flowing steadily from black-and-orange umbrellas. The room smells of wet plaster and damp wool. Sidewalks flood, forcing students to high-step through lawns already so sodden that each footprint fills with cold water. Soccer fields flood. Parking lots flood. Storm drains flood. Oak Creek runs high and muddy. I walk to school in the dark, walk home in the dark, and teach with wet feet, raising my voice over the din.

Meteorologists call this the Pineapple Express, because the weather rolls in from the South Pacific, loaded with water, and dumps half the ocean on our campus—a black freight train rumbling past the social-science building with sullen disregard, day after day after day.

> *place n : the point at which a reader left off*
> *<dropped the book and lost her place>*

For many years, I have struggled to understand my place in this academy. At first, I taught political philosophy and philosophy of law, even Great Ideas, from the perspective of the Western Enlightenment, separated from the times and places where my students lived. We read John Locke and John Rawls, page after page, and tried not to look out the window. When students asked if class could meet outside on the first sunny day, I always said no, asking them if sunshine could teach them anything about Liberty—knowing that it could, but knowing also that they couldn't tell me how. I taught Thomas Hobbes on weather (The day doesn't have to be rainy to be threatening, he wrote) but I made no connection to the rain coursing down the window (62). I taught deductive logic, wrote a book on Forgiveness, and everything went fine. As rain-drenched winters brightened to summers, I was tenured, promoted, named department chair.

All this time, I lived in two worlds: the world of Ideas, which thrilled me and paid my bills, and the world of rain and wind, which I loved. Weekdays found me in my office, where even the plants were dead; weekends found me out in the weather, carrying a waterproof journal, paying real attention to rain bouncing off rivers and running down creeks, sluicing past shining rocks, carrying the doomed little boats my children carved from sticks. For many years, it never occurred to me that the academic world and the wet, wild world could be—in fact, should be—the same place.

I can't say what prompted me to examine this divided life, to wonder if a life that lacks wholeness may ultimately lack integrity. It might have been the freedom that tenure provided me to define for myself what philosophy really is and where it ought to take place. It might have been articles written by other philosophers who were recoiling from Plato, arguing that there is no one Truth, but many truths; that every claim grows out of some grounding; that scholars should pay close attention to the situatedness (god forgive us for this word) of knowledge; that personal stories in particular places have truths no formula can begin to express. On the other hand, it might have been sadness, as I sensed that I wasn't doing the job I wanted to do; or it might have been guilt I felt, turning my back so decisively on a world I loved so much.

Or maybe it was rereading Dostoyevsky. "One must love life," he wrote, "before loving its meaning." One must love life, and some meaning may grow from that love. "But if love of life disappears, no meaning may console us." I began to wonder, sitting in the prow of a boat in steady rain, what meaning could grow from my love of the low light, the tracks of otter and mink, the smell of salmon, the golden floating leaves?—all this spinning, sliding world. What meaning can grow from a deep, caring connection to a place?

What if I tried to teach students to be attentive to what is beautiful and true in their own worlds? What if I tried to teach them to see, really see the place they live: to hold it in their hands, to learn everything about it, to listen to what it needs, what it seeks, what it sounds like at dawn? To learn the connections between places—between us and them, between near and far, between the mundane and the sacred. To appreciate the interconnectedness of people and places and the moral wholeness—the integrity—this calls for in us. Wouldn't this be important work? I believe that this kind of seeing, this kind of attentiveness to place is the first step toward caring. And caring is the portal to the moral world. Isn't this a professor's job, to lead students to this open door?

I knew I was moving onto contested ground, and at first I was frightened. Academic blood is shed in the dispute over whether knowledge is universal or place based. Take the losing side on this issue, write about crows in a department that writes about Beauty or write about Beauty in a department that writes about crows, and your work will be dismissed. All my professors taught that there are only two kinds of meaningful statements: those that can be deduced from first principles and those that can be disproved by empirical evidence. Despite their lessons, it was gradually dawning on me how much I lost when I banished stories, personal experience, even the landscape, the very ground I stood on, everything I really loved on the actual earth, from the philosophically meaningful world.

3. Squall

A squall has blown into campus from the coast range, a short-lived commotion of wind-driven rain. This is the kind of rain that moves in fast and hits hard, almost always during the time between classes. From my second-story office window, I watch one student running awkwardly through sheeting rain. Dressed in a T-shirt and jeans, he gallops with his head down, his notebook clasped to his chest. Another student strolls along the brick walk, completely oblivious to the rain. Two women cut the difference, hurrying across the space between buildings, their backpacks bouncing, their arms crossed, annoyance in their stride.

When you're caught in a squall without a parka, it's hard to know if you should walk or run. If you walk between buildings, the rain has a longer chance to soak you, flattening your hair and running in rivulets down your forehead. If you run, you shorten the time you're exposed to the rain, but you collide with the raindrops full force, driving them down your neck and wetting your pant legs, and this is especially miserable—jeans sticking to your knees, cold and clammy all through class.

place v : to earn a top spot in a competition

Even as I struggle to find my place in the university, the university's relation to its own place has become more and more of a quandary. In its strategic plan, a goal of my university is to place in the top tier of American land-grant institutions. Placing requires nationally ranked faculty, lured from other universities around the globe. It requires successful students, placed in positions of national prestige—New York, Cambridge, Bethesda, Palo Alto. In this heady world, time and space are pulled and chopped like taffy. A successful faculty member is far more likely to talk to a colleague in Washington than a neighbor in the next block. She is far more likely to fly to a conference in Prague than to float the river that flows by her town. The academic world is ridden with wormholes, shortcuts in space and time that transport ideas and reputations to Beijing or Berlin.

In this folded space, it's hard to know where a university is. Maybe the university has become a paradox, a place with no particular place. More likely it exists in a universal place—in a familiar geography of classrooms, restrooms, computer networks, and labs, where uncomfortable table-chairs and library shelves are an iconography recognizable around the world. This global University has a common language, shared ethical codes, standardized measures of status, and ingrained methodologies, economic systems, and taboos. What the University doesn't have is a meaningful relationship with a particular place—its absence the final achievement of the goal implicit in the word *university*.

Professors live simultaneously in two places. They inhabit the global University, while they live lightly in their own neighborhoods. Meanwhile, the people who proofread their papers and empty their wastebaskets, the students who take their courses, and maybe even their own children live in Albany or Lebanon or Salem—surrounding towns a twenty-minute commute away. There, rents are low, churches are thriving, and airport shuttles pause to pick up passengers on their way to the airport, where rain streams off the planes as they lift into the clouds—something many of my colleagues are unlikely to notice, waiting impatiently to reach ten thousand feet, where they can turn on their laptops and be back at the University again.

> *place v : to find a position for, as to secure remunerative employment*

As for the students, the most important address in the university is often the Placement Office, whose mission is to place students in positions of "responsibility and promise." *Place* is a fast-paced verb. It connotes strategic and narrow focus, a rapid pace, head down, looking neither right nor left. It connotes a kind of worry and self-consciousness, anxiety about measuring up for the right job. Students seek skills that can go anywhere, as the job requires. So for many—not all—of them, the university is not a home as much as it is a vehicle by which students move into the corporate world from the ranches and suburbs, their families' cigarette- or Polo- or juniper-scented houses. Not all, but many, students choose classes that will get them where they are going—to the extent that they can, bypassing the detours. In the express lane to economic success, students have no incentive, no time or occasion, to notice the complicated, richly populated and forested communities where they go to school. They are in training to become the new homeless, moving from place to place as the global economy requires.

4. Soft Rain

In other college towns, soft rain might be called drizzle, but that ignores the kindness of this rain. Soft rain falls at exactly the rate that can be absorbed by green mats of moss and sweet layers of pine duff; exactly the rate that Douglas firs and Sitka spruce can pull it into their shining needles, growing all winter in this soft rain; exactly the rate that water evaporates from a person's hair. You can stand in soft rain and never get wet. Meanwhile, all around you, grass fields grow green, trees lengthen and put on girth, frogs sing as if their hearts would burst, and along the roads, Scotch broom blooms in yellow heaps. Soft rain smells like apples. It tastes like pine trees. In class, against the windows, it sounds like somebody shushing a child.

You can lie on your back in soft rain, licking moisture off your face. When you stand up, there will be an outline of your body, light against dark pavement—a rain angel. Watching students—how they gather in small groups or sit down to wait for a friend—you won't know if it's raining or not. Soft rain doesn't quicken their pace or drive them indoors or bow their heads. Soft rain doesn't warp their books.

place n : a specific locality or cultural region

Even as it aspires to be a global University, Oregon State University, where I work, sits in the southern quadrant of the largest temperate rainforest in the world—or at any rate, in the stump-studded remnants of what once was the largest. Reminders of the ancient forest grace campus: giant Douglas firs, rhododendrons high as the rooftops, a grandmother maple with gardens of licorice ferns and lichens in the crooks of its branches. The College of Forestry manages the forests that ring the town and shapes forest-cut policy for the state.

The campus is Kalapuya country, a broad valley that the People burned each year so that camas would grow in broad blue fields and deer could fatten on acorns under spreading oaks. The meadows are largely replaced now by laser-leveled fields of grass grown for seed, a crop introduced to the valley by the College of Agriculture professor who once lived and died in my house. Campus edges up to the Marys River on the south and the Willamette River in the east, a mighty river now contained between walls of riprap but once spreading silver in braided gravel streams and marshes all across the valley. This is the Salmon Homeland, where red salmon crowd the streams to spawn—or did once, before the hatcheries and dams designed in part by OSU grads. Now Department of Fisheries faculty struggle to save the last of the salmon runs.

Corvallis, home to Oregon State University, sits in the midst of timber towns, or so they were, when there was timber. A person can't make a living from logging when the forests are gone, so the towns are ragged at the edges, sad Wal-Mart towns. The college town itself is a green, well-gardened place, an overgrown village of small white houses ringed by new, million-dollar homes in the hills. Retirees move here because of the rich cultural offerings of the university, even as the university hires fewer and fewer young profs who might create those offerings. So the elementary schools gradually close, and the population grows steadily older.

But enough. The point is that, no matter how the university might ignore or deny the importance of the fact, of course the university is in a specific place. That place is thoroughly shaped by the university. Moreover, the university is thoroughly shaped by the place. You can see it in the curriculum, the rangeland management and forest recreation and marine ecology and electrical engineering. You can see it in the plummeting budgets, cut year after year after year by taxpayers who don't understand why local people should pay the bill for the global University. You can see it in the students: Children of a green and gentle land, they are homesick maybe, maybe lost, but never cynical. You can see it in the buildings and the lay of the land, the covered bike racks and windowless classrooms, a campus so responsive to the rain that there is no place a class can meet outside. You can see it sometimes in the truth-claims of professors in service to the Western Cattleman's Association or Weyerhaeuser Company.

You can see it in an administration in various stages of denial and confusion, bouncing from the mission of a thoroughly located university putting its resources to solving regional problems to the vision of a thoroughly disengaged Cyber-university, existing in some ethereal, perhaps more profitable plane. Clearly, this is a university struggling to find its place.

5. Broken Sun

Here is the rain that falls like light through trees just beginning to green up. On a rare day of sunlit sky, white clouds ramble generally eastward, trailing showers. These are the days of rainbows, double rainbows, triple rainbows, arching over the entire campus from the grass fields in the south to the fir-clothed hills to the north. Sidewalks steam. The cupola of the music building glows white in storm light, and every fleck of rain shines like glitter, floating. I can hear a trumpet climbing the musical scales, up and up, and when a car goes by, the music is the Beach Boys.

The Weather Beaver, the little icon that forecasts weather in our local paper, calls this *broken sun*. I don't know why. It might mean that the sunny expanse of the day may be broken by showers, but these showers do no damage to the sun. I like to think it means that on a day like this, the sun, expanding, flies apart into a million flecks of light that drift onto the sports fields, the fir trees, the uplifted faces of the students.

place n : a proper role, a station and its duties

So what is my job as a teacher in a university that both is and is not in this place and time? Against all the forces that would uproot them, I have resolved to teach students to be acutely aware of where they are. Aware of the physical and temporal place, the rain and the ancient stones, the forests, the passage of time. Of the cultural place, the communities and libraries and histories—all the stories. Of the ecological place, which is to say, the relation of people to the great cycles of water and air, the great cycles of living and dying that sustain them. In the University, so far from home, it is easy for students to forget that they are part of deeply interconnected biocultural communities. This forgetting is a lonely and dangerous thing. Lonely, because it allows students to forget that they are created and sustained, one might say cradled, by long cultural traditions and ecological systems. Dangerous, because it encourages students to forget that their acts or failures to act have consequences in this place and future times.

"All ethics so far evolved," Aldo Leopold writes, "rest upon a single premise: that the individual is a member of a community of interdependent parts," a community that includes "soils, waters, plants, and animals, or collectively, the land," and the people, their hopes and fears for their children, their prejudices and practices (203). By reminding students of their membership in the community, by helping them understand it and rejoice in it, perhaps I can engage in a kind of moral education.

If I can help students understand the deep and complicated and comforting ways in which they are *in a place*, a community of interdependent parts, maybe I can help them acquire a necessary condition for the skill of moral imagination, the ability to imagine themselves *in another's place*. Empathy, sympathy, caring have their roots in moral imagination: Without knowing the biocultural context for their own hope and despair, how can students appreciate the hope and despair of others?—different from their own, but equally rooted in complicated, beautiful webs of relationship that grow from the place they inhabit.

Moreover, if students can learn how deeply, essentially connected they are to a place, maybe they will begin to question the consequences that their own decisions have for that place. This questioning is the beginning of moral responsibility.

I believe that this, at least, is my place in the university: to teach students that because their decisions (what to eat, where to live, how to get to campus, what to care about, what to love or despise) fundamentally affect the people around them and influence the well-being of the systems that sustain them, they have the moral responsibility to make decisions that are wise, caring, and deeply informed.

6. Mist

When I zip open the tent, I find that although bulrushes still nod and drip at the edge of the lake, the lake itself has vanished in mist, along with the reflections of the mountains and the sky. Soon, the mist will rise like stage curtains from the lake, revealing a sunlit, steaming world and fifteen students gathered for PHL 436—the Philosophy of Nature. Carrying *Walden* and a cup of tea, I will join them on the beach then. But for the moment, I settle back into my sleeping bag and let the morning mist do all the teaching. There will be time for words.

I'm not clear about where mist comes from, whether it falls from the sky or rises from the lake or materializes in place. Whatever its origin, it's a moisture thick and milky that softens what you can see, as it sharpens what you hear. From my sleeping bag, I hear mist sizzle against my tent, the pump handle creak, the thump of the outhouse door. A slosh as someone launches a canoe. Wood snapping, sticks breaking, and then the smell of woodsmoke on damp wind. Two women talk quietly by the fire. Gravel crunches as a jogger sets out on the trail, alert—I hope—for bear.

place n : a point in a set of relationships, a niche

So now I teach Philosophy of Nature. We go to the mountains for this course, camping beside a lake, a flotilla of students in little boats adrift in moonlight, asking what it is exactly that we value in this wild place and how we can find or create those values in our campus lives. I'm about to teach Environmental Ethics, and I'll teach this in the community. Don't know exactly how, but I'll give it a shot, sending my students into the suburban streams and soup kitchens. I teach Native American Philosophies, or I should say I raise the funds to invite other people—Native poets, musicians, storytellers, scholars—to lead students to examine what they most deeply believe about who they are in this place and time and what sustains them, physically, emotionally, and spiritually. I'm signed up to teach Critical Thinking in the winter term, and maybe this too will be a course in listening and seeing.

I'm insecure in this teaching, as you might imagine, wandering so far from the usual path that I wonder sometimes if I'm lost. I constantly ask myself, is this what students need? Is this what the world needs? But I find myself answering, yes and yes.

We are creatures of place, and our beginnings, our hopes, and our destinies rest on the health and wholeness of those places. Gary Snyder reminds us that spreading savannahs gave us our far-seeing eyes, "the streams and breezes gave us versatile tongues and whorly ears" (29). Does our ability to sing praises come from the beauty of the rain, our capacity to grieve from the short span of human life relative to the hills? And our ability to learn, is this a gift of complex and mysterious patterns of place and time that create the present in which we make our lives? If so, then our great educational systems should honor this gift in its entirety, protecting it and celebrating it in all its dimensions and with all our powers—not just to learn, but to listen, to imagine, to hope, to question, to celebrate, and to care.

As I finish writing this essay, I look down from my office window onto the flat roofs of campus—the Geosciences building, the Bioengineering labs, the porch of the Philosophy building. Water collects on those roofs, so each one is a lake, reflecting the brick buildings adjacent. Yellow rubber ducklings float on the water pooled above Philosophy's porch. I don't know where they came from, I don't ask. A robin is taking a bath in the Bioengineering lake. The bird shakes from its shoulders to its tail, lifting a chop on the water. Elm seeds drift onto the lakes, each seed with a hole where an evening grosbeak has neatly clipped out the nut meat. As the wind rises, the reflections of Biological Science and History shift and sway.

Notes

This paper grew from a long-term partnership exploring the topography of knowledge. Here, the complicated product of our comparative academic experiences is represented by a single voice speaking from a particular place.

1. All definitions are adapted from *Webster's Third New International Dictionary*.

Bibliography

Dostoyevsky, Fyodor. *The Brothers Karamazov*. New York: Everyman's Library, 1992.

Hobbes, Thomas. *Leviathan*. Ed. C. B. Macpherson. New York: Penguin, 1982. Pt. 1, chap. 8.

Leopold, Aldo. *A Sand County Almanac*. New York: Oxford UP, 1949.

Plato: The Collected Dialogues. Ed. Edith Hamilton and Huntington Cairns. Princeton: Princeton UP, 1961.

Snyder, Gary. *The Practice of the Wild*. San Francisco: North Point, 1990.

3

The Work the Landscape Calls Us To

Michael Sowder

May 2003. I'm sitting on "Winter-Tea Rock," looking down on the Cub River canyon as it descends into Cache Valley. In the distance, the Wellsville Mountains rise steeply into sheer, vertical peaks and ridges, Teton-like, blue and snow draped, forming the western rim of the valley where Jennifer, my wife, and I live and teach. At an elevation of 4,700 feet, Cache Valley sits between the Bear Mountains on the east, a range of 9,000 foot peaks, where I now sit, and the Wellsvilles to the west, a spur of the Wasatch range, which separates our valley from that of the Great Salt Lake. North to south, Cache Valley lies athwart the Utah-Idaho border in ecological defiance of political division, and like the valley itself, our lives too lie across the border. Teaching at Utah State in the southern end of Cache Valley, we live in the northern end in southeastern Idaho. We've been here for four years.

Krishna, our new puppy, is exploring the mountainside meadows. It's early summer, early June, the fields shot through with sunflowers (mules ears), avalanche lilies, yellow fawn lilies. Since spring began, Krishna and I have climbed this trail three times a week to Winter-Tea Rock, a narrow path rising steeply above the river, a small clear stream tumbling through the Bear Mountains over rocks covered with moss or ice. Jennifer and I discovered the trail snowshoeing. Over five feet of snow, we climbed the path for an hour until it opened onto a high sloping meadow, a shelf or bench above the canyon. At the high end of the meadow lay a large flat-topped boulder. We stopped and made tea in blowing snow and twenty-degree weather, warming ourselves from the inside out, and named the place "Winter-Tea Rock." Rangers have since told me it's not an "official trail," not "maintained," making it all the more inviting. In the last three months, I've encountered a solitary hiker on it with his dog and one group of horse riders. Rising steeply, it discourages weekend campers and, being narrow and unmaintained, wards off the ATVs in summer and snowmobiles in winter.

Breathing hard after the climb, I sit on the rock and take a look around. The dark green of junipers mixes with the new yellow-green of aspens and the red, smokelike blush of the red maples. Yellow warblers flit about, singing among the branches. Krishna, who knows she's on her own now for an hour or so, explores the woods. She flushes some grouse and then tears off across the meadow toward the next ridge where she's heard a deer. Part black Lab, part Australian shepherd, she has a shining, jet-black coat, longer than a Lab's, soft and feathered over her sleek body. With one brown eye, one blue, she looks a little otherworldly, so we named her Krishna, for the incarnation of God whose body was a beautiful blue.

I close my eyes and practice meditation, watching my breath, listening. Chickadees fill the air with chatter, and their occasional high lonesome *cee-be, cee-be* rises up from the gorge. A towhee sings out, *drink your teeeeea, drink your teeeeea*. Before long, the *quork* of a raven passing over. After twenty minutes or so, I open my eyes and look out toward the valley, out across the tumbling rims of the canyon. The mountains to the south roll out like surf, descending into blue foothills, flattening out into the valley floor. Sunflowers cover green foothills like gold dust. The valley was once the bay of an inland sea, an arm of the great prehistoric Lake Bonneville. I sip green tea and read poems from the T'ang dynasty—Tu Fu, Li Po, and the fourth-century Hsieh Ling-yün. I've also carried up here a book by Stephen Levine, a Buddhist teacher who works with the terminally ill and those in chronic pain. Levine describes a meditation that works to reawaken repressed traumas associated with parts of the body that have been psychically deadened. Gently letting the attention move through the body, allowing awareness to come to these hurt places, the meditation reawakens old wounds and often initiates deep grieving. The breaking up of frozen emotions that facilitates healing and the awakening of the body trigger a profound, global awakening of perception. One woman, a victim of childhood sexual abuse, began the practice twenty minutes twice a day and found it exceedingly difficult. After two and a half months of practicing, she reported, "A miracle happened the other day. I walked into the kitchen, sat down at the table, and looked up and saw the wall. I just saw the wall! I was just here in my body, in the world, in my heart. I saw the wall as if for the first time. I was just here. It was the most wonderful experience of my life" (138–39).

Emerson said, "Few adult persons can see nature. Most persons do not see the sun" (10). I think about the heightened, sharper quality of seeing that opens out for us at particular moments, taking us into a deeper level of "being-in-the-world," in which we become more present in the body, more present to the landscape, more awake, more alive. In such moments, seeing (and by "seeing" I mean to refer to all of the senses) becomes something more than perception. We feel things though our eyes. We participate in a tactile communication with things described by Thich Nhat Hanh as "interbeing" (54). The wall, the sun, the hawk, the stone, the flower are no longer inert objects, but presences in whose life we participate.

When I consider the theme of "landscape, work, and identity," I keep returning to this question of seeing—for landscape can inform our identity only to the extent that, day by day, moment by moment, throughout our ordinary lives, we truly see it. Yet how do we cultivate the kind of clarified seeing with which the woman in Levine's book saw the kitchen wall for the first time? Such moments seem to come rarely, almost as if by chance.

A hawk passes below me, twenty feet above ground, cutting the dew-drenched air above the meadow, checking us out. Krishna takes off after it. Silly dog. I feel the warm sun and the cool breeze. When it's time to go, I call for her, and she comes bounding. Realizing we're heading back, she's wild with joy and streaks through the meadow, head down, ears back, full speed into the woods, running in wild circles, leaping over logs, under bushes, thrilled we're going home, thrilled she knows the way. How I love this dog.

One summer evening in Athens, Georgia, years ago, I was sitting in the car with my wife, Anne, in the midst of a divorce. Two years of separation, two years of heartbreaking talks, accusations, anger, and tears behind us, and I was still trying, yet unable finally, to leave—paralyzed by ambivalence, self-recrimination, and fear. That evening, she asked me directly if I felt I really had to leave. I was silent. I looked inside myself and tried to speak truthfully. I looked out the window.

A tall stand of grasses not far from the car was moving in summer air and evening sun, long green spears holding gold seed tips. *I just saw them.* Crickets chirred in the pines behind the house, fireflies beginning to blink. I was seeing through a clarity that felt like a kind of intimacy, centering, and waking up, which seemed somehow to say to me, "Yes, this is who you are." I felt anchored in a moment where the terror that kept me caught in endless ambivalence seemed to flow away. This was it. I said, "Yes, I do."

Paying attention to *what is* is simple. But not easy. It is difficult, as it was for the woman in Levine's book, to sit and look out at the world for more than a few minutes without distractions like lunch, a drink, a book, a friend, some TV, or sex. We get uncomfortable. Start to itch, worry, fidget. Memories rise up. In a poem called "Black Oak," Mary Oliver stands in a forest looking up at the oak, as it starts to drizzle. She wants to stay and look but feels the itch to get going: "Listen, says ambition, nervously shifting her weight from / one boot to another—why don't you get going?" I too want to get up and get going. But if we can sit through the itch, the boredom, and the anxiety, which may come in a storm of feelings or a great wave, these also pass through us, returning us to the moment, to the landscape around us with a little more clarity. More space opens within us for seeing *what is*. We stop running away from what's inside of us and can begin to really start to have a look around.

September 2003. I'm sitting in the living room of an empty house, reading Thomas Merton's essay about the rain. His voice moves in a deep interiority, a calm reservoir of solitude. When I finish the essay, I go outside. Fall is coming. The trees are turning. Crickets sing with a hollower, lonelier sound. The air is cool. The sky a darker blue. A red-tailed hawk, resident of a neighbor's spruce, is crying out. Behind the neighbors' house, the land drops off into farm fields that spread off into the distance and then rise up into the mountains. The high-pitched screech seems more like that of a tiny bird than this winged monster who makes us fear for our cats when they're out too long. I get the binoculars and study it. Soon I hear another cry, off in the distance, answering.

I love the spring in this land of fierce winters, love the slow March melting of three-foot-long icicles. I have feared beautiful fall days like this as the gateway to the coming ferocity of cold. Burning fingers, sliding tires, winds that can blow a tractor-trailer off the highway. But today I love the fall again, that excitement in the blood that must hark back to our kinship with the great migrating animals, ancient nomadic days. I may yet learn to love the hard austerity of Idaho winters. But now, the wind in the maples has a different, a deeper sound. The barking of a dog, far off, comes out of some deep hollow. I think of wolves. The hawk's cry seems more insistent. It will not stop now. The horn of the valley train calls out of some forgotten memory.

Though I've long been enraptured by landscape, I've been a fickle lover. For while the woods were my childhood playground and the mountains and rivers have formed my sense of self as poet and writer, I've been harried, like many, by a sense of never having had any home ground, a place to stay. Having lived in twenty-one houses or apartments in eleven geographies—from Cincinnati to Birmingham to Charleston to Seattle to Athens and Atlanta to Ann Arbor to Idaho—I've followed a peripatetic life of my own mapping. I've tried to see my rootlessness in the best light, considered myself a "saunterer," a term Thoreau—that rooted Transcendentalist—defined in his essay "Walking." Finding it derived from a word for idle people who roved about the country in the Middle Ages asking charity under the pretense of going *à la Sainte Terre,* he thought of himself—and hence, I thought of myself—as wandering toward some Holy Land. That's what I was up to wandering the American landscape. Alternatively, he thought the word may have come from "*sans terre,* without land or home, which, therefore, in the good sense, will mean having no particular home, but equally at home everywhere" (657). Socrates said the same thing. He was a citizen of the world. I adopted this rationale as well. I was cosmopolitan, not of any provincial locale. But today, *Webster's* derives "saunterer" from a Middle English word meaning "to muse," and to be honest the musing I've done in my wandering has risen out of a hunger for home.

   Fueled by a struggle to find my right livelihood—a calling to worthwhile work—I'd begun four wildly disparate careers: classical guitarist, yogic monk, lawyer, and now poet and teacher. Being unsettled in work kept me from settling in a place where I could be still enough to begin to take a look around in a more sustained manner than itinerancy allowed. Two of these careers took me particularly far away from landscape and a sense of place. As a yogic monk, a *sanyassi* in a Tantric tradition I was pursuing during and after college, I would have been an itinerant teacher, traveling constantly, without a home, again ostensibly at home everywhere. But after several years I came to realize that this lack of rootedness only reinforced a focus on transcendence of the world, a belief that the phenomenal world is a trap—illusion, *Maya*. And the poet cloistered in my heart felt Frost's phrase was right, that "earth's the place for love." To be cut off from the earth was too high a price to pay, and so I never took my final vows.

My second career, lawyering, was little better, its rationalistic language rarely connected to the earth, rarely connected to feeling. For ten years I fought Atlanta traffic and at work wielded verbal abstractions, while on weekends I sought refuge in the north Georgia mountains, trying to get the kindling relit beneath a buried poetic life. I read Studs Terkel's *Working* and saw how few people of any race, class, or gender found truly fulfilling work. I read J. R. Krishnamurti, who maintained that the purpose of education is to help young people find what it is they love to do. And when one finds what one loves to do and does it no matter what the cost, he promised, one's work brings deep satisfaction. Now, years later, having found work that I love, I am just beginning to understand how much this settling down, this satisfaction, this sitting, allows us to move more deeply into the world. Feeling secure enough within ourselves allows us to be able to see the world more fully, more compassionately, to face its wounds as well as its beauty.

May 2003. Jennifer is working in her study. It's evening. We've had dinner. The dishes are done. I am out back putting in an herb garden. The sun lingers, saffron at the ridges of the west. The air cool. Krishna helps me dig. With her paws, she digs furiously, buries her nose, snorts, jumps up, runs around, barks, comes back, and digs again in the same place. I've turned over the dirt of an east-facing slope, taken out the grass, made three terraces, carried white river stones to support the terraces and make a border. Now I am breaking the earth with my hands. It is dark, cool, soft, and crumbly. I let it run through my fingers. A warm breeze moves through the garden, through this warm-cool evening in half-light drenched with some sweet ungraspable memory from childhood.

June 2003. I have hiked high above Winter-Tea Rock to the high ridges of the Bears. After a half hour of meditation, I open my eyes and look out over the valley. I realize I am beginning to think of this place, this valley, as home—beginning to accept the possibility that my transient life may have come to rest. I see how my finding home has been a molting—shedding false selves, false-hoods, cowls of one kind or another, letting go of fears. This molting reached a crisis one December night before we had Krishna. Jennifer and I were driving home late from a party in Pocatello, an hour's drive on two-lane Highway 91, mourning the loss of a close friend, Ford Swetnam. I had been teaching at Idaho State University and had become close to Ford, a fellow poet and hiker of the mountains. His death affected me profoundly. We were descending the long hill to the bottom of the Bear River canyon, beneath the otherwise flat plain bordered in the distance by Oxford Peak. The land was snow covered, the road relatively clear. As we started across the Bear River bridge, something leapt into the headlights. Before I could hit the brakes, it thudded against the front bumper and ricocheted against the rail of the bridge. We were stunned. Jennifer started crying, "We hit a dog! We hit a dog!" We pulled over, turned around, and drove back. It was still in the lane. I got out. Another solitary car stopped. We walked up to the dog. It was obviously dead. A big black Lab, already stiff.

"I hit it," I said.

"It must have died instantly," the couple reassured.

We pulled it over to the side of the road, and the young couple drove off. There were no houses in sight. A dirt road led to a cluster of trailers in a distant stand of trees, but it was dark over there. We decided not to go knocking on doors in the middle of the night. We drove home.

As I drove home, as we pulled into the garage, as we got ready for bed, as we lay together, the sense of the violence in the event grew inside me. The dog wore a red collar. When I was a child, we had a black Lab named Blackjack. I began sobbing. I lay on my side, Jennifer holding me, and I began to let out huge breaths, huge sobs. I cried and cried for that dog, and before long I was crying not only for the dog, but for Ford and for my divorce, for my abandoned careers, for friends I'd made and left, all the leave-takings I'd done. A channel of feelings broke open, and years of stored up grief came pouring out. I'd not felt tears pour out of my eyes like that since childhood. Today, I think these deadened feelings resurfaced and broke out as a result of the growing sense of security I was beginning to feel in finding a home here in Cache Valley. Feeling I'd found my home, I felt safe enough to release this powerful wave of feelings. And in turn, releasing such blocked emotions cleared out an opening in which I could really begin to see the place I've begun to call home, like the woman in Levine's book who finally saw the wall for the first time.

The next day I went back to see the dog. To see if I could find its owners. More snow had fallen. The morning was gray and chilly. I drove down the hill to the bridge. The dog lay there by the side of the road. Still wearing its collar. No tag. I pulled it farther off the road to an open place where it could easily be seen. A deep rawness moved inside me. A car pulled up. Someone from the trailers. I ask if he knew whose it was. "No. Sorry, Son." I felt hollow inside, yet a feeling of peace was there, too.

Standing by the bridge, I looked across the river and saw a historical marker I'd driven by almost daily for three years but never stopped to really take a look at it. The monument commemorated the Bear River Massacre—a massacre of a band of Shoshone Indians by the U.S. Cavalry in 1863. Today, however, I went over to see it. Under the command of a Colonel Patrick Conner, the cavalry committed one of the largest massacres of native peoples in the West, though the event received little attention because of the nation's preoccupation with the Civil War. I went home and began to do some research.

Cache Valley, this green jewel resting above the vast desert-wilderness of Utah, had long been home to the Shoshone. They called the Logan River "The River of the Cranes," and then, as now, sandhill cranes, along with a great population of resident and migratory birds, made the valley a permanent or temporary home. Mormon settlers began arriving in the 1850s, taking over the valley, cutting trees, irrigating, carving up the land on the strict Mormon grid of horizontal and vertical lines, building fences, farms, towns. Soon the settlers had appropriated all the land and all the water. The Shoshone were pushed north, out onto the less fertile, more desertlike northern end of the valley. Before long, some of the young Shoshone men began to strike back. After a number of raids and killings, the settlers raised a hue and cry, and the government sent Connor in to pacify the "hostile Indians." It is well to remember that here, as in other places in the West, military actions against native peoples were often not top-down government affairs, but actions initiated by the settlers, by ordinary folk.

At 6:00 a.m. on that cold January morning of 1863, Connor's troops attacked the Shoshone village. When a straight-on attack was repelled and twenty-three soldier casualties were suffered, the army circled, shooting indiscriminately into the village. Eventually the Shoshone ran out of ammunition. The soldiers moved in, slaughtering men, women, children, the elderly. Raping, mutilating, murdering. Afterwards, the settlers gave thanks, seeing "the movement of Colonel Connor as the intervention of the Almighty."

In Levine's book, a woman in chronic pain said two kinds of people came to visit her. One kind could never sit still, would keep moving about, shifting things around, sitting down, getting up, opening and closing the window, inquiring what she needed. "'But they couldn't stay long with my pain.' They had no room in their hearts for her pain, she said, because they had no room in their hearts for their own." Another kind didn't try to fix her or give her anything or take anything away, and if she were so uncomfortable she couldn't even be touched, they could just sit there with her silently. "They had room for my pain because they had room for their own" (10). Looking back on the night that I killed that dog, I can see how letting out that reservoir of grief I'd carried inside began a healing that opened my heart and enabled me to see other, greater losses around me. As the grief I'd carried was released, I had room in my heart to see the wounds in the land around me. When I stopped running away from my own pain, I could begin paying attention to the place where I was living, to open to *what is*—its pain and loss as well as its beauty. And once I started to see that pain, I started to ask how to care for the place I was beginning to call home.

June 2003. I close my eyes as Rae Ann reads her poem. The soft timbre and the falling cadences of her voice lull me to a place of great peace, and her poem as always ends with a powerful turn. The women around the table listen attentively. All praise when she finishes. Rae Ann is the best poet in the creative writing class I teach at the Pocatello Women's Correctional Center. She's been coming to the class for three years now. The first day I went to teach at the prison, she walked in wearing flat shoes, a long gray pony tail, and introduced herself, looking into my eyes with her bright, serene, gray eyes, and I thought to myself, "This woman must be a Buddhist priest." During the last three years, she has written powerful, moving, healing poems. She and the other women share horrifying traumas, terrible losses of children and family, conflicts, rages, bringing to the surface their grief and injuries, bearing witness to their lives, clearing a place for healing, for creativity, for seeing. There are many tears in the class.

I am learning that finding a right livelihood and a place to be may finally end in what we have to give. Making a home and doing one's work can meet in how we care for place. I become interested in how to protect the quiet trail to Winter-Tea Rock from the menace of machines, in how to protect the Bear Mountains, Cache Valley, Idaho, Utah, the Rockies. The arc of caring widens. Places to act appear everywhere. Frederick Buechner said, "The place God calls you to is the place where your own deep gladness and the world's deep hunger meet" (95).

November 2003. Krishna and I have hiked the trail to Winter-Tea Rock in seven inches of snow. Light comes late, and we have hiked under stars through moonlight. From above the Thorne Spring watershed, I see far out across the valley, the Wellsville Mountains in the distance white and blue. To come again and again to the same mountains, to take the same trail over and over, is new to me. I've watched the progression of wildflowers through spring and summer and fall. Now the aspens etch the blue peaks with gold, and the maples run red and orange down the nearly vertical streambeds. Snow lies around us, blue and white, and now that the sun has crested the mountains, it glitters with prisms in all directions. The sun warms my feet and body. The river roars. Clouds break on the high ridges like waves rolling in, cling to the canyon walls and cliffs—Tu Fu scenes, I think. The sky is clear to the north and west and shows blues of many hues—royal, pastel, seashell, blue jay, kingfisher. The whole world seems a great blessing of the dawn. I look right at the sun. Apollo crests the peaks, Aurora already fled. All is silence except for puffs of snow falling from a cedar. Our first sun in weeks. Krishna runs through the snow with joy, black against the white, then sits in the snow looking at me with her one blue eye, mysterious, lupine.

January 1, 2004. We are pulling into a rental car return at the Atlanta airport and get a call on our cell phone from our housesitter, a graduate student who's been caring for our house and animals for a week while we're in North Carolina. As I pull into the car return queue, Jennifer exclaims, "What? What? Krishna got hit by a car!" She starts to cry. *"Is she dead?* Oh, my God! Oh, my God!" She looks at me with desperate eyes. She gives me the phone. She gets out of the car. I get out. I speak into the phone. "Krishna got hit by a car?" Jennifer keeps asking, "*Is she dead? Is she dead?*" The Avis people are gathering around. I ask, "What happened? Is she dead?" A pause. "Yes." I repeat, "Yes," to Jennifer, and she starts screaming. Crying. Stomping on the pavement around the cars lined up at Avis. I try to hold her, but she keeps stomping around, crying, "*She's dead? How can she be dead?*" I tell the people our dog has gotten run over. Jennifer, who is so very tenderhearted, is almost hysterical, crying. "*Why? Why our puppy? Why our Krishna?*"

An Avis employee, a kind woman, offers to take us to the terminal in her car so we won't have to ride the shuttle. Jennifer cries the whole way. I've steeled myself, holding back my feelings, waiting through the long hours until we get home, until I have a place. On the way home from the Salt Lake City Airport I start to cry. We both cry for days. Remembering, naming all the things we loved about her.

The month before, I'd read *The Mind on Fire,* a biography of Emerson. After the death of his son, he said, "Home is where your dead are." But we can't even bury Krishna in our yard because she was disposed of in a local landfill before we could return.

June 2004. I'm home alone with Aidan, our three-month-old son. Pippin, our new border-collie, black-Lab mix, who "Four Paws," the adoption center, said was Krishna's brother, sleeps at my feet. A different dog. Krishna would get inside a UPS truck and happily wait to be driven away. Pippin, having been abandoned, mistreated, and picked up by the pound, is sweet beyond reckoning but fiercely protective of home. He stays by me twenty-four hours a day, unless Jennifer is nursing Aidan, and then he's there beside them, no matter where I am. If Aidan cries in his swing or crib, Pippin goes and lies down beside him, licking his face if we don't get there first to say, "Pippin. No licks."

I've warmed the milk Jennifer left for me and fed Aidan. When he's taking his milk, he stares into my eyes without looking away. We play for half an hour. Now he's tired. He's crying. I think he cries too much. Then, I remember how recently he's come from the womb. I remember how Terry Tempest Williams said our mother's womb is the first landscape we inhabit (50). I think of how Aidan was connected to the landscape of his mother, a place of utter interbeing. How our own connection to our landscape is really no less total, if less visible. I hold Aidan to comfort him. I think of how we learn to be accommodated to isolation, separateness, aloneness. How we then have to unlearn this alienation on our path and open the gates of healing, to resuture our bond with the earth, with each other.

August 2004. I watch my breath. The morning air warms slowly, returning from its thirty-degree diurnal swing. Aidan sleeps on his blanket beside me and Pippin beside him. I watch my breath, entering the space that opens out within, breath poured into the universe like milk poured from a pitcher to a bowl. A vast place beyond the limited self, a place of healing, of pure being, union, of ecstasy. Words fall apart. After a time, I open my eyes, see the world, and write in my journal.

Above Bear River

High among canyon cliffs, sunflowers
follow the sun, sway against junipers, sage.
Early summer air. Mountain
bluebirds, yellow warblers flit above us.
On his fourth hike, Aidan, three months old,
sleeps on a blue blanket. Pippin, our border collie,
stretches out beside him after his puppy chow.
Already we've seen a doe with fawns, swallows
arcing down cliffs, white pelicans on the Bear River,
heard coyotes on the pass.
Aidan starts to cry. I change him,
then read him some
Hsieh Ling-yün.
The Tao opens,
like a sunflower and we are
floating,
three feathers
through canyon splendor.
I gather up our things
hoist Aidan up in his backpack
and we pick our way

down the rocky, dusty slope,
Aidan's temple at my chest,
new eyes bright toward a new world
of orange cliffs, blue peaks,
blowing clouds,
his little ears learning
the sound of the Bear roaring below us.

Bibliography

Emerson, Ralph Waldo. *Nature.* 1836. *Ralph Waldo Emerson: Essays and Lectures.* New York: Library of America, 1983. 5–49.

Fleisher, Kass. *The Bear River Massacre and the Making of History.* New York: SUNY, 2004.

Hanh, Thich Nhat. *Essential Writings.* Maryknoll, NY: Orbis, 2001.

Krishnamurti, J.R. *Think on These Things.* New York: Harper, 1989.

Levine, Stephen. *Healing into Life and Death.* New York: Anchor, 1989.

Madsen, Brigham D. *The Shoshoni Frontier and the Bear River Massacre.* Salt Lake City: U of Utah P, 1985.

Oliver, Mary. *West Wind.* Boston: Houghton, 1997.

Richardson, Robert. *Emerson: The Mind on Fire.* Berkeley: U of California P, 1996.

Terkel, Studs. *Working.* New York: Random, 1984.

Thoreau, Henry David. "Walking." *Atlantic Monthly* 9 (June 1862): 657–74.

The Utah History Encyclopedia. Ed. Allen Kent Powell. Salt Lake City: U of Utah P, 1994.

Williams, Terry Tempest. *Refuge: An Unnatural History of Family and Place.* New York: Vintage, 1992.

4
Valley Language

Diana Garcia

What do I remember, and why do I choose to remember it? I am in my senior year of high school, waiting for word on whether and where I will go to college. A heavy fug of manure and alfalfa drifts through the windows. Sweaty adolescents strain to follow algebraic logic. Or is it chemistry? If it is chemistry and memory betrays me, it is for good reason. I never mastered the slide rule. Less than fifty yards away, on the other side of a fence, the water company's cattle chew alfalfa and sprawl on native grasses. Their deep lows of contentment serve as bass to the audible and frustrated sighs of classmates. We are responding to a quiz. It might be a Wednesday. I do not sigh. I am the nervous plodder, trying to erase the stigma of being labeled "Zero" Garcia after my first geometry quiz my sophomore year. Theorems and quadratic equations: for the rest of my life, I will argue I do not need to know them. I will never enter a profession that requires either skill.

At this moment, though, I dream of attending UC Santa Barbara, a place of natural beauty and fresh coastal breezes. I will read fine books beneath protected stands of pine, indulge in fresh seafood on the pier, and meditate on the beach at sunrise. The dream I do not have is that of marrying and having children. I am aware that, unlike my friends, I do not write "Mrs. Juan Mendoza" in my binder. I do not talk about weddings or how many children I will have. Instead, in my dreams I travel to distant continents where no one speaks English or Spanish. Too bad my dreams don't indicate how I will pay for all this travel.

The dream I never share with anyone is that of attending Brown University in Rhode Island. I imagine myself following the steps of

Hiawatha and Thoreau, losing myself in second-generation forests, wandering alongside a burbling creek, descending to the mouth of roaring rivers. This East Coast mystery of green and water is nothing like the San Joaquin Valley with its endless stretch of numbing dirt, sky, and sun. Only in winter, when the tule fog lifts and swirls through reconfigured orchards of misshapen and denuded fig trees, does the valley come close to my imagined fantasies.

But back to reality. Here, the valley begins to sweat in ninety-degree weather by 10:00 a.m. The only coastal breezes with which I am familiar are those on the Monterey coast, quick day trips we take midsummer when the heat gives the younger of my two brothers a bloody nose. I can't imagine my parents letting their teenage daughter move clear across the continent. I can't imagine living on the East Coast either. Afraid to stray too far from home, in August I will enroll at Fresno State College, fifty-five miles away. In a quirk of cosmic irony, I will get pregnant a year later, become a single mother on welfare. (Perhaps it's just as well; I might not have experienced motherhood otherwise.)

I will move to San Diego, get off welfare, and get a job at Children's Hospital; I will join the working poor on half-hour freeway commutes. When hunger for soil and brindled cows overwhelms me, I will drive an hour east to the Cuyamaca Mountains, take deep breaths of meadow and sage. During all of this, I will spend sixteen years taking courses at San Diego State before I finally graduate with my BA. It takes me that long to believe in my own dreams. Years later, I will tell students in my courses, may this never happen to you.

Return to an earlier time when I spoke Spanish. In the farm labor camp where my parents lived and worked when I was born, my aunts and uncles, my godparents, my cousins, everyone I knew spoke Spanish. Consigned to small cabins perched on the banks of the Bear Creek, it was hard not to feel a strong connectedness to soil and water. Ripening peach orchards on one side and tomato fields on the other, guitars strumming in the background, I knew who I was—*mija*, beloved daughter. That language of familial love was the litany of daily life, the sounds of the creek, the scent of ripening fruit, all part of the valley's own liturgy.

But that life, that sense of connectedness to valley and community, changed at age five when I became Karen, not Diana. Having experienced their own share of racial discrimination when they were in school, at my birth my parents had given me a first name they hoped would spare me some of the humiliations their own first names—Manuel and Tomasa—had engendered. At home, my family called me by my middle name, Diana, pronounced "Thee-ah-nah," accent over the first *a*. Sometime before my first day in kindergarten, my mother must have explained to me that when I started school, I would become Karen. She must have told me something like, "When the teacher calls the name 'Karen Garcia,' raise your hand and answer 'here.'" Dutiful child, I'm sure that's exactly what I did.

Years later, when I ask my mother why they gave me the first name Karen but always called me Diana, she explains that they thought Karen sounded more American, more professional. At age five, I must have pondered these changes. No longer surrounded by family at the labor camp, we had moved to Merced, to a house not far from my grammar school. Nestled in a swing I'd make by twisting together lengths of branches from the weeping willow in our backyard, I'd shoot up, lean back to study an expanse of sky, clouds I could transform into specific shapes even as I contemplated my own transformation. I did not know why I needed to become Karen to start school, but even at such a young age, I must have realized there was something not right about being Diana, something you did not want to be. I must have sensed that being Karen was better. Of such small but critical moments do we develop initial perceptions of a self. Instead of feeling self-confident and comfortable entering school, I must have felt a dissonance between my home life and my school life, between being my parents' daughter and becoming a student, between living in the labor camp and moving into town.

As if it weren't enough that I had to leave the comfort of the camp, then change to fit the name Karen, I also had to undergo the transformation of speaking English instead of Spanish. I had learned English well enough to make friends on the monkey bars my first day of kindergarten, but I was raised a proper Mexican American child; I answered in the language in which I was addressed, and at home, this was in Spanish. As a result, my conversational Spanish was better than my conversational English. Also, I had been raised to be respectful to my elders, to cast my eyes down and not speak unless directly addressed. My kindergarten teacher had feared that my silence and timidity during class discussions was a symptom of deeper learning problems. At the beginning of first grade, I was shocked to learn I had been placed in junior first, a half step between kindergarten and first grade. When my mother learned what had happened, she marched me back to school and made me read aloud in English. I was reinstated to a proper first grade, but my parents never let us speak Spanish at home again. Although my father was more comfortable, more articulate, more poetic in Spanish, we became an English-speaking family.

Again, I cannot explain the process that occurred. I barely remember the moment I became Karen at school—Karen, a name centered somewhere north of Scandinavia; not Diana, redolent of sage cracking through dirt in August. I've lost the memory of a time when I spoke Spanish and English both at home and in my neighborhood but then switched to an English-only life beginning in first grade.

To understand what happened during those early grammar school years, I draw on my relationship to the San Joaquin Valley. In summer, the valley stretches endlessly, bordered by coastal hills to the west and the Sierra Nevada foothills to the east. Standing motionless in the middle of a cotton or a tomato field, I must have felt what the French scientist and philosopher Gaston Bachelard describes as that "[i]mmensity . . . within ourselves" in his book, *The Poetics of Space* (184). That "inner immensity" allowed me to focus on the smallest details of a fig orchard canopy, how it loomed above and around me, yet spit me out to that expansive valley at the end of the day (185). At another level, I drew on my experience of tule fogs—how, if I walked three feet in any direction, I lost all sense of where I had been. The valley cocooned me and obscured me, swallowed me and challenged my imagination.

Not surprisingly, in a region of such cultural and geographic extremes, reading became my crutch and my escape. By third grade I was a classic bookworm. When I read, I became one of the characters in the book. I was present. I could visualize each scene, hear the accents and intonations each character used, breathe the scents of a world of foods coming from each kitchen.

My first experience with a library was the small stone building next to the Merced County Fairgrounds. I fell in love with the smell of books lining old bookshelves and the odor of furniture polish lifting from the checkout counter. The children's section was in back, two steps up from the rest of the building. Two small windows offered a pale light blocked in part by a mature pine to one side of the yard. The adult section was in front, the first section I saw as I walked through the door. That was the section I yearned for, with books over a half-inch thick and no pictures to get in the way of the ideas and images. One of the first books I read from the adult section was Pearl S. Buck's *The Good Earth*. I can still smell the steam rising from the rice bowls, feel the shape of the bowl in my hands. From John Steinbeck's *Cannery Row*, I learned to envy a life spent collecting marine samples from Monterey Bay, marine life as diverse and interconnected as those of the local residents whose stories he also told. The scent of seaweed and drying mollusks filled my nostrils.

I checked out three, four, five, six books at a time, the numbers increasing as the librarian became familiar with my passion for reading. I was voracious. I read before and after school, before bed, after lights out. My parents refused to let me read during meals. In fact, my reading became a worry for them. They began throwing me out of the house, ordering me outside into the sun and fresh air. I learned to sneak a book under my shirt, then climb the apricot tree in the backyard where I could read without interruption. From my perch, I selected the ripest, rosiest apricots, their perfume thundering up my nose and mouth. I had a bird's-eye view of the comings and goings in the alley behind our house and in our neighbors' yards. Or, at least I might have if I had had better vision. Instead, I guessed by size and shape who was coming out of Helen's back door, who was coming to Sammy's house, which brother was chasing which sister directly next door. The neighborhood goings-on became the backdrop for my growing relationship to writers and their books.

All that reading, all those disparate bits of information that filtered through these books quickly paid off. Beginning in fifth grade, I was bused east of the first set of tracks to attend a program for gifted children. Ostracized by my brothers, cousins, and old elementary school friends for leaving our side of town, I rode the bus with my grammar school friend, Victoria. We collected at the bus stop each morning, relishing the crisp October air and despairing in January's damp fog. This passage from the west side to the east side of town delivered me to an almost-all-white class. All the other children on the bus, including Victoria, were going to the MR class—that's what my friends and busmates were called, mentally retarded.

From that bus, we filed past the talented jeers of students, some my new classmates. I veered right, into the gifted classroom. I was protected from the longer walk my busmates took, a walk the length of the school to the portable classrooms parked on the former basketball court. I remember my sense of relief at the spared embarrassment from the vicious humiliations. It was bad enough that the larger student body considered those of us in the gifted program a bunch of brains, that my own brothers and cousins ostracized me. It was bad enough that my new classmates tolerated my presence but never invited me into their social circles. After all, I was not a member of their Brownie (later, Girl Scouts) troops; I did not attend any of the grammar schools they attended on the good side of town. Thank goodness, I thought, I was not one of the mentally retarded students as well.

That first year on the bus, Victoria and I whispered about our catechism class, about the nuns who directed us in choir. She told me who got her first kiss behind the parish hall, who climbed the water tower and panicked halfway up. I remember her descriptions of ghosts shaped by fog—this one a boy looking for a dog, that one a dog hiding from a boy. Hers was delicious gossip, frightening stories, possible endings that unnerved me in brightest daylight. I admired her sharp dissection of some of the students who lined the sidewalk. She kept her head up, her back straight, as we walked from the bus, hand in hand. When the time came to separate, I'd watch as her shoulders slumped. The contrast pained me. She was the most beautiful girl in my grade.

Now I'll tell you two facts: Victoria, my friend and bus companion, was not dumb. She was smarter than I was at math. Next, her family spoke Spanish. Hers was a formal and hierarchical tongue: the *Ud.* for parents, elders, anyone in authority; *tu* for the rest of us. Victoria was raised to stay silent when spoken to unless commanded to speak. She was raised to keep her head bowed, to keep her voice low, her eyes averted, not to appear challenging or aggressive when confronted by adults. Unlike Victoria, at my parents' insistence, I had learned the language of parity: there was no formal *you* in English. I did not know how to teach her what I had learned. Years later, the first time I saw an oystercatcher, its glossy black feathers reminded me of Victoria's hair. What was not to admire? Her Indian features, her dark skin, her slight build, hinted at ancestors older than mine.

The classmates in my gifted class knew nothing about Victoria. Their fathers were dentists, mayors, judges. They would graduate, move away to college, marry well (or not), and succeed (or not). Sometime in eighth grade, Victoria disappeared. She left school, and I never saw her again. The taunts and humiliations shamed her. At home, she was a good girl, respectful, honest, hardworking. At school, she was the girl whose accent and diction proclaimed her dumb, not worthy of more than the barest attention. I imagine her in class, lifting her head to study the shape and silence of fog, study how she might disappear into it.

Children of those who walk in heat and soil, offspring of those with little or no education, have no connection to a language that speaks to them from radio and television, from the mouths of those who stand in front of a classroom or behind the counter at a bank. Heads bowed, eyes lowered, their body speaks of respect for those in authority. Authority does not recognize their primal language of survival.

Victoria disappeared. I almost disappeared, too. A teenage pregnancy, welfare, single motherhood ahead of me, I was little different. What gifted me was the importance of hard work, modeled by both my parents. What inspired me were the memories of books I'd read, universes I'd devoured, information to be learned. What saved me was knowledge of tomatoes ripe on the vine, how fine bristles prickle when you lift them, unlock those last fruits steamed in heat, soil, rot. The message of meadowlarks and red-winged blackbirds nurtured me, the beauty of a valley's sunrise, the sharp sting of snowmelt as I drifted the Merced River, waves of lightning hitting Half Dome in the distance. This valley and the sierra to the east taught me a focused gaze and close attention to detail. I learned to raise my head, look teachers in the eye, pattern the cadence of my voice to theirs, read and write in precise, calculated words. I could imagine a world beyond the valley, peopled with characters as complex as any I had savored in a book.

In my midthirties, now living in San Diego, my intermediate-composition professor told me I was one of the best writers he had had in years. (Perhaps it was my glowing review of Woody Allen's film, *The Purple Rose of Cairo*. I admit, I'm a sucker for fantasy.) He recommended I take an introduction to creative writing course from a colleague, a well-known poet. I took that advice the following semester, and the universe opened itself to me. Although I always had enjoyed writing, no one had ever told me I was a gifted writer. That first creative writing course was the greatest gift—apart from family and friends—I had ever received.

I spent the semester in an avalanche of creativity, churning out draft after draft towards each assignment, goading myself to find the precise words to express an idea, develop each image, flesh out my characters. I peopled my stories with the valley's soil, the mute fog, the dense stillness of a field at dawn. Tomatoes ripened on the page, rose from a bowl of salsa, bathed in a steaming canning jar. Despite the intervening years, the transformation from Diana to Karen, the loss of Spanish as my home language, the loss of Victoria and others like her, despite all the numbing jobs, I had retained an elemental relationship to the valley. My nostrils stung once again with memories of dry soil on a hot August afternoon. I had found my way home.

Before dawn each morning, from my dining room window I shared my writing space with the skunks, raccoons, squirrels, and foxes that roamed my yard, seeking an overlooked avocado. I'd spy as the day's raccoon hauled his find to the leaking sprinkler and carefully washed the dirt and white fly residue from the peel. Skunks peered through the window, reassured themselves that I wasn't planning to give chase. Through the dappled light that shifted through the avocado's canopy, I contemplated a future of such mornings, hours of writing that would stretch into weeks and books of poetry. The blue plumbago glowed as if lit by black lights, and the eucalyptus spread its incense over the house. I knew myself blessed, rough drafts spread across the table, surrounded by the fruit of my own tree, spied on by the denizens of the canyon below.

At the end of the semester, the professor approached me outside of class to tell me I had written "the best damned stories in the class—the shittiest poems but the best short stories." He asked me what my major was. At the time, I was personnel manager for an electronics research, development, and manufacturing firm in San Diego's Golden Triangle. Out of necessity a practical individual, I was a business major with an emphasis on business psychology. Before that, I'd been a journalism major, before that, a Spanish major, and before that, an English major.

Now he said to me, "You should be a writer." I felt as if I were standing outside my body digesting the words. The planet had sprouted beneath my feet, exposing a whole other world, one I never imagined existed for me. I heard myself ask, "But how would I survive?" Again, practicality before dreams. And he said, "You could do what I do." He couldn't have stunned me more than if he'd hit me with a full-on tackle. This tall, burly man with silvery hair, his bright cheeks and blue eyes a perfect model for Santa Claus, was making an outrageous assertion: I could do what he did. How could I do that when I had placed him—along with other accomplished writers and highly regarded professors—on a pedestal? These were larger-than-life individuals. I knew they didn't shop for groceries or jump-start their cars.

After all, this was 1986. The only Chicano writers whose work I'd read were Alurista, Gary Soto, and Richard Rodriguez. My literary godmothers—Ana Castillo, Pat Mora, Denise Chavez, Sandra Cisneros—were unknown to me at the time. A part of me must have wondered who would want to read what I might write, who would be interested. Another part of me must have shouted, *Yes! Finally, someone will want to read about the lives of people like me and my parents, the generations-long struggle for respect and equity.*

I took a second course, a fiction workshop, the following fall. At the end of the semester, I called my professor at 7:00 a.m. and announced I was changing my major to English with a creative writing emphasis. A decade later, she would tell me that her heart stuck in her throat when she took that call, thinking to herself, *What have I done? This woman has a wonderful job. Headhunters are approaching her with amazing offers.* To her credit, she bit her tongue and instead gave me advice on courses to take in the coming year. A year later, at the suggestion of this same professor, I would travel to El Paso and interview Pat Mora. I would search out the *comadres* whose work would become my touchstone. Eventually I would earn an MFA in creative writing and produce an award-winning collection of poetry.

I think of the composition professor and the two poets at San Diego State and wonder if they realize the depth of my gratitude to them. I visit my former poetry professor every few years, the one who told me I wrote "the shittiest poems," and update him on my latest adventures. What I've never told him, what I want to tell him, is that for thirty-five years, I struggled to find a place for myself in the universe. Then, when I wasn't looking, when I had resigned myself to plowing the fields of industry, he and his colleagues offered me entry into the world of writing and, by extension, the world of the academe. Much like finding my life's partner after dating dozens of people, in the end, a chance observation offered me the opportunity to take all I had ever learned and experienced and apply myself to what might become an unexpected and highly fulfilling venture.

In 1994, I finally realized my dream to live on the East Coast. At Central Connecticut State University, where I taught for four years,

I stood beneath a copper beech in autumn and let the amber tones highlight my skin. I learned about pignut and mock nut and shagbark hickory. The closest I came to Hiawatha's setting was when I canoed the Farmington River and picnicked beneath Connecticut's iconic oak. In one of my braver moments, I rock climbed with a group of students and learned the allure of traprock. I survived one hundred inches of snow my first winter and drove forty miles in an ice storm to buy the ingredients for making tamales on Christmas Eve. Who knows? If I had stayed, I might have become an avid cross-country skier. I never paid a visit to Walden Pond. I never overcame a deep homesickness for the scent of sage on a summer day.

I am now at California State University–Monterey Bay, a one-time army fort, where cypress and pine bend to the wind while scrub oaks wave mossy beards in the fog. We traded army recruits for students, guns for books. Once faculty and students alike survive the initial cold, wet, stormy shock of this spot on the peninsula, we learn to take pride in our transformed surroundings. We imagine harnessing stories of war, earthquake, and the Monterey coast to produce an academic culture as sturdy and flexible as the surrounding maritime chaparral.

Teaching in the university's Creative Writing and Social Action Program satisfies my deepest desire: the desire to teach students whose backgrounds render them invisible in high school; students willing to address the shame and embarrassment that come from living lives of poverty; students willing to dream and be ambitious for themselves and their communities. Each time a young woman from Michoacán describes her academic journey, how no one had ever suggested she could go to college until a high school counselor or someone from a college outreach program approached her, I think of Victoria. I couldn't save my childhood friend. I refuse to let any of my students disappear.

In fall 2001, I taught a course called "Pesticides and Beyond: Policies and Practices Affecting Area Farm Workers." In that course, students were required to spend thirty hours at a field site in the greater Salinas Valley—either a legal assistance center, a public health clinic, or the United Farm Workers (UFW) research center. Their service learning brought them to the lettuce fields at dawn, wind and drizzle a stark introduction to the toil faced by the workers they would interview and photograph. They watched as a group of men heated tortillas on a *comal* that, days earlier, had served as the cover to a 33-gallon drum of toxic oils. My students were shocked into realizing that, even as they were rising from their dorm beds to head to the beach for a half day of surfing, these men were rising from sleeping bags soaked from fog, their only shelter tarps strung between an old van and a rusted truck.

In addition to their site work, students read about the toxic legacy that pesticide use imposes on field-workers and their children. Three of the eighteen students in the class were themselves the children of farmworkers. Their shock and dismay when reading the assigned nonfiction books and research studies were palpable. They remembered signs similar to those depicted in black-and-white photographs illustrating chapters on pesticide poisoning, signs reading *Peligro: Se Prohibe Entrar*, like the signs posted at the edge of fields where they had worked and played. The assigned short stories, poems, and essays reconnected the entire class to the decency and humanity they needed to complete the course. Their time at their service-learning sites bonded them to the Salinas Valley, its expanse of just-disked fields.

In addition to their service learning and their extensive readings, they wrote several original pieces—poems, short stories, creative nonfiction—using details from their service work to document the struggles their characters faced. At the end of the semester, we held a public reading at the Salinas Community Complex. Attending were the medical director of La Clinica de Salud del Valle de Salinas, the largest public health clinic in California; the head of the UFW Research Center; and the directors and codirectors of the two legal clinics, California Rural Legal Assistance (CRLA) and the Watsonville Law Center. We lined the walls with oversized black-and-white photos of farmworkers, their children, and their homes. The students read their stories, poems, and essays, bringing voice to their own and the workers' experiences.

The immediacy and applicability of this kind of learning yield practical and long-lasting results. One student was hired upon graduation as a research assistant for the Watsonville Law Center. He intends to go to law school. Another student produced a sample brochure on the care and treatment of asthmatic children for the health clinic, combining and updating materials from all seven satellite clinics. She is now in an MFA program in creative writing. A third student worked as a community liaison for an area state assemblyman before leaving for a graduate program in public policy. Two of these three students are the children of farmworkers; both intend to return to the Salinas Valley. They want to help change the policies and practices affecting farm workers, but they also write that they miss the seasonal crop rotations, the fields of newly sprouted strawberry and lettuce shimmering against purpling hills. I assure them that if they write the stories, describe the conditions, claim a relationship to the soil and the right to speak out against the injustices, they will never lose this sense of place. The valley's air thunders in their hearts.

You can't put a price on the impression such images and experiences can make. When students visit me in my office, I pay close attention to those who pay close attention to the books on my shelves. I listen for the hunger in a voice that asks, "Are these all yours?" and then, "Have you read all of them?" Like food, I want to say, each book is like food. Hopefully one day they will all have banks of books to feed that hunger. Even more, however, I hope more students will have the opportunity to witness the lived realities of those who toil to make our lives easier, to be able to draw parallels between what they witness and what they read and write.

A longer time ago, before my grandparents arrived in the San Joaquin Valley, early explorers wrote of inland lakes so large that waves rose and fell with the tides. Waves gave way to tule rushes. Rushes gave way to meadows of wild iris and blue-eyed grass. Banks of golden poppies studded with stands of shooting rockets flanked lupine sloping east. In spring, vernal ponds teemed with fairy shrimp. Much of this landscape has disappeared, replaced by irrigation ditches, canals, and rows upon rows of melons, artichokes, peppers, and garlic. These early explorers and settlers spoke and wrote in Spanish, their words translated into English centuries later, our only record of what has been lost. No one taught these explorers' diaries in my classes. Their descriptions and stories still are not taught in California's kindergarten-through-twelfth-grade history curriculum, a stunning example of insensitivity in a state whose culture and history are indelibly marked by Spanish and Mexican settlement.

The San Joaquin Valley tried to teach me slide rules. The lessons never stuck. What stuck was the reality of hot days measured by rows of cotton and expanses of fig trees awaiting harvest. What stuck was that to survive in this culture, the language of privilege is English; success is measured in dollars and how many influential individuals you know. How do I survive knowing the loss of so many without influence? How can I survive knowing how little value we place on the environment that nurtures us? How will all our stories survive?

One day, I tell myself, a woman my age, a bit shorter, straight-haired, will stop me on a downtown street. She will salute me in Spanish, glance up to see if I have recognized her. When that moment of recognition occurs, I will take her hand the way I did when we were ten years old. We will walk to the nearest bench. We will mourn the years apart. We will weep the losses—deaths of old friends, breasts and ovaries destroyed by too many pesticides, brains burned out from too many drugs. We will toast our triumphs: healthy, mouthy children who speak out even if they are not addressed. We will dig our toes in soil and reclaim the stories of those who stayed in the fields, those who drifted away in the fog.

I was the lucky one. I almost lost my Spanish but regained it years later, never as well as when I was a child. I was shamed once for speaking Spanish, for having friends who spoke Spanish but who never learned English. Never again. This valley and the people who toil in the fields, who build the freeways and secure the foundations, who send their children to the schools so they can succeed—for them, the lesson of the valley is survival beneath an unyielding sun. I remember Victoria and Xavier and Porfirio and so many others. Their names and faces stay with me. I search for long, raven hair whenever I read my poems in front of a Spanish-speaking crowd. My eyes mist when I spot a small-faced, dark-skinned woman in one of my creative writing and social action classes.

For my part, I place the lessons I learned about survival beside those my students share in my classes. I remind myself that if I am to remember the lessons of the San Joaquin Valley, I must remember them well. Ours was a landscape of cattle and fairy shrimp. Blackbirds rang the willows. Once upon a time, a girl with raven hair told me stories about the fog, then disappeared. I survey my memory's landscape for all those ghosts in the fog.

Bibliography

Bachelard, Gaston. "Intimate Immensity." *The Poetics of Space.* Trans. Maria Jolas. Boston: Beacon, 1969.
Buck, Pearl S. *The Good Earth.* New York: Washington Square, 1999.
Longfellow, Henry Wadsworth. *The Song of Hiawatha.* Boston: Godine, 2004.
Steinbeck, John. *Cannery Row.* New York: Penguin, 1992.
Thoreau, Henry David. *Walden.* Boston: Houghton, 1995.

5

What I Learned from the Campus Plumber

Charles Bergman

Gawking and awkward, we shuffled across the concrete floor between two huge metal tanks. One was a metallic blue, the other silver, and each connected to color-coded pipes that disappeared into the ceiling. We were in a room below the basement of the University Center. We had descended to the guts of the campus, and the tanks reminded me vaguely of two enormous, artificial kidneys.

Ross Winters was waiting in the space between the tanks. Beneath his Fu Manchu mustache, he grinned with a self-conscious smile. Ross is the campus plumber, a trade he learned during his stint in the Navy. "These tanks are boilers," Ross told us as we settled down. "They boil water into steam. These yellow and red pipes carry the steam underground to the buildings."

The pipes supply hot water to five buildings on campus. Ross named each building. He explained that the tanks heat water to 235°F at fifteen pounds per square inch (psi). Ross had brought us here to show us how we heat our classrooms and offices.

It was the first time I'd seen this room. Ross himself has worked for our university for over twenty years. Ours is not a big campus—about seven hundred faculty and staff—but I had never met Ross before this morning. Apart from the information Ross gave us, I found myself with a strong visceral response to the pressurized tanks, gleaming in this dark room. Ross and these tanks opened up a whole dimension of the campus—its physical operations—to me in ways I'd never before imagined. The tanks of pressurized water embodied the material realities of our lives at the university.

As Ross spoke, I found myself with a new perspective on the place I work. For most of us at a university or college, the campus is a picturesque backdrop for our teaching and learning, more or less attractive, more or less accommodating. College is where we, as students and teachers, go to give and take courses. Perhaps because students pass through colleges and universities and are by nature transient, campuses are not typically viewed as places in their own right. Nor are faculty likely to think of the campus itself as a part of the education we offer students. In this tour with Ross Winters, I realized from these tanks that we can learn not only *at* a college campus, but *from* a college campus. For the first time, I thought of the campus itself as a form of pedagogy.

Like the boiler tanks in the basement of the University Center, the campus as a whole—the campus as a material reality—is a silent syllabus in which the college gives ongoing, unremitting tutorials in who we are and what we value. Faculty and students are likely to privilege the college classroom as the iconographic image of a place of learning: it is metonymic for the campus and its central purpose, educating students. Yet it is perhaps the lessons that are encoded in the campus itself that have the deepest reach and most long-lasting effects on the students, because, like the heating systems in our classrooms, these lessons are inescapable and all the more powerful for being unspoken. They are taken in every day, all day, through the body—pervasive lessons that, like the ambient heat created by these huge water tanks, are unseen but shape the conditions of the lives we actually live on campus. Buildings are books, bearing mute testimony to a campus's lived, as opposed to professed, values. If a campus teaches a way of life, usually that means lessons in displacement and disconnectedness.

I first began to realize the meaning of place at our school in pondering the impact of a 700-person community of employees—faculty, administrators, and staff—on local resources. Add to this some 3,600 students, about half of whom live in residence halls on campus. Given these numbers and competing pressures, we have realized there is an enormous, unexploited educational opportunity encoded in understanding the campus of the university as a place. In *The Nature of Design*, David Orr focuses on architecture and buildings when he writes, "The curriculum embedded in any building instructs us as powerfully as any course taught in it" (128). Yet there is a hidden curriculum in every feature of a campus—the heat in our classrooms, the paper we use, the food we eat, the electricity in our lights, the water we flush in toilets, and the irrigation for grounds.

Those of us in the boiler room were part of a Campus Sustainability Workshop. Some years ago, I had been asked to chair our new Campus Sustainability Committee. Though I had been active for decades in our Environmental Studies program and write frequently on natural history and environmental issues, nothing in my background had trained me in the scientific and technical details that characterize much of the work on sustainability. My PhD, in fact, is in the English Renaissance—a far cry from the architecture and chemistry and engineering degrees that decorate the names of most of the people I've met who are leaders in the field.

Nevertheless, I've had a long-standing interest in environmental issues and environmental writing. Right out of graduate school, I began writing on environmental issues for national magazines. It's a passion I've followed, leading me to write books of creative nonfiction on endangered animals and other topics. My most recent book is on water issues in the West. Called *Red Delta: Fighting for Life at the End of the Colorado River*, the book describes the efforts to save and restore the abandoned delta of the Colorado River in Mexico—once one of the great desert river deltas in the world. In the process, I came to be deeply interested in water issues in the American West and, more broadly, as a major global issue for the coming century. Though experts warn of global conflicts over access to dwindling water resources, I discovered that we don't have to go to China, or India, or North Africa to discover pressing questions of conservation and ecological justice with regard to water.

In fact, I came to realize that even in the Pacific Northwest, water is a major issue. My school is located in this wet and green part of the country. Most people associate the state of Washington with abundant water: it's a state defined by beautiful waterways like Puget Sound and by its abundant rain. Yet the state is already at the limits of water use. And so I found my own environmental interests in water and in place intersecting on my own campus, where I live and where my professional identity has been largely shaped. As my interest in sustainability has grown, I have felt called to make my values inform my life and to work to live more directly. I wanted my own writing and scholarship to inform the way I live, even at work. And so, in our Campus Sustainability Committee, we early on focused our efforts on making the campus into a model of water sustainability among colleges and universities in the region.

We secured a series of significant grants that totaled $110,000 from a local foundation—The Russell Family Foundation located in Gig Harbor, Washington. The foundation emphasizes water sustainability and the protection and restoration of Puget Sound. Our committee dived into both sustainability and water.

One of the advantages of teaching on a relatively small campus like Pacific Lutheran University is that you have the chance to make a difference. In my years at the university, I've helped organize a number of interdisciplinary workshops, largely in Writing across the Curriculum. Yet our sustainability workshops have been quite different from anything I'd ever done before, and not just because they include information on the number of Btu's in the University Center boilers. It's because, in addition to faculty and students, we included staff who literally work on the ground. We included Ross Winters and many of his colleagues in Facilities Management: irrigation specialists, groundskeepers, print shop workers, plumbers, electricians, and more.

As important, we made these people our teachers. This tour of the boilers, for example, was the first item on the workshop agenda, after introductions. That was intentional. We wanted to make a statement, particularly with faculty, who are used to thinking of themselves as the ones who know and who, frankly, are likely to dominate discussions in a workshop. Most of the people in Facilities Management are invisible to faculty, part of the unnoticed background, almost like the water tanks. Yet these are the people who, like Ross, could teach us about the campus as an actual place: how it creates the material conditions of our lives.

At the heart of our workshops are our tours of the campus, with plumbers and groundskeepers and recycling people leading us in tutorials on the unseen campus. These walking tours have been among the most popular elements of our very successful workshops. Participants feel they are learning the campus in startling new ways. In part, this is because faculty are being schooled by people they may never have seen before on campus, but who make the place run and who know the place intimately. In part, this is also a function of simply walking the campus. It is like seeing the place for the first time, though many of us have worked here for years. Walking becomes a way of knowing the place in new ways.

The tours show us the campus as a living place, a place where we live as well as work and study and teach. For a person trained in poetry, the field of sustainability can seem highly technical, driven by data and statistics. Even the word *sustainability* sounds like jargon. To be placed is to have a sense of who you are and where you belong. It is a trope, I believe, of inhabitation. Thinking of sustainability in terms of the trope of place, of dwelling, gives a sense of heart and purpose to our work on our campus.

Wendell Berry offers the definition in *The Unsettling of America* that, more than any other, guides my own thinking about place and the back-and-forth that it implies between culture and nature:

> *We have given up the understanding—dropped it out of our language and out of our thought—that we and our country are part of each other, depend upon one another, are literally part of one another; that our land passes in and out of our bodies just as our bodies pass in and out of our land; that as we and our land are part of one another, so all who are living as neighbors here, human and plant and animal, are part of one another, and so cannot possibly flourish alone; and therefore our culture must be a response to our place[;] our culture and our place are images of each other and inseparable from each other, and so neither can be better than the other. (22)*

As we walk the campus and hear from Ross and others, we find ourselves opening up a conversation with parts of the campus we had not thought much about before. We're really just getting to know the neighborhood and our neighbors. If we have not exactly repressed an awareness of how we live, we have certainly ignored the consequences of our lives on a campus, as if colleges and universities can live without ecological consequence and responsibility. As if work and study are somehow separate from living.

I love our campus. We have ancient evergreen trees where barn owls roost. We have wetlands where green herons nest. I have invested so much time in campus sustainability because I believe that, if you care *for* something, you also have to take care *of* it. In the rest of this essay, I'll describe how at Pacific Lutheran University we've learned to make the unspoken lessons of the campus more explicit—how we've linked the hidden curriculum of the campus to the explicit curriculum of our courses. Before that, I'll deconstruct one of the underlying metaphors for a college education and a college campus, one that makes us think of the campus as an ecology of the mind, rather than an ecology of place.

Academic Pastoral

Ivy-covered walls are the iconic image of a college campus. They symbolize the "hallowed halls" of a college education. Ironically, in the Pacific Northwest, where my university is located, ivy is a problem plant. It is not a native species. It is an invasive species that overruns everything else. Our grand native evergreen trees, like Douglas fir and western hemlock, have no defenses against the ivy that grows up their trunks, slowly chokes them to death, and topples them.

The ivy that grows on our campus is English ivy. It's the same type of ivy that defines the campuses of higher education in England and Europe, as well as on the East Coast of the United States. It serves as a useful metaphor that reminds us that the East is the intellectual center and that we in the West remain the colony. Just as early settlers carried cows and viruses to the colonies, which overran and extirpated local flora and fauna, intellectual settlers carried their alien ivy—a symbol for overrunning local knowledge. Ivy on the buildings on our campus is a statement. Its quiet message is that education is something imported, something transplanted, something foreign to our own particular campus. It is the image of an education that is alien to knowledge of our own particular place.

Ivy is a bane on our campus. One of our projects to restore the campus is to rip out the ivy. It is hard manual labor, another physical way of knowing the campus. As we rip out the ivy, we are also deconstructing the traditional idea of a campus landscape. Ivy is part of the iconography of what I have come to call the academic pastoral. Ivy has been one of the principle plants through which a campus speaks. What ivy says is that the campus is a privileged location in the "landscape of the mind."

The pastoral genre is a shaping figure in our conception of the college campus and of academic life. As an inheritor of the medieval church's monastic ideal, the scholastic life invites us to see the campus as a place set apart from the real world, a refuge and a retreat into contemplation. As a principle locus in the contemplative life, the university campus is traditionally imagined as an idyllic retreat, sequestered and cloistered. Under sheltering trees and within its ivied walls, the academic world is a retreat that parallels a pastoral retreat. Both offer a contemplative retreat into a nature whose topography is defined by its place in the mind. In the

Renaissance, Francis Bacon made the connection between learning and the pastoral explicit. An education, according to Bacon, is not simply the learning of facts and information. In *Of the Advancement of Learning*, Bacon addresses the ways in which a contemplative life can produce virtue in the active life. It's a complicated argument, which we need not go into here. What is interesting is that he thinks of this education as taking place through an education in the "Culture of the Mind" (134). Culture here is not only a noun, but a process. The mind is a landscape, which an education cultivates. Bacon exploits the pastoral metaphor in his language, describing an agri-culture of the mind. The mind is figured as a ground or soil on a farm. By careful tillage and husbandry, it can be made not simply to know but also to acquire the virtues that will prepare it for the active life of, say, civic engagement.

Bacon calls this process of mental cultivation "Georgics of the mind" (134). These Georgics are a direct reference to one of the pastoral poems of Virgil, the Roman poet, treating life on the farm. Bacon points out that the ancient poet "got as much glory of eloquence, wit, and learning in the expressing of the observations of husbandry." The rural life, the life in connection with soil, produces the culture of the mind:

> *And surely if the purpose be in good earnest not to write at leisure that which men may read at leisure, but really to instruct and suborn action and active life, these Georgics of the mind, concerning the husbandry and tillage thereof, are no less worthy than the heroical descriptions of Virtue, Duty, and Felicity. (134)*

For Bacon, the culture of the mind is a kind of magical process, like the tilling and husbandry of soil, producing its crop of virtue in the actual life of the student. These metaphors still inform our notions of pedagogy. We still think in terms of teachers cultivating the fertile soil of young minds. In the rhetoric of the learning, the university is a topos for the contemplative life as a temporary retreat that prepares students for active lives in the world.

The trope of the pastoral typically treats nature as a place for learning, often focusing on self-knowledge and the virtues of the good life (as opposed to the court or the world). However, the pastoral genre may locate its lessons in nature, but it is not naturalistic. It does not locate its characters in specific places. The pastoral is not a field guide to actual places and creatures. The pastoral provides a topography of an imaginary nature. It is an ideal space. The pastoral is a venue for learning in a green world of the mind.

Both Shakespeare's Forest of Arden and Petrarch's Arcadia present an ecology of ideas, not of life in nature—a "landscape of the mind." Whether thought of as escapist or as retreat, the pastoral is the site of "remarkable symbolic richness," according to Helen Cooper in *Pastoral*. She writes, "The landscape becomes an extension of [the poet's] mind, and means of exploring it. . . ." (5). As Sukanta Chaudhuri says, in reference to one of the great pastoral poems, Shakespeare's *As You Like It*, "The centre of the pastoral state has passed within the mind. . . . The mind reacts to the landscape out of its own resources, producing a state of mind very different from what the landscape, directly interpreted, would induce" (361).

The most powerful and beautiful description of the pastoral as landscape of the mind is found in Andrew Marvell's seventeenth-century poem, "The Garden." The literal site or location is an aristocratic garden, the mind cultivated not on a farm but on a country estate. The impulse to withdraw into the mind, described in this poem, is vaguely Platonic:

> Meanwhile the mind, from pleasures less,
> Withdraws into its happiness:
> The mind, that ocean where each kind
> Does straight its own resemblance find;
> Yet it creates, transcending these,
> Far other worlds, and other seas;
> Annihilating all that's made
> To a green thought in a green shade. (lines 41–48)

Nature is an image of the mind, and pastoral withdrawal becomes an expression of the impulse for self-contemplation. This version of pastoral encourages us to think of nature not as a place, but only as an echo of the human mind.

"A green thought in a green shade": the mind does not simply transcend nature, but it "annihilates" it. This pastoral is more than a metaphor, more than a trope. It is a stance toward the world, particularly when we remember that the global environmental crisis has been perpetuated by highly educated people for whom nature is a reflection of human desire.

If the archetypal ivy-covered university campus looks like a cross between a medieval cloister and a country estate, green in trees and lawns, that is because its landscaping and architecture embody this garden of the mind, this academic pastoral. And if education has connotations of retreat and escapism, they can be traced to this intersection of contemplation and pastoral. The only plumbing in this intellectualized version of the pastoral as a place is in the unplumbed consciousness. All the photographs in college recruitment catalogs of classes outdoors, reading on the campus green, participate in this image of college not as its own place, but as a more or less generic landscape of withdrawal into a mental green world. It is the natural habitat not for creatures and people, but for various species of mind. It is from this tradition that my own university draws its sense of the education we impart. The planning document for Pacific Lutheran University states that "the practices of the life of the mind [are] placed at the center of the community" (*PLU 2010* 14).

My quarrel is not with an education in the life of the mind as such. My quarrel is with the way the academic pastoral removes our work—teaching and learning—from our lives. The landscape of the mind at a university converts nature from a specific place to an intellectual abstraction, where even plants and animals are "resemblances" or thoughts. It is like an intellectual theme park. Insofar as the academic pastoral teaches us that place and nature can be ignored, or are important only as a reflection of ourselves and our ideas, it teaches that only people matter, that the culture transcends nature, and that nature is an accident of consciousness.

The pastoral as found on the college campus is not so much an ecology of place as it is a psychology of space—an ethic of self-referentiality and, ultimately, self-indulgence. One message of the pastoral genre is that nature can provide, or is the site of, an education. But the academic pastoral everywhere teaches that nature itself is not quite real and that the particularities of our lives in a place are unimportant. Paradoxically, this retreat into an academic pastoral reinforces the constant messages of the larger culture, with its nonstop indoctrination in the values of privilege and consumption without consequences.

One further obstruction is likely to prevent academics from thinking of the campus as a real place where real lives are located. Humanists may be particularly susceptible to the blandishments of this temptation, one that is closely related to the poetics of the academic pastoral. The academy is a place that privileges language, that imagines itself not as a place but as a discourse. Or, perhaps more accurately, as a site of multiple and conflicting discourses of knowledge. In his influential essay, "Inventing the University," for example, David Bartholomae writes:

> *Every time a student sits down to write for us, he has to invent the university for the occasion—invent the university, that is, or a branch of it, like History or Anthropology or Economics or English. . . . Or perhaps I should say the various discourses of our community, since it is in the nature of a liberal arts education that a student, after the first year or two, must learn to try on a variety of voices and interpretive schemes. . . ." (511)*

The emphasis on "inventing" the university in discourse is revealing, since it suggests that the university is an idea, or series of ideas. That is, it is not an actual place, with an ecology of living beings both human and "other-than-human." Rather, it is conceived as a discursive ecology, an epistemological ecology. And it is not an ecology at all, really, but a political diversity. In such a conception of an education, students do not learn to place themselves in an ecology of place, but rather in an abstraction whose primary reality is linguistic. Locating yourself is imagined in metaphorical terms only, within an academic discourse. Students and faculty learn disciplinary commonplaces, but they do not learn anything about their common place in the university.

It cannot be surprising, in such a pedagogical context, that universities can be such highly literate places, but ones which more or less ob-literate their own sense of place. Through the guided walks in our workshops, much of the power lies in simply reintroducing ourselves to the neighborhood. It is part of making the campus—and our lives on campus—real. Of connecting our students' lives to their education and our lives as faculty to the place where we work.

The Campus as Pedagogy

After visiting the hot water tanks in the University Center, participants in our workshop broke into small teams. I stayed with Ross Winters, the plumber, who led a group of five of us to Stuen Hall, one of the residence halls on campus. We went straight to one of the bathrooms, tiled in pale green that gave it a vaguely hospital feel.

We turned on a faucet in one of the sinks and let it run into a bucket. In one minute, we filled a five-gallon bucket. The faucet had a flow of five gallons per minute (gpm).

Ross reached into his equipment bag and pulled out several aerators—devices that look like small baskets, about the size of a nickel. We fitted one onto the end of a faucet.

We measured the flow again for one minute.

This time, the bucket was less than a third full. In fact, the aerators reduced the amount of water coming out of the faucet to 1.5 gpm.

Ross invited us to imagine how much water—and money—we might save if we did a plumbing retrofit for the entire campus.

In fact, that's exactly what we were doing as part of our sustainability on campus.

The problem with the way we live is that we think water comes from the faucet. We think that light comes from the switch on the wall. And we think that food comes from the grocery store. These delusions are particularly self-serving.

Every shower, for example, provides our students with a daily education written in water. Many of the dorms on our campus were built in the 1950s and 1960s when bigger meant better. The faucets were profligate in their use of water. With old shower heads that sloshed about ten gallons per minute over the bodies of the students, a ten-minute shower used one hundred gallons of water alone. Ten minutes? That's a short shower for most Americans. The typical toilet uses about five gallons of water per flush. Where is all this water coming from? Not from valves and pipes. On our campus, it comes from Parkland Light and Water, which taps wells into local aquifers. In Tacoma, the water comes from rivers that have to be dammed (with implications for salmon runs). Where does the water go when we're done with it? It flows into Puget Sound. According to a series of articles in the *Seattle Post-Intelligencer*, every day two billion gallons of untreated water are dumped into Puget Sound.

As part of our workshop exercise, we computed how much money the campus would save if all the faucets and showerheads were changed out with aerators. We also asked what would happen if every student took a shower that was two minutes shorter per day. The result would be an annual savings of $137,000. At our campus, that constitutes a half percent raise for every faculty person each year.

In fact, in our program of retrofitting both the aerators and plumbing in all residence halls on campus, over a series of years we have seen clear trends in water conservation. In several residence halls now, we have changed aerators. (It turns out they have to have "locks" on them or students will remove them and use them for smoking drugs.) We have also redone plumbing. The pipes and underground valves have been changed, which have their own effects at reducing water consumption. The toilets now flush with three gallons, and we are experimenting on campus in some places with waterless urinals.

Working with Facilities Management, one member of our Campus Sustainability Committee has calculated the effects these changes have had on campus water consumption. Rose McKenney has a joint appointment in both Geosciences and Environmental Studies. She provides the following numbers. In the academic year 2000–2001, the campus as a whole used almost eighty-three million cubic feet of water (740 gallons per cubic foot). Almost half of that water usage (thirty-six million cubic feet) came from the residence halls; the rest is consumed in irrigation, gyms, the university cafeteria, and academic buildings. Even though we have had an increase in student enrollment, in the last five years we have reduced water consumption in the residence halls by nearly 25 percent. It is down now to twenty-seven million cubic feet. Through various other conservation methods, we have reduced total water usage on campus to fifty-five million cubic feet—down over 33 percent (McKenney 6).

Changing the plumbing in the dorms may seem prosaic, but in fact we're replumbing students' lives. We are rewriting the implicit education they get every time they take a shower. What's more, it's a private education, an education in the restroom, not the classroom. What is the lesson of a ten-gallon-per-minute shower? What's the lesson of every shower, every day, with the old showerheads? Mostly the shower is an exercise in waste and excess. Not only is the long shower okay, it is desirable.

Must students know that they are flushing low-flow toilets for them to be receiving an education? One of the central principles of the sustainable efforts on campus is that we won't put anything in the dorms that we would not also use in our own homes. In other words, we want green plumbing that is so good that students might not even notice that it's been changed. That's not hard to do, by the way. Yet we want students also to be aware of what they are using—because we want them to realize that they have choices when they leave PLU and have their own houses. To make sure students are as aware as possible, we've consulted with the people in the residence halls—the students, their resident-hall assistants, and the leaders in Student Life—before the plumbing retrofits began. More important, we are developing a campuswide campaign of interpretive signage that let's everyone know about our sustainable initiatives. We want everyone to know that they have choices. It's part of the education on campus.

The shower stalls illustrate the ways in which every element of the campus is a pedagogy. Unfortunately, in most instances, what the campus teaches contradicts the values that the professors and administration profess. The mission of our university is to "empower students for lives of thoughtful leadership, service, inquiry, and care—for other people, for their community, and for the earth." Our work on sustainability is an effort to understand more fully what it means to care for the earth. We also understand it as an effort to make the university walk our talk. The university should be model of an environmentally conscious life.

David Orr insists, "Design is pedagogy" (126). The whole campus tells a story. Students read the story unconsciously, and it structures or reinforces their desires. We may try to teach students about global environmental crises, but if our campuses do not reflect an awareness of place and ecological integrity, what are we really teaching them? As Orr writes, "Students begin to suspect, I think, that those issues are unreal or that they are unsolvable in any practical way, or that they occur somewhere else" (128–29). In fact, the displacements built into a college campus may teach that the task of the educated life is to displace as many costs, and as many problems, as possible onto other cultures and other creatures. Or it can illustrate the possibilities of a new relationship to nature and place.

A Campus Story Written in Water

Our emphasis on plumbing at Pacific Lutheran University is not accidental. We chose it intentionally as a way to give us a focus in working with the campus. We want to become a model of water sustainability among college campuses. A number of considerations led us to choose water.

The campus once had a stream that flowed directly through our campus, Clover Creek. Not that long ago, people in Parkland, the local town, caught large salmon in it. About fifty years ago, Clover Creek was diverted from campus through culverts and concrete channels. The old channel of Clover Creek is still visible on campus, though not many recognize it. The channel is near an area on campus we are working to relandscape and restore as a signature project.

Plus, water defines the Pacific Northwest. As rain and river, as sound and ocean, water shapes our lives and sculpts our landscapes. Ironically, though we think of ourselves as having too much water, experts say we are at or near the limits of our water resources. Water is also one of the ways our daily lives intersect with global environmental and political issues. Many experts believe that fresh water will be the biggest environmental issue of the coming century. And finally, water is a vessel for potent cultural significations. Water carries meaning. It figures in theology and philosophy. Heracleitus used the river to describe the flux of things. It is a poetic symbol, as in Shakespeare's "sea change." We live in a floating world. Even our brains float within our skulls.

We are rewriting the story of the campus as it is written in water. In our campus workshops, we have had two goals. One has been to plan and prioritize sustainability projects on campus—to redesign the campus as a place. The other has been to link curriculum to campus operations. The goals reinforce each other, and we have been importing the campus itself into the curriculum. The campus has become a 140-acre laboratory for research and experimentation.

I want here to illustrate how we are using the curriculum to understand the campus and how we can better care for it. In introductory courses, for example, student research into the use of water—or power or trash—gives a local habitation to questions of resource use, resource waste, and resource conservation. As a result of our workshops, for example, religion professor Kathlyn Breazeale redesigned her lower-division course to look explicitly at the role of water in various theologies. The relationship between water consciousness and water ethics—between awareness and behavior—comes home when she asks the students to research specific questions about their own water use. The questions include the following: Where does the drinking water on campus come from? Where does the sewage go from campus? Where does other wastewater on campus go, and can you trace the routes? How many vending machines on campus sell bottled water? Which buildings on campus have low-flow toilets? Which residence halls on campus have low-flow showerheads? Which buildings on campus have aerators on the faucets? Who are the leaders on campus in sustainability? What effects does the campus have on its watershed?

Other questions could address irrigation on campus, use of pesticides and herbicides, and storm water runoff. In all these questions, students begin to discover that their own lives are implicated in water.

At a higher level in the curriculum, several students in the Environmental Studies program have conducted their senior research projects on the campus. A number have focused on water use on campus. A year ago, for example, Eric Friesth conducted a study of student water attitudes and water behavior. He called his study, "A Drip in Time: Water Audit and Survey of Environmental Attitudes of Students in Pacific Lutheran University Residence Halls." Eric surveyed student attitudes toward conservation and water use. Some two billion people on the globe currently do not have adequate access to clean water. UNESCO predicts that within the next half century, every individual in the world will have about one-third less water available to him or her. Our students are probably typical of American attitudes more widely: Eric found that PLU students do not believe that water scarcity affects them. They do not worry about the availability of drinking water. Overwhelmingly, students believe that water conservation is important. According to Eric's survey, however, only 29 percent turn off the water when brushing their teeth.

For our students, the environment is an abstraction. They do not understand how water issues apply to their own lives. Eric concludes that technological solutions to water issues are not enough. Students need to understand how their attitudes must change. He urges PLU to become "a model of how to use water."

Both these models of campus research—lower-division introductory classes and senior-level capstones—reengage students with the campus. The students also discover new teachers and new experts on campus. To conduct their research, they have seek out people in Facilities Management. Eric Friesth had to work closely with David Kohler, director of Facilities Management, and with Ross Winters, the Campus Plumber. Students answering the questions in the lower-division religion class had to seek out people in Facilities as well. We not only now ask students to seek them out to learn from them, but we also increasingly bring them into our classes to give presentations. Barbara McConathy directs the vigorous recycling program on campus and has won several awards for her work. She also does a wonderful classroom presentation on campus trash. We produce about 180 tons of solid waste per year. Under her leadership, we now have one of the highest recycling rates among colleges and universities in the region—over 60 percent.

This increasingly visible role of people from Facilities Management has been one of the most rewarding features of our work. These are the people who know the most about how the campus as a campus actually works. David Kohler, for example, has been one of the three faculty mentors on several senior capstone projects. What's more, faculty members are learning from students and their research. We have asked students in both workshops to make public presentations based on their capstone research.

Perhaps that is the strongest value of our work in sustainability. Not only has it enriched our sense of the campus as a living place, but it has also expanded our notions of community. To enter into anything like a deepening dialogue with the campus and how we live on it, we have had to involve people who have been largely invisible. The people from Facilities Management have a kind of knowledge not displayed by the faculty. It is not as highly prized by the academy, but it is crucial. It is local knowledge. These are the people who know the campus as a physical reality that they tend and care for daily, not as an abstraction in the landscape of the mind.

Every Campus Needs a Wilderness

I'll conclude with a story of local knowledge and expanding community. As I mentioned, we have an area on campus near the University Center where the old Clover Creek once flowed. When the University Center was built about thirty years ago, long after the creek was rechanneled, several faculty members from natural sciences put an artificial pond in the area. The idea was to create a natural area on campus. Over the years, however, the area has fallen into neglect. Overgrown and dark, it is now widely avoided and even reviled.

The area has no official name, though we now call it UC Pond. Students and faculty consider it dangerous. Groundskeepers consider it a problem area. Yet one of the main paths from upper to lower campus passes right through this pond, across a small bridge and through the woods. Nothing has ever happened in the area. No one has been mugged—or worse. But it's seen as a crime scene waiting to happen.

Our Campus Sustainability Committee has more or less adopted the area. Safety provides the compelling rationale for the university to restore the area, and we want to make it a signature statement on sustainability.

For some time we have been developing plans for this space, incorporating it into the Campus Master Plan. The goal is to remake it into a sustainable native garden and an outdoor learning space. It will be planted with native plants, using storm water runoff from nearby buildings. In one workshop, we were discussing ideas for this space, when one of the groundskeepers in the workshop stood up.

Her name is Yvonne Butler, but she prefers to be called Wulli (pronounced Woolly). She is another person I had only just met in the workshop.

"I wanna remind you that there're animals livin' there," she said.

Wulli talked particularly about a green heron nesting in the trees in the woods. It was a testimony to a textured and precise knowledge of the campus and its community. It was a defense of the space as a wildlife area and a reminder that our pastoral campus—our place—supports many species of animals other than humans. Surely part of knowing a place, of caring for a place, is attending to the lives of creatures as well as humans. We make our lives in their geographies, their territories, as well as our own. It was immediately clear that we needed to conduct an inventory of the plants and animals we have on campus. One of our two Sustainability Fellows (who are undergraduate students) is developing this inventory over the summer. We will use this knowledge to help build a sustainable wild place on our campus.

Wulli spoke with a passionate commitment to our campus and its rich fauna. Her voice provided a local knowledge that the rest of us lacked. She was a spokesperson for the many invisible and secret lives all around us. She reminded us that we need to care for the many other creatures, like the green heron, with whom we share our place. Sharing our campuses with other creatures must be as important a message about our place in this world as we can share with students.

Bibliography

Bacon, Francis. *The Philosophical Works of Francis Bacon.* Ed. John M. Robertson. London: Routledge, 1905.

Bartholomae, David. "Inventing the University." *Literacy: A Critical Sourcebook.* Ed. Ellen Cashman, Mike Rose, Barry Kroll, and Eugene R. Kintgen. Boston: Bedford, 2001. 511–25.

Bergman, Charles. *Red Delta: Fighting for Life at the End of the Colorado River.* Boulder: Fulcrum, 2002.

Berry, Wendell. *The Unsettling of America: Culture and Agriculture.* 1977. San Francisco: Sierra Club, 1996.

Chaudhuri, Sukanta. *Renaissance Pastoral and Its English Developments.* Oxford: Clarendon, 1989.

Cooper, Helen. *Pastoral: Medieval into Renaissance.* Totowa, NJ: Rowman, 1977.

Friesth, Eric. "A Drip in Time: Water Audit and Survey of Environmental Attitudes of Students in Pacific Lutheran University Residence Halls." Unpublished essay, 2003. <http://www.plu.edu/~sustain>.

Hebel, J. William, and Hoyt H. Hudson. *Poetry of the English Renaissance 1509–1660.* 1929. New York: Appleton, 1957.

McClure, Robert, Lisa Stiffler, and Lise Olsen. "Area's Defining Waterway Is a Cesspool of Pollution." *Seattle Post-Intelligencer* 18 Nov. 2002. 24 Nov. 2002 <http://seattlepi.nwsource.com/local/95872_sound18.shtml>.

McKenney, Rose. "PLU Water Budget." Unpublished lab exercise, 2005.

Orr, David W. *Earth in Mind: On Education, Environment, and the Human Prospect.* Washington, DC: Island, 1994.

———. *The Nature of Design: Ecology, Culture, and Human Intention.* Oxford: Oxford UP, 2002.

PLU 2010: The Next Level of Distinction. The Long-Range Plan of Pacific Lutheran University. 2003.

Snyder, Gary. "The Place, the Region, and the Commons." *The Practice of the Wild.* San Francisco: North Point, 1990. 25–47.

6

M-I-Crooked Letter- Crooked Letter

Katherine Fischer

I learned that the earliest language was not our syntax of chained pebbles but liquid, made by the first tribes, the fish people.

Margaret Atwood

As I write, my front yard is turning liquid. By next week, the basement will flood. Catfish carcasses, mud, rubber tires, and condoms left over from last summer's season will drape the bottom step when the water recedes.

Other springs, the river runs through my living room. Then, so much depends upon a dinghy tied to the back doorknob; it's my only deliverance to higher ground. I live on a backwater slough that oxbows off the main channel of the Mississippi River. If there's anything wild left of this engineered, locked-and-dammed river, it's here in the backwaters where no dredge boat can squeeze through and no barge cares to travel.

You've seen clips on the national news in May and June. You remember—the footage of a house sailing downstream with some poor Holstein standing helplessly on the roof, stock still, not even swishing her tail. Our stories appear on the front pages of your newspaper, too, with the heroic rescue of a frightened tot found aboard a houseboat just moments before it capsizes, crashing against limestone bluffs. In the weeks following the flood, you hear experts on National Public Radio argue over the drawbacks of floodwalls. When a community agrees to certain government regulations about flood insurance and building regulations, FEMA buys out people like me to move us up the hill, safe from the disaster of floodplains.

But I dig my heels into the sand. I won't go. I may evacuate, but I'll return. The river that runs in through my front door and out the back is the same as the river that runs through me—cantankerous, wild, relentless, unpredictable, meandering, and blessed.

This is not fiction. There's no Huck Finn or Mary Loftus in my narrative. This is true.

What is also true about living on the third largest river in the world is July when the cottonwoods snow down on island beaches as my children make castles of sand and "dig to China." Sultry August afternoons, I arm-over-arm the Mississippi and flip with the fishes as twilight softens beneath an early autumn moon. By December, I'm walking on water, my skates gliding across the surface. Frozen midwave, tiny fish are embedded in the ice, their hearty souls stalled by winter's onslaught. I've counted sixty-four hungry bald eagles in the trees that border the beach of my front yard when dead fish rise to the surface, winter softening into spring.

Under layers of knitted wool, I've also bristled against river winds. With pants legs rolled, I've waded along the shore as early as March, goosebumps cobbling my legs. With spring thaw, too, come billions of dead shad emitting the inescapable odor of rotten eggs and rotting fish flesh. The backwaters are not for the faint of heart, the inflexible, nor for those who must stack life neatly in alphabetical order.

But I didn't always live here on the floodplain. I used to be an uplander.

Having grown up on the Wisconsin side of clear blue Lake Michigan, I once approached the muddy Mississippi with as much enthusiasm as someone embracing roadkill. We became neighbors then, this dark turgid river and I, once I left behind my Wisconsin homeland. I'd come into its territory by way of career moves with my family, but I did so with my heels dug into the mud. I was sure that beneath that brown surface unspeakable things lay waiting to grab my legs, pull me under and down to where I would choke on the slick bottom, mud flooding my gullet. But as much as I feared this river, so unlike the sapphire waters of my native lake, still the mystery of it, the layers of mud and story, of a river that moves faster and farther than any Great Lake, pulled me in. It was hate-love at first sight.

I'd heard stories. Before I made my first true communion with it—went "on the river," as it is called in these regions when you become a river person—I'd listen to anyone around me who had a Mississippi tale to tell. Each fall, students returned to my Iowa high school English classroom and told of catching enormous catfish with eighteen-inch whiskers and of high times swinging out over limestone river bluffs before dropping in. Faculty colleagues gathered over lunch recounting the saddest tales of all, those of young people who had slipped beneath the surface and whose bodies were churned up farther downstream. Listening, I would hold my breath as long as possible, the way you'd do before letting your lungs fill up if you were drowning; then I'd shake my head, thinking of what the river takes.

Even as a child, I knew that where adventure was involved, Lake Michigan came up shallow in contrast to the Big River. North of Milwaukee, where I grew up, the lake coastline is either rocky and impassable or tame and sandy, holding little to explore other than dune grass and an occasional "crick." Yes, there were stories about ships lost during a seiche when air pushed downward on the center of the lake like a thumbprint, causing near tidal waves at the shore. There were mariner tales of hulls torn open when even lighthouses couldn't steer navigators safe. But these mostly involved commercial or military craft with women and children taking little part in such horrific narrations. Those adventures were only for grown-ups, mainly men who worked the Great Lakes. I loved the lake, but for me it wasn't a river of dreams—or of nightmares, for that matter.

What I knew about the Mississippi, on the other hand, mostly involved Huck Finn. (This is the part where he comes in.) Back in fifth grade at Milwaukee's St. Eugene School, Sister John Mary jibbed the skirts of her habit midcalf as she read how Huck climbed into his canoe to escape Pap's drunken beatings. Sister crouched behind the podium as she described Huck and Jim hiding out on Jackson Island, eluding townspeople searching for their lost bodies.

During quiet reading time, I'd chant to myself, "M-i-crooked letter-crooked letter-i-crooked letter-crooked letter-i-p-p-i" as I pretended to trace the course of the river on my wooden desk. I'd imagine rafting with the likes of Mary Loftus and Mary Jane Wilkes, women "full of sand," who could navigate the roughness of shanty river towns as well as (or better than) any man. I even searched through *The Adventures of Tom Sawyer* to find the one passage in which Twain writes of a girl boarding a steamboat. As Becky Thatcher strode up the gangplank to brave the Mississippi, I was right alongside her.

At home after school, I fished Milwaukee's storm ditches for catfish and pretended to smoke reeds behind the garage while balancing on a plywood raft "afloat" rain puddles. Mine may have been rivers of shoal water, but in my play, Huck's islands and my own were the same. Like the Mississippi itself, a mile wide at points, here was a riverscape of imagination wide enough to include rapscallions as well as the rich, children as well as oldsters, women as well as men, teachers and students, all.

I grew up and left Lake Michigan behind, moving to the prairies of Iowa to begin my teaching career. Dubuque is a river town: the great Mississippi sweeps past it on the east, rolling down from the north. It serves as the watery border between Iowa on the western bank and Illinois and Wisconsin on the eastern shore. Surrounded by water, however, I spent years in dry dock. My time was taken up raising five children as well as navigating a writing and teaching career. There was no time for the Mississippi. Or so I'd convinced myself.

One day I found I was gazing down hundreds of feet of limestone bluffs at lock and dam eleven, where I had driven on sudden impulse. I heard the towboats pushing barges through the lock, their horns calling to me like sirens. I saw an island within a mile of the dam. There was a rowboat tied to one of the cottonwoods at the tip. Before I knew it, Becky, Huck, and I were again running through those cottonwoods, climbing, and swinging out over the river from low-lying branches yelling, "Last one in is a dirty yeller bottom-sucking catfish!"

In the next minute, shedding the scales of educator, mother, and writer, I stood shoulder to shoulder with Captain Bixby in the pilothouse steering our course clear of sawyers and sandbars. The Mississippi called to me in a voice muddled yet familiar, like the voice of one's mother heard from underwater.

From that moment on, I was full steam ahead to get on the river. I taped photographs of Evinrudes, Larsons, and Carvers to our refrigerator, dreaming of one day motoring out on the river at the helm of my own boat. Crossing the Iowa-Wisconsin bridge on one of our frequent trips to visit family back in Milwaukee, I would utter the scene in breathless awe: "Look at the surface today . . . it's like chocolate silk in a breeze, don't you think?" I thought of myself as a siren, calling to my husband and children, *Come, dive in.*

I took to watching our children float plastic boats in their kiddie pool and feeling regret over my poor parenting. How could I be raising youngsters without the advantages I'd had growing up on the lake? What great natural truths would they never stumble upon, staying safely far from the river's reach? What fantasies would they fail to develop, what metaphors never internalize? Fantasy and metaphor, adventure and my own yearning heart—these were too important to neglect. One afternoon in mid-July, I packed sunscreen, inner tubes, buckets, shovels, and bright orange lifejackets along with the children and drove to Finley's Landing, the only beach close by that was accessible by car back then.

There we built houses out of sand and then swamped them, imitating the force of spring floods. We swam out to the diving raft and floated on our backs, doubtless looking like an assortment of drifting tangerines in our lifejackets. Then we lay on the beach, inhaling the carpy river and watching the sun go down. I knew it still wasn't enough.

Next time, I hauled notebook and pen along and sat leaning into the page, trying to find the river in my longhand. The children played at the water's edge digging deep enough until the river rose up in the gorge they'd created.

I stared through the "snow" of the cottonwoods floating down on a jetty of rocks near the far edge of the swimming beach. I tried to imagine twelve feet of flood—realizing, of course, that we would all be several feet underwater if this were the spring of 1965. The thought of being part of the river, part of its mysterious underwater world, was enough to do it.

"Let's buy a boat," I finally said to my husband. I'd pasted the pictures of boats up in the kitchen, yes, but I had never actually said the words to anyone but myself. What I didn't say was that I knew I needed to get much closer, into the Mississippi's very atmosphere, if I wanted to breathe river. If I wanted to teach and write the river, I would need to get beneath its skin into its soul.

What I didn't know was that he was already talking with the marina up north about buying a sweet nineteen-foot Larson runabout. "It would be a source of everlasting regret to live so close to the Mississippi River and never have a boat," he offered by way of persuading me to make the deal. My only everlasting regret was that I didn't speak up much earlier.

By the time we bought the boat (and later river property), I was eager to take on this river that runs the length of a nation—and of a nation's imagination. That first summer, I mangled the Larson's prop, much to the amusement of local marine mechanics, "Musta been flying, lady, to do that much damage." What did I know of wing dams?

When I asked him why in heaven's name anyone would construct such stupid dangerous structures, he explained patiently the need for a deep channel. I stared at him with my mouth agape. No Lake Michigan tale had ever involved anything as deceptively whimsical sounding as a *wing dam.*

Wing dams were created in the nineteenth century. These stone and willow mat underwater walls jut out from the shore like arcs forcing currents toward the main channel. This early attempt at channelizing the Mississippi, engineers hoped, would cause the river to flow faster, thus scooping out a deeper bed.

The opposition of the two words magnetized me. How could something be both as airy as wings and as burdensome as a dam? But in fact, they are. Shaped like wings, these matted walls give flight to the current, sending it to the center of the channel in order to scour it out and make it deep enough for navigation. Too, wing dams are the safe haven for bottom-feeders like catfish.

I forged on despite the wing dams. Excited to discover hidden inlets that even old river rats might have failed to explore, I caused the runabout to flounder in underwater stump fields or to beach on sudden, thinly submerged sandbars. Local boaters, shaking their heads, kindly oared in for the rescue, flung me a line, and towed me out of harm's way. My husband kept a spare pair of mudshoes on board in order to hop out of the boat and lift us off whatever sandbar I'd beached us on.

Together my husband and I figured out how to rev the outboard in order to churn our way out of mud and to avoid the snarl of water lilies and discarded tires. Yet it would take years before I could "see" the landscape under the river. River folks were tolerant. They taught me to read the river the way you read the dark in a room familiar to you without stubbing your toe even once.

Upon first coming to the Mississippi, I envisioned it as it appears in textbooks, one long, wild river, snaking its way to the Gulf of Mexico. Instead, today's river is anything but a flowing blue highway. "Pool," on the Mississippi north of St. Louis, refers to a stretch of river between two dams. The Army Corps of Engineers began constructing locks and dams back in the 1930s to hold water back in order to ensure a nine-foot channel, deep enough for barges and boats to navigate. Because of the lock-and-dam system, the Upper Mississippi is actually a series of pools rather than a continuous flowing river. The dams are the end "walls" of the pools.

Locks provide a means by which boats can move up- and downstream without having to leapfrog these walls. Much like a watery elevator, a lock allows boats to enter on one side of the chamber and then closes its chamber door. Once the chamber is closed, the water is raised or lowered, depending on whether you're moving up- or downstream. Once the water level reaches the same height as the next pool, the gates at the other side of the chamber are opened, and boats go on their merry little way.

Before locks, dams, floodwalls, and levees, the Mississippi meandered off course, shifting as much as ten miles to the west down near Vicksburg. In low-water Septembers, you could walk across the riverbed without getting a drop on your toes. Nowadays, however, satellite readings register automatically in the Corps's data system. If the system doesn't like the river level, lockmasters are directed to throw a switch and either hold more river back or let more river flow into the pool.

Floodwalls and levees have been constructed along the Mississippi to girdle it in, to keep things under control. But when you hold a flooding river to a tighter corridor, it rises higher. Go ahead. Try it yourself. Let the spigot flow freely onto your yard, and it'll disperse water thinly across the grass. But contain water in a narrow trough and before you know it, your knees will float.

Floodwalls are impenetrable fortresses of concrete that protect cities and farmlands from the Mississippi's powerful floods. Destructively, however, they also cause water to rise higher and more forcefully farther downstream until the lower river suffers irreparable damage, loss of wetlands, and ultimate desecration. The loss of such wetlands and their ability to absorb high water in Louisiana were particularly evident in the surge that came up from the Gulf of Mexico and wreaked havoc on New Orleans during Hurricane Katrina. For the most part, floodwalls were constructed back when we didn't know any better. "Something there is that doesn't love a wall," Robert Frost claims.

Levees often have the good manners of being overcome regularly by high water. There's a levee system on the Mississippi girdling it for hundreds of miles. While these levees may result in dryer towns in the short run, they damage the environment in the long run. They lure people to settle in behind the false security of earthen walls. Developers establish residential neighborhoods—later leaving people homeless in the wake of The Big One. Wetlands that provided habitat for many species have dried up. High water can't spill onto natural floodplains, so the toxicity in the river builds up until all those chemicals and hog runoff flow down past New Orleans into what is currently termed the Dead Zone and Cancer Alley. If Robert Frost were still around today, he'd write, "Something there is that doesn't love a levee."

After boating the river for years, we moved down the bluffs, through the woods, and onto the floodplain. My natural environmentalist tendencies became more radical as I daily witnessed the results of the engineering of the Mississippi. At the same time, I marveled at human ingenuity in controlling such a powerful waterway. No single feat garnered as much of my wonderment as wing dams. Although these underwater brush and stone walls were built over a hundred years ago extending from the riverbank toward the channel, thousands of them still exist today. Most of the time you can't see them unless you know how to read the river. The water over a wing dam furls back upon itself in a line with small waves breaking on the surface perpendicular to shore. You can spot them frequently by locating a red "nun" buoy and scanning the surface between the buoy and the shore.

Here on the Upper River where folks know exactly how many inches their boats draw (how much depth they need to navigate a slough or the main channel), we attend to websites and Army Corps of Engineers broadcasts to track levels on any given day. Contrary to popular belief, the system of locks and dams was not created in order to control flooding; still lockmasters affect depth by holding back water or allowing some of it to flow into the pool south. In low water, wing dams are the bugaboo of boaters, who risk both propeller and keel unless they attend to river charts.

Pontoon boats, johnboats, houseboats, runabouts, and the magnificent Delta Queen sternwheeler—all boats with more than a two-foot draw—make their way downriver minding the wing dams that jut out silently underwater, unseen. Not all of them appear on Quimby's river charts either.

On the other hand, collectively these dams prevent the channel from cutting new paths as it did for centuries before human engineering. Along with floodwalls, levees, locks, and dams, wing dams are also responsible for drying up wetlands. Gone are the piping plovers. And those bottom-feeders hoping for a resting place? Every fisher worth her bait knows fishing off the downstream side of a wing dam is a sure bet for walleye. Throw 'em a line. Hoist 'em. Hit 'em over the head with a wooden mallet. Scale 'em. Eat 'em. What kind of safe harbor is that?

Schooled in education departments of the early 1970s, I believed that if I poured flowing streams of lessons and sage advice into student heads, their knowledge would flow downstream like a contained river—kept neatly to its shores. The right words would rise up from their mouths until bubbling into white water rapids. Back then, I thought I understood teaching and learning *precisely*. Back then, I thought the Mississippi was controllable. Channel student ideas into the nice flowcharts of Maslow's hierarchy. Comingle the backwaters of deconstruction, tagmemics, and behavioral modification. Wait until the spring rise, and students would certainly flood with inspiration. It would be like those lovely solutions I'd learned in calculus class—predictable and measurable.

Then reality bit. I entered the chalk dust world of secondary education, teaching five classes of Mass Media five days a week. As a college student, I'd charted Hemingway's stylistics and categorized Dickinson's images. I knew how to write a sonnet. I'd studied Milton's hell, but I never expected to feel the heat of it in the classroom. Now, I was faced with thirty students in a class, who expected me to teach plugs and wires, to use a "portapak" (the 30-pound, strapped-to-your-hip, reel-to-reel forerunner of video cameras and lightweight video disk cameras), and to numerically represent their progress in grades. It felt as though I were ensnarled by a spaghetti of wires. I wandered the aisles of study hall searching under desks for literary criticism, predictable paradigms, and sure signs of self-actualization. Instead, all I found was chewing gum.

On top of this, the administration expected me to teach foreign courses like Composition. Although I could easily identify parts of speech and diagram any sentence, now I actually had to teach students to write. I was an English major of the 1970s. I didn't know nuthin 'bout teaching writing. Junior Class Moderator, I tried to assist students in constructing an evening of prom fantasy out of crepe paper saved from the previous fall's homecoming float. Worse, I was expected to explain why Heather and Juan hadn't jumped fourteen points on the verbal section of standardized tests in a single year. Parents wanted my advice on how to cure their teenager's addictions to rock music and beer. My carefully mapped-out lessons for what *I'd* teach them were drowned out by what *they* needed to learn. I grabbed for any piece of driftwood in the pool.

Worried over whether I'd do a good job, I wanted sure signs by which to steer my course as an educator. My early teaching invested in locks and dams, measures to steer student learning and my own proficiency and to keep us safe from scraping bottom. I latched onto every theory and educational buzz trend that came down the pike. I made grids for students to chart their writing progress. I created lesson plan checklists and never strayed. I took copious notes at in-service workshops, thirsty for that watery elevator that would raise me through the lock chamber into the next channel. That was in the early days before I moved to the river.

The floodwalls and levees I'd built in my teaching life by following verbatim certain theories and prescribed methods weren't holding. Sure, my students held to the middle channel, but every once in a while, all hell broke loose, and I had to admit they weren't learning much. The wetlands were drying up. Students could memorize lists of terms and apply them to passages I'd given them, for example, but they couldn't transfer the knowledge in useful ways. In short, I wasn't teaching them to think. Although theory informed my classroom practice, I hadn't yet made it organic to me.

During years of high school teaching, I suffered the dams and floodwalls of prescriptive models. One year it was Madelyn Hunter's thumbs up/thumbs down method of assessing student response. I followed her advise solidly, asking my students to hold thumbs up if they got it, down if not, and to the side if they weren't quite sure. All the teachers in my high school had attended the same workshop. By the end of the week, several students entered class with their opposables cartoonishly bandaged as they chanted, "No More Thumbs! No More Thumbs!" They were right. Applying a single method so rigidly was reductive when it comes to the rich art of teaching and learning. Still, what I learned from the Madelyn Hunter method was the importance of focusing on what students received versus what I thought I'd taught.

Next, it was Behavioral Objectives, a practice many of us came to refer to as the B.O. of education. I dutifully memorized the hundred verbs to use in creating B.O., but again I found that focusing too narrowly on one theory took on an aroma matching the name we'd so glibly given the theory. Important values and qualities learned in the classroom couldn't be adequately defined within the dammed pool of Behavioral Objectives.

I was stuck in the middle of the channel, unsure which shore to swim to. On Private Me Island, I loved both literature and writing with passion, for how they make us more richly human. But on Teacher Island, I'd been informed by current literary theory that only intellectual reader responses counted. "Gut reaction matters when it comes to art," Private Me Island tugged. "What sets us apart from the beasts is our ability to apply critical theory to literachure," Teacher Island yanked back.

Attending the symphony in Dubuque one night, my epiphany arrived as clear-cut as twilight on the river separating light from darkness. Yes, of course, aesthetic criticism enhances appreciation, but to ask folks used to dressing in overalls to suddenly don tuxes, evening gowns, and lorgnettes in order to enjoy music originally produced for the masses is a tedious exercise in stripping away passion. I resolved to find a way to reconcile the fops and chicken bone-slinging audience of the Globe Theater with the elegance of Shakespeare's plays in my teaching life. Surely one didn't have to be sacrificed for the sake of the other. After all, as a second-generation American, my own roots were in the beer halls and horse stables of Milwaukee's Miller Brewing Company; yet here I was at the front of the classroom. Perhaps opposites *should* attract.

What was there to lose? I no longer wanted to be part of girdling in my teaching or student learning. It was time to blow up the wing dams I'd constructed. We'd dig to China in my classroom, I imagined. Yet I worried. If students jumped out of the boat, could they swim? Could I?

Fortunately, I became the English department chair at the high school where I was teaching, and along with the appointment came more flexibility. Living on the floodplain, I learned from the neighbors about dealing with the spring rise. Some install pulleys on sofas so they can be hoisted up when water flows into the living room. Installing your furnace in an upstairs bedroom closet and elevating the water heater five feet off the ground leaves a person with a practical sense of humility—and humor. Life, I realized by living on the floodplain, was neither a bowl of cherries nor of pits. It's a bumper-car rink. If the river rises too quickly for us to pull up the carpet beforehand, then I tear up the muddy mess later, pitch it, and live with painted plywood and scatter rugs for a few years. Failed classroom experiment? Bump back and try, try, try again.

I entered college teaching through the back slough. First, while still teaching high school, I served as a nighttime adjunct in the degree program for nontraditional students at Clarke College. Later, I substituted for the writing lab director on leave one year to finish her PhD. I had no intention of staying. University life, however, and my new colleagues challenged me even more to experiment, to risk, to sink—and to swim. Now that I was heavily involved with river revival efforts and riparian cleanup, I found the college's invitation to enter into full-time college teaching irresistible. Furthermore, asked to develop the core required course for Clarke's honors program, I knew students would write, research, and write some more. But how? What?

I fretted for months over methods to engage smart students in ways that might also provide service to the community. Sitting on the dock at our boat slip one July afternoon with my big toe dangling in the river, I stared down into the surface. Only my own image reflected back at me out of the muddy water, and then I knew. The river would be their textbook. Its surface would be their writing tablet.

The local river museum was researching fish, wildlife, and environmental concerns in preparation for the forty-million-dollar National Mississippi River Museum and Aquarium it would construct within a few years. The director and curator agreed to partner with us and developed a list of topics they needed more information about in order to write exhibit scripts. Since some of my students had grown up along the Mississippi and since all of them were now living within a mile of its banks, they dived in head first, eager to get to the main channel.

Researching the disappearance of Higgins' eye mussels juxtaposed with the onslaught of zebra mussels, examining the poor results of mitigation banking as an excuse to destroy wetlands, and investigating even legal levels of chemical pollution on our stretch of the river, students learned creative methods of scholarly research. Of course, museum curators and the director performed the lion's share of research; yet these students played significant roles in finding background information. When students presented their findings to the museum's director and board and grappled with their questions, they gained a sense of place more expansive than the four white Sheetrocked walls of our classroom. They knew their research, filtered through exhibits, would eventually inform millions of visitors touring the National Mississippi River Museum and Aquarium. Even now years later, these same students return to visit the Museum/Aquarium commenting frequently, "I remember when we did the water quality tests and recorded our data" or "They're finding new ways to deal with those dratted zebra mussels."

Feeling the river running through me, its wildness and unpredictability, I've also been drawn to teaching and writing forms of the essay first introduced by Michel de Montaigne. Often meandering, multiple-voiced, associative, and self-reflective, Montaigne's work contrasts with Francis Bacon's locked-and-dammed thesis-driven compositions. People like Kathleen Yancey, Wendy Bishop, Michael Spooner, and David Starkey welcomed me into academic writing, not in spite of my alternate essay forms, but because of them.

After several years of teaching and being on the river, I drove up to Lake Itasca in Minnesota north of St. Paul. Only here, north of the lock-and-dam system and levees, would I find the river in its natural state, its primitive existence predating human engineering. Over 250 tributaries drain more than forty percent of the United States. These tributaries stretch from the Rockies to the Appalachians. Its official source is tiny Lake Itasca. Barely ten feet wide and not more than two feet deep, the small stream that flows out of the northern end of the lake builds to nearly a mile wide and one hundred feet deep at points during its journey to the Gulf of Mexico. There at Itasca, where the Mississippi begins modestly, barely bubbling out of rock, I felt a reverence for small beginnings that, in time, amount to greatness. Why should teaching be any different?

Stepping carefully onto slippery rocks in the shallow cool water, I imagined the same drops streaming over my ankles in their journey down to St. Anthony's Falls near Minneapolis, down through Dubuque, down to Cairo where they'd commingle with other drops from the Ohio River, and finally all the way down to New Orleans through to the Head-of-Passes at the Gulf of Mexico. Only there, at the Itasca headwaters, did I appreciate fully the Ojibwa naming of this "great river," this "gathering of water," this "Meche Sepe." My waterscape identity gathers in me the river's energy, beyond stereotype and myth. Ultimately, mine is the story of how the nature of the Mississippi connects with the nature of oneself.

Over all, I've discovered that the chief difference between the Mississippi and Lake Michigan—and all oceans, lakes, streams, puddles for that matter—is how it *moves*. Lakes and oceans have tides and waves, of course, but it is the Mississippi's current that leads Mark Twain to reiterate Heracleitus's assertion that no one "steps into the same river twice." It travels. Thus many of us take up residence on houseboats, our homes vehicles of floating migration, metaphor for the wandering nomadic life.

So, too, is it metaphor for my teaching life. As paradoxical as it may be for a stiff, bespectacled, lesson-planning academic to reside in harmony with wildness and caprice, it is so in my case.

So constant is the rhythm of the river's movement that it becomes, oddly, its only stable quality. No matter when I swim out to the main channel, I know the current will take me willy-nilly if I let it, so I use caution. I never shore my boat without tying a bow *and* a stern line.

Ever present in our profession is change. A ten-year span of critical theory and composition practice regularly gives way to new theories and practices, oxbowing off the main channel. Mine is a recursive practice as well, which may return to previous methods in the classroom only to give way to something newer. Still, I never enter the classroom without a plan. When it suddenly strikes me midlesson to ask students to get out of their desks and waltz as we recite Roethke's "My Papa's Waltz" in order to feel the rhythm of the lines, however, I'll follow that current. In both my life on the river and in the classroom, the very unpredictability is the only predictability. I have only to steer my course—and to navigate the wing dams.

    I
    be
    co
    me
    wat
    er
    be
    co
    m
    e
    s
    m
    e

Notes

Part of this chapter is excerpted from *Dreaming the Mississippi* by Katherine Fischer, published by the University of Missouri Press in the fall of 2006.

Bibliography

Atwood, Margaret. "Fishing for Eel Totems." Uncommon Waters. Ed. Holly Morris. Seattle: Seal, 1991. 179.

7
On Frogs, Poems, and Teaching at a Rural Community College

Seán W. Henne

My father grew up on a dairy farm along the Flint River in Michigan's Lapeer County. His father raised and milked cattle, and his mother taught Longfellow and arithmetic in a succession of local schoolhouses. Those two rhythms—the particular, deliberate rhythm of country life and the equally organic cadence of community learning—form a strong, double-thudding heartbeat at the core of everything I do. Thinking of the Flint River now, I see the sugar shack my uncle built along its banks to house his evaporating pans for boiling off maple syrup and his huge cider press for the pressing of cider in the fall. The "shack" is actually several large rooms encased in wood from barns that are no longer barns, though we all know their stories. There, every fall and every spring, my family gathers to extract the sweetness from the woods and orchards around us. And there, every gathering features both the lively music of our Irish American heritage and deeply wrought teaching stories. Of my dad's siblings and their spouses, six are or have been teachers in Michigan's public schools. In that sugar shack, over the twenty years it has been sending clouds of steam rising over the river flats, knots of teachers have stood alternately raising their voices in song, taking a turn pouring off the rich liquids we distilled, or unraveling for each other the integral intersections of their lives with the lives of literally thousands of students from schools across the state. Students sing and play and work there, too. My uncle's four children all encountered his high school

English courses, and many, many other current and former students of his and my aunt's show up at the shack to bring a load of apples or firewood, to collect sap, to stand in the sweet steam listening to Uncle Paul discourse on sugaring in as lively a voice as ever he used to help them into Beowulf. This student-teacher pattern is repeated throughout the shack: my own mother taught me and my two brothers high school English as well, and I am only one of several of my cousins who has chosen the profession that we saw enacted, in classrooms and kitchens and on the banks of the Flint River, throughout our childhoods.

My parents left the farmland of southeast Michigan for the north a year or so before I was born. They now live on a farm of their own on the north shore of Lake Charlevoix, that slender finger pointing two of northern Michigan's rivers the way into the greater lake that so strongly patterns life on the west side of the state. Although I spent much of my early years on the ancestral farm in Lapeer County, I actually grew up and came to understand my own identity in the north woods, among the beech and maple of my folks' forty acres. Seasonal change is dramatic across Michigan, but in the north it is endowed with special significance, and along Lake Michigan the drama of the seasons is fierce, relentless, and terribly beautiful. I learned to mark the changes with the movement of geese, with a bushel of seed potatoes, with the angry snarl of chainsaws in the fall and the special pleasure of dressing by a woodstove on frosty mornings. I've seen waterspouts dance across the big lake in a summer storm and followed the twisted architecture of ice along the dunes in the winter, and these regional realities have led me to yearn, always, for the part of the state where I experienced the challenging beauty of such things. It is not surprising, then, that I now develop my own teaching stories at West Shore Community College, on a campus where out my window I can just see a portion of the Lincoln River nodding to me as it runs the last ten-mile stretch to Lake Michigan. I have tried living elsewhere—in a central Wisconsin mill town, in Boston, in Ann Arbor. But the rhythms of these places couldn't satisfy the hunger I have to know what the big lake looks like on a blustery fall day or to walk into a local grocery store or gas station and know that some of my students will likely be working in the building.

Choosing to work at a rural community college isn't all about environment, of course. I teach five courses a semester during the regular school year, meaning I work with between 100 and

130 students each semester, a load very similar to that faced by high school teachers like my mother and uncle. The small community aspects of my job are countered somewhat by this load: intimacy and familiarity are encouraged by the close environment but simultaneously challenged by the large number and endless variety of students with whom I spend my time. My course load also makes it more difficult for me to do *this*, to share my ideas and reflections with an intellectual community through writing. When I am immersed in the current of a semester, however, I like to think that I am living as deeply as one can the life of this region. Because I have so many students and because they come from all over the district and from so many backgrounds and have experienced such a range of what west Michigan has to offer, I truly feel more aware of where I am. To a large extent, this is because I rely pedagogically on reflective writing in all my classes. I ask my students each semester to live writing lives, and one of the consequences of this is that I am made more strongly aware of how their various experiences shape their understanding of the courses we run together and how these courses might, in turn, be affecting their experiences of the landscape and community we inhabit. Working at a community college, then, deliberately puts me at the heart of the community, or at least in a place where the multiple currents of being human hereabouts dramatically intersect.

I drive to work seven miles down dirt roads through cornfields and stands of alfalfa for dairy cows. The residences I pass are misshapen old farmhouses, trailer homes, newer homes from the 1990s whose suburban look feels a bit alien, isolated as they are among the oaks and maples of the Manistee National Forest. This is a world that I've celebrated ever since the first time I drove a spile into a maple tree, ever since the moment of joy I had when as a third grader I read to my class a personal experience essay about cutting Christmas trees. For me, it is relatively easy to relax into joy about where I live. I have a good job and even some time to spend freely in a canoe or with my dog in the dunes. My students, though, have a more complex relationship with this landscape. The district served by the college has one of the highest unemployment rates in Michigan, and a sense of isolation, of being cut off from the dream of a good job and a real future, runs its riptide through our campus. The landscape here can seem a wasteland where the rusted-out Chevy and the rotted woodpile stand in sullen recognition of cold winters and cold prospects. But my students, like me, also are aware of the uncanny brilliance of a sunset over the lake, of the sudden rushing white when trilliums fill our springtime woods, of the quiet cold of October mornings when an arrow connects hunter and deer in an ancient ritual. The landscape here is not, or not merely, romantic idyll, because it creates livelihoods for many who are able to stay, but it often offers a very difficult hope, the succulence of a morel mushroom it took agonizing hours to find. Some teaching stories ache with helplessness or throb with violence. Even here, in a world I've always known to be beautiful, or maybe especially here, the frustrations of poverty and parochialism can be suffocating, and the college writhes with such tensions as often as it lights with creativity and hope.

> *Place, a physical place, shapes us and inscribes our writing. It inspires us or saddens us or angers us, and it draws the story out.*
>
> Lorraine Anderson

Lorraine Anderson is an editor at the *Traverse City Record Eagle*, a fine northwest Michigan institution. I like this quotation of hers because it emphasizes the very active role of place in the writing process. For Anderson, as for me, our region is not merely a place we write about but rather is a landscape that draws forth our words. Up here the geography requires, even demands, response. Wildly Socratic, it continues to ask challenging questions of its denizens, and we decline to answer at our peril. I came to work at West Shore in part because there are certain questions that are asked here in patterns delightfully familiar to me, about when to plant tomatoes, about where to move several feet of snow, about knocking back aspens to let wild apple trees catch the sun. But there are other questions asked by this landscape that I'm just beginning to frame answers to, and I know I have a long way to go. The main town in Mason County, the county that holds both West Shore Community College and my forty acres, is Ludington. Ludington is most noted for its presence on the lake and the car ferry that takes passengers to Wisconsin. It has some of the most magnificent beaches in the country because of the undulating dunes that luxuriate unimpeded north of here through a popular state park and a wilderness area. Accordingly, Ludington pushes tourism and has been making a concerted effort to develop its considerable lakefront with parks and luxury condominiums. Across the street from the crown jewel of such development, however, sits an abandoned factory and warehouse complex. When I ask my composition students to write descriptive profiles of place, this old factory proves to be a magnet; I've taught eleven sections of composition since I've come to West Shore, and in six of those classes, a student has decided to tackle the complex as a subject. The rusted hulk casts a deep shadow over the harbor and on the consciousness of my students. In revision, I try to get them to imagine the possibilities—what could happen to that space, how might the factory be rehabilitated. But they are reluctant to travel far down this road. For them, the question raised by this misshapen oddity of the harbor front isn't so much what do we do next with it, but how do we get out from under its shadow. Borrowing from Lorraine Anderson again, such acquiescence to the terrible inertia of symbols like the factory complex is what "saddens" me about the physical place I inhabit. My students accept a great many things about themselves and their places, and their resignation is a frequent answer to the hard-edged dramas of our shared environment.

Last spring a newly married and very young couple took one of my writing courses. Both of them were very bright and engaging and wrote exceptionally well; they also stood out from the other students in part because of their relationship but also because the bulk of the rest of the class consisted of dual-enrolled high school students even younger than the newly married couple. Observing them in compassionate and earnest engagement with their younger classmates, I became convinced that they could very successfully develop their talents in the teacher-training program. When I suggested that they consider taking a few education courses, though, I met with considerable resistance. I suppose that I have worked in teacher education long enough and have felt the need for good teachers keenly enough that I am sometimes more evangelical in such circumstances than I should be: there is considerable presumption involved in anyone, no matter how experienced or careful and well meaning, interfering with vocational decisions. But when I read the young woman's fine and thoughtful research paper on attention deficit disorder and the young man's equally insightful comparison-contrast essay on teaching styles, I redoubled my efforts. Of course, I'm discovering an awkward prejudice here as this paragraph lurches towards a lament about some students' "acceptance" of an associate's degree as terminal. Telling this story now allows me to worry back to how well I listened to the stories they brought to me, whether I quieted the roar of my enthusiasm enough to let their needs and interests surface. I do expect this young couple will live profoundly involved and fulfilling lives in any careers they choose. But the reason that their story comes to my mind now is that neither of these promising young folks believed, at the time of my earnest promptings, that they *could* become good teachers. Something analogous to Ludington's old hulk of a factory had cast its shadow over their understanding of their abilities and talents.

At a community college, as with any small institution, employees wear many hats. Although the bulk of my teaching load consists of composition and literature courses, I was actually hired to develop the education program, because a great many of West Shore's students transfer into schools of education in Michigan's universities. This means that some of my courses are introductory-level education courses where students explore whether and how teaching might be a vocation for them. About half of my education students are traditional eighteen- and nineteen-year-olds not quite sure yet of their road. The other half tend to be women aged twenty-five to thirty-five, most of them with families, many of them single. They already know a good deal about children and about the realities of the region, and they bring strong, direct, purposeful questions into my classroom. The concerns of these mothers, working students all, are sincere articulations of what this region asks of its inhabitants. My students know about child support, child abuse, alcoholism, welfare, and children having children. They have firsthand knowledge of the legal system, of racial and sexual discrimination, of the alienation from school that comes from poor self-esteem and a culture of resignation. I have students who want teaching to be not just about answering their own considerable needs and interests but also about addressing important local and social concerns. My curriculum, then, is partly directed by such concerns and issues, which are not particular to our part of Michigan, of course, but are definitely exacerbated by the relative isolation, and the relative poverty, of a largely rural district where winter bites hard and employment can be desperately seasonal.

Trying to frame my own answers to the tough questions, I seek solace in the pieces of landscape that remain familiar to me. I am sitting right now in my library at home. Behind me are two of my favorite artifacts, one of them a huge oak bookshelf from the high school library where my mother brought hundreds of students, including my brothers and me, to research term papers long ago.

She is now the librarian in a new building, but she made sure I received this old bookshelf, which still proudly bears the word FICTION, during the move. Next to this shelf is my great-grandfather's teaching chair. He, like his daughter (my father's mother), taught in a community school not far from the Flint River. A picture of him standing with his class in 1902 sits on a library shelf next to several books of poems by Robert Frost, a favorite poet of all the language teachers of my family. This room has a huge bay window, looking west, lakeward. Right now the sky is gray and heavy, but warm; the last of our snow washed out in the rain last night and with the pond free of ice, frogs of all kinds are not waiting for evening but are filling the afternoon with jubilation, just as I imagine they are on my father's farm where he pauses to listen beside his black iron cauldron of boiling sap. The frogs rejoice in "these flowery waters and these watery flowers / from snow that melted only yesterday," as Frost wrote in one of the few poems crafted during his Michigan sojourn (lines 11–12). Out of such things—the shelves of poems that connect me to my mother and to learning to love words, the chair in which my great-grandfather sat reading student themes, and the long, gray warmth of sky drawing forth excited frogsongs—out of such things I find words and images to use in building a reply to the harder demands of my physical place.

This essay can't be about solving the problems of poverty in rural places like the district served by West Shore Community College. I can't use frogs and Frost poems to stem the tide of violence against women and children or correct inequities in education and opportunity across my region. But this essay can be about valuing place and allowing the richness of a community to invigorate not just my writing, but also my curricula. The point of the frogs in this essay is that I can hear them, right now. They are a part of my conscious mind as I type, and they are performing, at this moment, rituals that are important to me beyond their considerable inspirational value to my psyche. Amphibians are indicator species: they are more susceptible to pollutants and dramatic changes in environment than other species are. Hearing them in such abundance is, in part, a signal that the natural world I inhabit is functioning richly and powerfully, that the play of life is working as it should be. The frogs and the maple trees and my students and I are denizens of a community in which we all depend in some measure on each other. This ecological reality is a good way to frame a curriculum; my students, all of them, bring into my courses webs of connection to each other and to environmental realities both inspiring and challenging. In my place I can't afford not to hear the frogs singing or the songs and laughter, anger and tears in the questions of my students. I need to let the realities of my place have a role in my classroom. Most of my education students will become teachers. Many of them will be teachers, if not in Mason County, at least in places very like it, and one of the many, many things I will ask of them is that, as teachers, they learn to listen to the realities of their places, to let the curriculum be about what their students are about. I can't use frogs to fight inequity, but I can learn to listen to students in the way I've learned to identify a cricket frog's chatter and know what it means to me in physical and spiritual ways. Hearing frogs, right now, reminds me that my curricula need to be aware of the realities brought into my room by the other inhabitants that share my space; their needs are in so many ways my own. I know this as surely as I recognize now that when my teaching relatives brought teaching stories into their kitchens and into the sugar shack, they were *working*. Telling stories about teaching, especially the difficult stories, is a way of working out the problems, embodying them in a place where they can be carefully handled.

This summer I will teach a course in Michigan writing to interested undergraduates. A great many and a great variety of artists have wrestled with the environmental realities of Michigan, and my own students and I, of course, will be Michigan writers, too, our words reflecting on our place and on others who have similarly reflected. I will use Native American stories, the words of French missionaries who canoed our coastline, and a wry, exploratory novel of Michigan's frontier by Caroline Kirkland to set a foundation. From there we will wander into the recent century and an explosion of words, some of them grim and some of them celebratory, all of them attempting to reply to the exciting, challenging peninsulas that draw their stories out. I suspect I will sneak some Robert Frost into this course, at least "Spring Pools," the poem I excerpted above. I'll do this because this exploration of Michigan writing is, for me, an organic development of what my family has delighted in doing for generations, sharing words in a community of learners. My mother, my uncle, my grandmother, my great-grandfather, I myself, and so many others connected to us by blood, by love, by the realities of a classroom's walls, have carefully chosen words that reverberate, froglike, in the places in which they are shared. Saying poems is a way to share the joy I feel in where I live, a place I've been learning how to inhabit well all of my life. The curriculum I will teach this summer is important to me, in part, because it courses like maple sap with a powerful love of language that I have felt since my mother first read to me, since I first heard Uncle Paul recite a Frost poem or describe his sugaring process, since my father first gave me the specific names of the trees in his woods and the frogs in his own wetland. This course will be important also because it will allow my students and me to learn from the variety of ways Michigan's writers have responded to where they are. We will read bruised, brokenhearted words and bold, exuberant prose. We will face hard questions and hear delighted songs, and we will have, before us, a challenge to raise our own voices in chorus. Reading and writing poems communally can allow us to discover, together, language for the personal and communal responses to the geography insistently tugging our stories toward the surface.

Bibliography

Anderson, Lorraine. "Writing Me." *Peninsula: Essays and Memoirs of Michigan.* Ed. Michael Steinberg. East Lansing: Michigan State UP, 2000. 1–3.

Frost, Robert. "Spring Pools." *The Poetry of Robert Frost.* Ed. Edward Connery Latham. New York: Holt, 1969. 245.

III
There

8

Levittown Breeds Anarchists! Film at 11

Kathryn T. Flannery

Everybody comes from someplace, and the places we come from—cherished or rejected—inevitably affect our work.

Lucy Lippard

My mother-in-law used to joke that she needed a separate address book just for my husband and me. Married while still in college in the late 1960s, we have since moved from place to place to place, rarely staying in any one place more than a few years. From Ohio to upstate New York, New York to Virginia, Virginia to Massachusetts, Massachusetts to North Dakota, North Dakota to Pennsylvania, Pennsylvania to Indiana, and now back to Pennsylvania, we have been restless nomads, not content to stay put, and even when "settled" in one geographic locale, we've fixed up an apartment or a house only to move on to another one in the same town. And yet, in over thirty years of wandering, we have managed to avoid returning to the kinds of places where we grew up: we've managed, that is, to avoid returning to the suburbs. Even so, we trail the suburbs behind us, not as some psychological leg-iron that we'd rather lose and forget, but as a knotty rope of expectations about place, about home. Most of the time that knotty rope bumps along, fraying as we move farther and farther away from childhood. But every once in a while the knots catch on something and jerk us back.

We live in a city now, on a mixed-use block as urban planners like to say: some rentals, some owner-occupied dwellings, a commercial property or two. This is an ethnically and racially diverse "border" neighborhood, marking a just-visible line between Pittsburgh proper and the next urbanized town over. We've had a hard, bearing-down-on-you kind of winter, with snow that kept buried the accumulating layers of urban detritus. Until, that is, a first thaw exposed it all. That's when, once again, I got the itch to move. Nomadic tribes move to give the land a rest, letting the land reabsorb the waste and grow back what the domestic animals and the humans have grazed down. Maybe this itch to move is some sort of atavistic urge—except I wasn't aiming to leave my own mess behind, but someone else's careless trash. There is only so much of someone else's mess I want to pick up before I become more than a little irritated and restless to move. So I set out to look—just look—for an alternative place to live. Driving through a nearby town, farther and farther from the sights of the rusting postindustrial city, I began to notice how other drivers yielded the right of way, how a hulky SUV, gas-guzzler though it surely was, courteously pulled to the curb to let me pass through a narrow lane. I began to relax. I found my way to a tidy neighborhood, tidy yards, no visible trash, no obvious piles of dog feces, and as far as I could tell, no cigarette butts or assorted fast-food containers decorating the defiant hydrangeas. This wasn't technically a suburb, but a small town, and yet I read onto this landscape what I remembered from childhood—not bland uniformity but a largely untrumpeted sense of joint purpose, of interconnectedness and mutual responsibility. Not a lawn-nazi-world where men take pride in creating the monoculture of poisoned turf, but a neighborhood that assumes rather simply that one picks up after oneself. I was feeling the need for this sort of (albeit righteous) tidiness, for a bit of what I remembered as home. And that's part of what I mean by the knotty rope. It snagged on tidiness.

The trouble of course is that tidy can seem to depend on sameness. Christine Frederick, an early critic of suburban living, rejected what she saw in 1928 as "neat little toy houses on their neat little patches of lawn and their neat little colonial lives, to say nothing of the neat little housewives and their neat little children—all set in neat rows, for all the world like children's books" (qtd. in Lippard 226). But is that the inevitable formula? I grew up in Levittown, New York, in the 1950s, a place and a time that would seem to confirm the simple calculus, having come to represent in the cultural imaginary all that is most troubling about America.

Although not the first planned community, Levittown was the largest—17,447 houses in all—and it thus took on the role of prototypical post-WWII cultural uniformity, serving as the subject of sociological studies that set out to diagnose America's ills and as literary counterpoint to what America was thought to have been (or thought that it should be) (Kelly 3). The feminist art historian Lucy Lippard observes that after World War II, "planned obsolescence and consumer culture took hold in earnest" with "the first Levittown [leading] the way to plastic supernormality" (226, 232). In his fictional memoir, *Tidewater Morning*, William Styron refers to "the legion of bleak Levittowns" that stand in stark contrast to the village of his narrator's youth, a village figured as a "more agreeable, far prettier place to grow up in than the mass-produced high-tech eyesores that overwhelmed the landscape in later decades" (115). Although at least some part of my academic training (as well as my political commitments) inclines me to hold consumer capitalism responsible for these "eyesores," for the human-made blight evident almost anywhere one turns in the United States, I cannot say that I recognize my own childhood in Lippard's "plastic supernormality" or Styron's "bleak Levittowns." There is something more to the story than this familiar metonymic critique suggests, something paradoxical that has to do with complex relationships between order and sameness on the one hand and freedom and change or flux on the other.

    I cannot say that having grown up in Levittown gives me greater access to some "truth" about the place, but rather the experience of having been made the subject of scholarly attention adds a certain kind of personal edge to my academic work. As a historian of literacy practices, I have been drawn to stories "from below," in the spirit of the social historian E. P. Thompson: those stories that do not fit readily into the larger, grander stories that history and the social sciences want to tell. I cannot say that Levittown taught me such historiography, but learning as an adult that scholars and social critics had held such families as my own under their academic lens was sufficiently alienating to incline me to seek out alternative forms of intellectual work. What happens when the "subject" speaks back? Whatever the time frame of my research, even when it is remote in time, there is thus something personal for me in wanting to think about how ordinary people don't simply do what the planners and politicians and the social critics—and academics—think they should do. This then is an intellectually anarchic counterweight to my desire for tidiness: I am drawn to the messy parts of history, the parts that run counter to the dominant stories, and those instances that remind me of how ordinary nonconformity can be. The joke is that places like Levittown can indeed breed anarchists.

As Lippard argues, "one reason to know our own histories is so that we are not defined by others, so that we can resist other people's images of our past, and consequently, our futures" (85). Levittown was not and is not a single place, nor can it be held in amber. The point is not that my memories of childhood can override what I now know about the official histories of that place. At the same time, my memories lead me to be skeptical of scholarship that figures the human actors as dupes or pawns or easily categorizable types. When I ask students in my classes to conduct historical research, I ask them to test out what they read "on the pulse": given your personal experience, does this public account make sense? If it runs counter to your sense of things, what sense can you make of the disjuncture? I don't want to say that personal experience, personal memory, automatically carries more weight—sometimes our experiences are exceptional, our memories at best partial—but it is to say that dissonant sites where personal and public stories are in tension may well be precisely the places that need to be explored, opened up, reexamined, that tell us something we have overlooked about the past, but also something about the investments of those who have had the power to tell the stories. It is sometimes in these cracks that open up in the dominant stories that we get some inkling of the unheroic nature of human agency.

My family, like others who lived in Levittown, both fits and fails to fit the terms that have been applied to them. If, as Barbara Kelly argues, Levittown was grounded in a notion of environmental determinism—that is, a properly designed place was expected to produce a better citizenry and, thus, Levittown as garden community was expected to produce good yeoman citizens—then the primarily young families that initially peopled the place somehow failed (mercifully) to fully conform to expectations. Their lives were not so easily engineered, not so easily mass-produced as the houses. The residents made and remade homes, as they made and remade their lives, not to produce a utopian community but also not in the paternalistic image of the eponymous founder. When Levittown was first built, it may have been "clean and quaint and hopeful," but it very quickly began to change into a "multifaceted place that reflects difference, the lives within it, and the social forces that form it from without, even when such a reflection exposes some ugliness" (Lippard 231). Levittown was not the ideal community promoted in the developer's advertising, nor was it the model for *The Truman Show*. The relationship between place and people, between intention and actuality is more complex, more ambiguous than that. Levittown can thus stand for the mismatch between what traditional scholarship "from above" has to say about a place and what those who live and work in the place have to say.

It would be no surprise to my father to learn that Levittown's developer William Levitt shared in a widespread belief that, if citizens owned their own homes, they were less likely to engage in subversive activities. "No man who owns his house and lot," Levitt contended, "can be a Communist [because] he has too much to do" (qtd. in Kelly 49). My father was no fan of Levitt, whose business tactics my father held in disdain. My father was a Roosevelt New Deal Democrat, and, for him, Levitt represented the kind of self-serving capitalist who took advantage of post–World War governmental programs for his own gain rather than for the good of the commonweal. At the same time, my father was no fan of communists. Before the war, before he enlisted in the Army Air Corps, my father had worked in a tool and die factory in Brooklyn. He tells two kinds of stories about that experience: one has to do with standing up to the bosses and the other has to do with standing up to the "commie goons" who threatened to take over the union. The latter story has to do with my very skinny father wielding a very large wrench in the "goon's" face. The former story has to do with my father beating the boss at his own game by more efficiently reaching the expected production quota in shorter time, to either earn more money or earn more time off. My father would agree in principle with Levitt that a man should be able to own the roof over his head and that hard work should by rights be rewarded. But he would have categorized Levitt as a "boss," someone who could not be fully trusted and, therefore, someone to outwit. Just as working for a boss was a fact of life, buying a home from someone like Levitt was understood to be a practical, if not wholly savory, necessity.

Levittown can be understood as having been created as an "intentional" community with an ideological agenda, a place planned to "structur[e] the social order" (Kelly 44). Levitt was not inventing the plan, however, but was following the prescriptions of the Federal Housing Administration that reflected "a growing consensus about the nature of the American character and about the role of the house and home in its formation" (42). Not a new set of ideas, of course, as Barbara Kelly observes,

> *an ideology of house and home had been part of the American political culture from the colonial days through the founding of the Republic and into the reform periods that followed it. Expressed from the top in the form of land grants and voting privileges for the landed, and from the bottom in the form of a restless wandering in search of a better piece of land, the consensus was rooted in the theory that the privately owned homestead was the most appropriate form of housing for the republic. (42)*

More immediately, in the wake of World War II and against the backdrop of the rise of communism, Levitt capitalized on the federal government's efforts to address a significant housing shortage (and thereby ward off political upheaval).

Some sixteen million GIs had returned from duty only to find insufficient housing. Depleted construction supplies, a labor shortage, and the building industry in decline meant that new housing had to be created quickly. One report has it that ex-GIs and their families across the country "were living with their parents or in rented attics, basements, . . . unheated summer bungalows [and] some even lived in barns, trolley cars, and tool sheds" (Levittown Historical Society). In this regard, my parents were fairly typical. After my father was discharged from the service, he and my mother and my older sister, then an infant, moved in with my mother's parents on Staten Island, the most rural of the boroughs of New York City. But when I was born, the need to find a place of their own became acute. Neither of my parents came from money, and so they had to depend, in prototypically American fashion, on their own pluck and luck. My father found work as an air traffic controller at LaGuardia in Queens and that meant moving closer to his work. At the same time, my parents wanted more privacy for a growing family and greater independence to craft a life not bound to the Republican and conservative expectations of my mother's family. With little money, they had few options. For them, Levittown never appeared as selling out to cultural uniformity. They did not have the luxury to think in such terms. Rather, Levittown represented the only way they could afford to own their own home and to escape what Peter Hales refers to as the "relentless self-replication" of apartment-house living in one of the city's boroughs (5). In that sense, the unlikely Levitt house represented promise and possibility, "a new form of ideal American life, one that combined the idealized middle-class life of the prewar suburban communities, with the democratized life of younger, mainly urban-raised GIs and their families" (3).

In 1950, my parents bought one of Levitt's basic four-room Cape Cods with an unfinished attic and no garage. This was the first model in the development, and it was designed with cement-slab construction. What I remember as sweaty floors were a result of building the house not on a basement foundation but on a cement base in which were placed heating coils. When the heat was on, moisture would condense on the tile surface, making the floors a slippery hazard. The surface was hard on my mother's feet and hard on anything that happened to fall. Glass baby bottles were especially vulnerable. The floor plan was simple: essentially a square divided into four sections, a living room and kitchen in the front of the house, two bedrooms in the back, with a small section of one bedroom "square" taken up by the bathroom. Levitt later added ranch models, still on the four-square plan, but with slight variations in color, window placement, and roof line. Although my parents were seeking privacy from their parents, the Levitt house itself provided little space for privacy for family members. No "master suite" separated parents from the children; initially only a single bedroom was shared by whatever number of children; everyone used the one bathroom; and no playroom, no basement, no spare space allowed family members to hide away from other family members. The physical space required a literal rather than sentimental family togetherness. Strictly enforced naptime gave my mother some respite, some private time. Whether we slept or read in our bedroom, it did not matter, as long as we were quiet and left my mother alone for one hour—one hour to herself.

Whatever the social or psychological cost, the Levitt house was economical. Economies in mass construction made it possible to build houses that "a group on the lower edge of middle-class life—in effect, a prewar tenant class with a median income of little over $3000" could afford to buy (Taylor 1; Levittown Historical Society). Having learned cost-cutting techniques during the war, Levitt continued to perfect the mass production tract house that has now become so familiar. Cheap land, cheap building methods, nonunion contracts, and modifications in building codes together made it possible for Levitt to produce houses assembly-line fashion, averaging, when fully operational, thirty houses a day (Levittown Historical Society). This may not seem so remarkable today when blap housing developments sprout like toadstools after a spring rain. But it was remarkable then. My father's father had been a house builder on Staten Island before the Crash, but in his day he was thought "progressive" because he could work on two or three houses at once—not to complete these few houses in a day, but to work on building them over several weeks, or even months. My grandfather was a craftsman who built "from scratch" on site. Levitt, on the other hand, developed on-site, factory-like techniques—technically not a prefab process—that depended on the delivery of precut lumber to the construction site and the greater availability of standardized building materials such as sheetrock panels. Teams of workers moved from house site to house site, "completing one stage of construction before moving on to repeat that stage at the next site" (Kelly 26). Levitt bought directly from manufacturers when he could, and when he could not—as in the case of a nail shortage—he built a factory on the building site (27).

I doubt that my parents had much sense of Levitt's goal to create a "complete, integrated, harmonious community" for people thought of as occupying something called a "tenant class" in order to "provide a pleasant and wholesome social life" for this lower order of humans (Levitt qtd. in Kelly 36). I doubt that my parents had any sense—or would have accepted the designation—that they were part of a tenant class. Rather, they were drawn to the possibilities in the physical place, limited as it was, not to a philosophy based on class-oriented "uplift." Not elegant, the Cape Cod was nonetheless solidly built and came fully equipped—unusual for the time—with stove, refrigerator, cabinets, and washing machine, the latter tucked under the staircase going up into the unfinished attic. My father would later make money on the side by repairing the hundreds of Bendix washing machines that inevitably broke down after a few years' use. All Levitt houses had the same brand appliances, leading to a cottage repair industry. Later model houses included a built-in television set, also tucked in under the staircase, but this time on the living room side of the stairwell (Levittown Historical Society).

Each small house sat on a proportionately large lot, providing physical distance and relative privacy from neighbors, a remarkable luxury for those accustomed to urban life. Each lot was planted with four trees. I remember two apple trees on our corner lot, an improbable mimosa with its feathery pink blossoms, and a peach tree that at maturity produced enough peaches for my mother to can, and, after a hurricane, littered the yard with rotting, fermenting fruit. To this day, I cannot stomach the smell of ripe peaches. The sandy soil that had once supported potato farmers soon supported lawns and gardens. My mother said she could just tuck a cutting into that friable soil knowing that almost any plant would root and grow without great effort.

Interior lanes curved through the development designed to keep major traffic to its periphery. Sidewalks along quiet streets meant that as child I could ride my bicycle safely as far as the parkway or I could walk to a playmate's house within the development without adult supervision. Indeed my mother sent me off on the first day of kindergarten to walk the few blocks to school with no other companion than another five-year-old in the neighborhood. Such independence depended on the expectation that we were safe to go off on our own. Although so large that it spilled across two towns and drew on the services of several municipalities, school districts, and fire stations, Levittown was nonetheless crafted to feel like a small town, arranged as it was around a series of "village greens," an echo of some English pastoral landscape. We could walk to the store, to the free public swimming pool (one of nine provided by the developer and open except during polio scares), and to school. Churches, synagogues, public libraries were all close at hand. The librarian knew me, knew that I liked to read, and set aside books for me. On the edge of the development, but still walking distance for my sister and me—on what we called the "turnpike" and urban planners would call "strip commercial"—were an ice cream parlor, bowling alley, roller skating rink, and movie theatre. I could not walk to the turnpike alone because it meant crossing a heavily traveled road, but my older sister and I could go together, or we could all go as a family. For all the ways in which the suburbs are now inextricably identified with the automobile, Levittown was designed—as were more affluent planned communities such as Radburn, New Jersey—as if it were still possible to do everything one needed to do by walking. Because my father drove the one car to work, commuting along one of Long Island's parkways, much of the time walking was the only means of transportation for the rest of the family. Without mass transit, my mother had to wait to use the car on those days when my father either carpooled or worked nights. Or she depended on neighbors. While I remember Levittown as a safe place for children, a place I could explore without close watch, I also know that it was in many ways a confining place for mothers, for my mother.

We have become suspicious of such places, of course, suspicious of the idea of manufactured community, of enforced domesticity that keeps women in the kitchen and out of the workforce and hides social difference and dissent behind the facade of sameness. Criticisms arose, in fact, before the first Levitt houses were built. Some feared the creation of an exurban ghetto with the influx of a tenant class that was not expected to know how to tend to property; others found the development aesthetically abhorrent with what appeared initially as "relentless homogeneity, the cramped quarters of its interiors, and the raw, unfinished quality of its landscape" (Hales 4). Still others assumed that in purchasing affordable housing, the primarily young buyers were also being "initiated . . . into a postwar climate of 'conformity and privatization'" (Taylor 1). It is no doubt true that by helping to finance home ownership through such efforts as Levitt's, the federal government was giving access to lower-income citizens who would otherwise have been excluded and, in the process, was expecting that these new homeowners would, as Barbara Kelly puts it, have a stronger stake in American society. Rather than overtly or explicitly dictating a set of bourgeois values, however, such social policy provided incentive for the "traditional values of cooperative individualism, industry, and thrift" through underwriting home mortgages (Kelly 168). But, for all the ways in which both the developer and the federal government had crafted a plan to reshape the so-called tenant class, the homeowners themselves, in varying ways and degrees, proceeded to remake much of the plan.

In renting or buying a Levitt house, families initially agreed to build no fences, agreed to limit the colors they would paint their houses, agreed to install no "laundry poles or lines outside the house, except the one portable revolving laundry dryer" provided by the developer, and that only in the rear yard and only on weekdays. Almost immediately, residents began the process of disrupting the uniformity of the houses, building fences, adding dormers, building garages, painting their houses outside the approved colors—and hanging laundry when they needed to. Following the war, do-it-yourself home improvement was a necessary response to the general labor shortage, and home decorating and handyman publications proliferated, providing assistance to new homeowners (Kelly 71). My father was not unusual in building a garage and finishing off the so-called expansion attic. He did not want the garage for the car—and in fact, he never built a driveway to make it possible to drive the car into the garage—but wanted a large workshop for the power tools he used to build furniture and to create additional living space for a growing family. Although local newspapers and magazines featured such transformations of the basic Levitt home, showcasing residents' handiwork, not everyone was so impressed. Ironically, even though critics continued to condemn the uninspired uniformity of Levitt housing, the sociologist William Dobriner criticized what he saw as do-it-yourselfism run amok. What was once "clean," "quaint," and "hopeful" in Levittown was soon marred through "individualism, indifference, neglect, and taste good and bad":

> *Do-it-yourself paint jobs: red, aqua, chartreuse, cerulean and pink trims. Jerry-built dormers stagger out of roofs. The expansion attics are all fully expanded. You see a half-finished carport, patched concrete, broken asbestos shingles, grime and children's fingerprints ground into a peeling light-blue door, a broken picket fence, a dead shrub, a muddy trampled lawn. . . . (qtd. in Lippard 231)*

The black and white wallpaper my father put up in the bathroom would no doubt have appalled Dobriner as much as it embarrassed my mother, with its cartoon depictions of people bathing. No nudity, mind you, just a repeated pattern of bathing scenes, a head peering out from above a shower curtain or an improbable third arm appearing with scrub brush in hand. The decor was always a compromise between what my mother envisioned and what my father actually carried out as the resident handyman. My mother sewed curtains, slipcovered sofas and chairs, and braided rugs, but the work of remaking the physical space was left to my father. However successful or unsuccessful the collaborative effort in anyone else's estimation, my parents assumed that the house was theirs to do with as their budget and time would allow, as both a matter of necessity—two children were now four children—and as a matter of personal aesthetics.

The art historian Peter Hales has argued that critics of Levittown tended to judge the place "from an older, more elite standpoint—they were, themselves, idealizing an American landscape inappropriate to Levitt, to his constituency, or to the moment in which Levittown came to be" (4–5). Such critics took as their reference point upper-middle-class, nonurban, individualized, custom-built housing, possible only for the few before the War and certainly not possible for those Levitt (or the Federal Housing Administration) referred to as the target market. In response to the kind of criticisms raised against Levittowners' handiwork, Lucy Lippard suggests that it would be well for us to consider how "human and hopeful" it is "when an artificially happy-face facade has given way to a multifaceted place that reflects difference." Levittown might then be viewed not as the "epitome of suburban self-abnegation" but as "a tribute to the ineradicable drive for self-expression" (231).

The physical look of the place, as Lippard suggests, reflected on some level a degree of human diversity. From the outset, Levittown was more diverse in terms of ethnicity and religion than the surrounding Long Island communities, especially the historically exclusive WASP enclaves of the North Shore. The relative physical proximity of different ethnic groups in a city can make us forget how enforced the lines dividing neighborhoods—and peoples—could (and can) be. But my parents were part of a generation dislocated first by economic depression and then by war. Many of the men of their generation had, thanks to military service, come into contact with people they would never have known in their old neighborhoods. What military experience began, Levittown continued by housing in one neighborhood people who were unlikely to live together if they had returned to their former lives on Staten Island or in Queens or Brooklyn. Relatively diverse in ethnic background, they were nonetheless similar in age and socioeconomic status. Most of those who crowded the development office early on to rent or purchase a Levitt home were married couples in their twenties and early thirties, some with small children, and most of the men were veterans (Kelly 59–60). Primarily blue-collar workers—many employed in the nearby aircraft industry, as well as some, like my father, "in the recently emerged white-collar middle class, wage-earning people whose work was clean, but not well-remunerated"—the first residents were for the most part people who before the war could not have afforded a home. They may not have measured up to dominant cultural norms in terms of "wealth, education, or social standing," as Barbara Kelly observes, but they were clearly looking to move up (45).

It is clear that the socioeconomic status of residents changed as did the physical environment. And yet, there was from the beginning one troubling constant, troubling especially because not unusual. In the earliest deeds, William Levitt included a racial covenant barring any owner of a Levitt house from selling to anyone other than "members of the Caucasian race."[1] At the time, Federal Housing Administration guidelines recommended against mixing "inharmonious racial or national groups." The federal agency advised that "if a neighborhood is to retain stability, it is necessary that properties continue to be occupied by the same social and racial classes" (Mohan 1; see also Chappell). While Levitt did in fact mix nationalities (whether or not "inharmonious") in apparent opposition to the federal recommendations, he nonetheless cited the FHA to support his decision to bar blacks, justifying his action on the grounds that it was "a business decision." Segregation was the norm and sanctioned by federal authorities, he contended, and to run counter to that norm would mean that other businesses would beat him in the marketplace. The language of the covenant is telling: "The tenant agrees not to permit the premises to be used or occupied by any person other than members of the Caucasian race. But the employment and maintenance of other than Caucasian domestic servants shall be permitted" (Mohan 1). The obvious racism here is married to the ludicrous notion of servants for homeowners categorized as part of a tenant class.

The FHA may have wanted to address the housing shortage for returning GIs, but that did not include the 1.2 million black Americans who had served in the armed forces (Raines 2). And yet, this oversight could have been a very brief chapter in the history of Levittown. The Supreme Court ruled in 1948, well before all the Levitt houses were built, that such covenants were "unenforceable as law and contrary to public policy"; and a year later the FHA revised its policy to no longer back mortgages that involved racial covenants. Subsequent deeds for Levitt houses did in fact omit the racial covenant, but Levitt continued to reassure the public that he would not sell homes to blacks. Only later, when faced with legal and political pressure, did Levitt relent (Mohan 2). And yet, the taint of racial discrimination together with the larger racism of American housing practices insured that Levittown would remain—continues to remain—largely white.[2] No doubt for some whites who purchased Levitt homes, racial segregation was a selling point. For others, however, especially early on, it was not necessarily a matter of active choice. Unlike gated communities today that attract the economically advantaged, who can choose where to live and actively choose (at least economic) exclusivity, the white sector of the so-called tenant class had fewer options. At the same time, the returning black GIs had fewer options still, with African Americans losing ground—literally—throughout the course of the twentieth century so that fewer and fewer blacks owned property.[3] Levittown managed on some level to break down ethnic and religious barriers but did not and has not managed to break down the racial divide that seems now, if anything, more, rather than less, definitive of American culture.

I don't know whether my parents' deed included a racial covenant. By 1950 when they bought their house, the Supreme Court had already ruled, and so it would be unlikely. But they could not have failed to notice the racial make-up of the development, even though I don't remember this fact of segregation to have been a topic of conversation between my parents or among the neighbors. Racial segregation was no doubt such a fact of life in much of the North that it could go unremarked, but consciousness of racism could not be kept entirely out of view. I remember a dinner at my mother's sister's house—they lived in one of the small fishing villages on the North Shore of Long Island—when my uncle used a racial slur. My father stood up from the table, said he did not want his children to hear such language, and marched us all out of the house and drove us home, back to all-white Levittown.

The contradictions of Levittown make clear that place alone does not determine lives but represents a set of limits and possibilities. Human actors who people a place are never wholly free to shape the environment or their lives but have to improvise from the possibilities at hand. In the dynamic interaction of place and people, change happens, but never fully as the planners plan it or as ordinary people intend it (to echo Marx). Thus Levittown does not stand for a single ideological formation, nor can it offer a fully predictable judgment about the American character. It is, as Lucy Lippard suggests, multicentered even as—or perhaps especially when—its limitations are exposed. For my parents, Levittown gave them a place to begin independent lives with a degree of distance from the conservatism, and, perhaps paradoxically, from the racism of their upbringing. Even as my mother's life was hemmed in by the limited expectations her family had for girls and the domesticity of Levittown, she worked to insure that not just her sons but also her daughters would go to college. While raising a family and crafting a home, she continued to teach herself skills that later—after we moved from Levittown—would lead to rewarding work outside the home. My parents tended to support liberal causes closer to the interests of their primarily Jewish friends than to their Protestant families. I remember when they banded together with other parents in the neighborhood to remove anti-Semitic materials from the elementary school curriculum. They raised their children to distrust "systems" and "bosses," to assume that if one is not part of the solution, one is part of the problem, and to believe that houses and communities and places of work and lives are all revisable. We were raised to think the world could be changed, and we had a responsibility to contribute. Indeed, to let things be is slothful, wasteful; above all, independence means doing it yourself. When they could afford to do so, my parents moved on, eventually leaving New York altogether for the wilds of Ohio. My family never lived in a planned community again, and we never lived in a wholly white community again—but we also never moved back as a family to a city.

Even as this long winter very reluctantly gives way to spring, my need to flee the city has passed, at least for now. We have begun this summer's restoration project on our hundred-year-old house. We begin to work the year's compost into the depleted urban soil and coax still more plants to grow in this small urban lot. Indeed, our house and yard seem more amenable to fixing up than the labyrinthine bureaucracy of the large research university where I teach. Like my parents, I have had to make compromises with my environment, to change what is within my compass but never quite to make peace with systems and bosses that seem so impervious to change. As long as the system, imperfect as it is, can make room for the work that matters to me most—that is, in teaching and in scholarship, but also politically, in figuring out how human agents manage and can manage better in relation to structures most often not of their own making—then I can see my way clear to stay a little longer.

Notes

1. Restrictive covenants were only one way to prevent blacks from buying property. Covenants in general "are a way to enforce some requirement in perpetuity, no matter how often the property changes hands." Any subsequent buyer is expected to abide by the terms of the covenant that "run[s] with the land." Initially racial covenants were thought to be unaffected by the Constitution (which was understood to address only government action) because such covenants were treated as private agreements between individuals. But in 1968, the Fair Housing Act outlawed racial discrimination in housing even by private individuals and specifically outlawed racial covenants (Gerber 1).
2. Geoffrey Mohan of *Newsday* reports that "into the 1980s, and today, [Levittown] remains 97 percent white" (2).
3. According to Franklin Raines, in 1920, blacks owned about "15 million acres of land [but by 2002], they [held] only 1.1 million acres" (2).

Bibliography

Chappell, David L. "If Affirmative Action Fails . . . What Then?" *New York Times* 8 May 2004. A17–A19.

Gerber, Eve. "George W.'s Racial Covenant." *Slate*. 20 December 2003 <http://www.slate.msn.com/id/1003204>.

Hales, Peter Bacon. *Levittown: Documents of an Ideal American Suburb*. 9 September 2003. <http://tigger.uic.edu/~pbhles/Levittown.html>.

Kelly, Barbara. *Expanding the American Dream: Building and Rebuilding Levittown*. Albany: SUNY P, 1993.

Levittown Historical Society. "Levittown USA: A Brief History." <http://www.levittownhistoricalsociety.org/history.htm>.

Lippard, Lucy R. *The Lure of the Local: Senses of Place in a Multicentered Society*. New York: New, 1997.

Mohan, Geoffrey. "Levitt's Defenses of Racist Policies." *Newsday*. 20 December 2003 <http://www.newsday.com/estras/lihistory/hsievrac.htm>.

Raines, Franklin. "40 Acres and a Mortgage." *Sojourners* (Sept.–Oct. 2002). 20 December 2003 <http://sojo.nci/archives/magazine/index.cfm>.

Styron, William. *Tidewater Morning*. New York: Vintage, 1993.

Taylor, William. Foreword. *Expanding the American Dream*. By Barbara Kelly. Albany: SUNY P, 1993. 1–2.

9
Living in a Transformed Desert

Mitsuye Yamada

It is a simple equation: place + people = politics.
Terry Tempest Williams

I noticed in my peripheral vision from the passenger seat where I was sitting a yellow pillowcase wriggling on the backseat of the VW van. Flo, an environmental biologist, and I were carpooling to Cypress College where we worked.[1] Flo and I were both veteran teachers of more than ten years, I in the English department and she in biology.

"What's that in the pillowcase?" I asked her warily.

"Oh, that's a little snake I picked up in the Mojave Desert last week to show to my class. I have to return it this afternoon."

"Return it? Where?"

"Don't worry. She's really quite harmless, just a little disoriented. I need to take her back this afternoon after my classes to the spot where I found her in the desert."

"Why?"

Patiently, Flo explained that, in order for her students to develop a sense of respect for the creatures that live in nature, it was necessary for them to see the animals as living beings, not just as pictures in books and films or specimens in jars. Therefore, she had been taking these trips into the Mojave Desert twice a year to pick up whatever creatures she could capture, show them to her students, and then return them in a few days. It would seem an intrusion on natural processes, but it was the only way most of her students could see these creatures close up, short of physically taking her whole class out into the desert.

But, I asked, wouldn't it be more sensible to keep the snake alive in a terrarium in her classroom so that she didn't have to do this twice a year or at least let it go in the hills near where we lived? What difference would it make to the animal, I wondered aloud.

"A big difference," she said, "because the animals live in close symbiotic relationship with other animals and plants that are particular to the area." Her explanation became somewhat technical, and my mind began to wander.

It had been eighteen years since I had driven through the Mojave Desert when my husband and I moved our family westward from New York to California for his new job. I remembered the numbing hours and hours of traveling through the vast uninhabited desert areas while trying to keep our restless children in the backseat occupied, and I was concerned about Flo driving into such a desolate area by herself. Impulsively, I offered to go along to keep her company. I made hasty telephone calls to my husband at work and my mother who would be caring for our children. After our morning classes, Flo and I, with her "little snake" in tow, were on the freeway for our four-hour drive towards the Providence Mountains in the Mojave Desert.

As she drove, I told her that I remembered living in the desert years ago. "Nothing is going on out there; the desert is such a sterile and nonproductive part of our country," I mumbled, as I looked out the window into the dry landscape seemingly devoid of all living things. This comment brought out the biologist in Flo. I should study the ecology of the desert, she said. I would then learn there is a great variety of living things in the desert. Furthermore, she added, they depend on each other for survival. Glancing towards the wriggling pillowcase in the backseat, she returned to my earlier question about why she must take the snake back. Just think, she said, if people picked up animals and depleted the population of certain species, it would upset the whole balance of nature in the desert. That seemed unlikely to me, but I was intrigued by her explanation of how this snake contributed to the ecological balance in her environment, even, cruel as it may sound, as food for another animal. This is important, she said, because they all live on limited resources and must share what little there is in an amazing kind of symbiosis.

We stopped, in the middle of nowhere it seemed. This is where she found the snake, she said, this area south of the Kelso Dunes. We walked a short distance from the van with the pillowcase to find "the spot" where Flo might have found the snake. The reptile, released from its cloth prison, was stunned at first but quickly adjusted to the warm sand and slithered away into the shade of a dry creosote bush. Miles of sameness wrapped around me. There was no sign of life anywhere, I thought, only dusty bushes as far as my eyes could reach—just like the area that surrounded the camp near Minidoka, Idaho, where I was sent in 1942 along with 120,000 other Japanese nationals and Japanese Americans a few months after the outbreak of World War II.

I had spent a year and a half in what was called an "assembly center," then moved to an Incarceration Camp in the Idaho desert; I have never been comfortable with desert animals or anything associated with the desert since then. The Japanese immigrants and their American-born children living on the West Coast were removed from their homes by presidential order and found themselves trapped in an inert part of the country, surrounded by barbed wires and watchtowers where armed U.S. soldiers stood guard over them. After leaving Idaho for college, I moved often and always lived in the urban areas of the country. As a resident alien, I never really felt settled anywhere, but I had always felt more at home in places like Chicago and New York City, large cities as far removed from the desert as possible. When my husband made a career change and we moved our family to Southern California, it took me years before I became acclimated to our new home with reminders of camp life: lizards in our backyard and cacti growing wild in uninhabited areas of the neighborhood. Furthermore, compared to New York City, the cultural and intellectual life in the suburbs where we lived seemed barren to me. On that day with Flo, I was back in the "real desert" for the first time in decades.

As we stood there, I noticed a certain orderliness in the way the plants grew in this desert wilderness. They were evenly spaced, as if someone had planted them that way. I thought I could actually smell the dry, clear air. I felt a heightened sense of awareness and spiritual calm as the penetrating midday sun seeped through my pores. The sound of our shoes crunching on the dry earth echoed in the stillness. The hushed silence was a welcome respite after a full schedule of classes and conferences with needy students that morning. We spent less than an hour in the desert before we started back to "civilization," but, in that short time, I sensed that this was a whole new world I had never known before.

On our drive back, I told Flo that a section of my first book, *Camp Notes and Other Poems*, depicted a rather grim view of the desert. I had written the poems in 1943 while working the night shift in the camp hospital. In "Desert Storm," one of my poems in this collection, I recounted my sense of besiegement in the desert climate:

> Near the mess hall
> along the latrines
> by the laundry
> between tar papered barracks
> the block captain galloped by.
> Take cover everyone he said
> here comes a twister.
>
> Hundreds of windows
> slammed shut.
> Five pairs of hands
> in our room
> with mess hall
> butter knives
> stuffed
> newspapers and rags
> between the cracks.
> But the Idaho dust
> persistent and seeping
> found us crouched
> under the covers.
>
> This was not
> im
> prison
> ment.
> This was
> re
> location.[2]

The desert had held no romantic images for me since my days of incarceration in a camp in the Idaho desert, and yet on that day when I was standing in the middle of the desert in California, I felt strangely moved by the sights, the silence, and the feel of the desert. Flo, a committed nature lover, smiled when she heard me express this. That is what is called the "mystique of the desert," she said. She reminded me that we Southern Californians live in the desert, but we don't realize it because our well-watered and manicured gardens have been transformed by importation of water from miles away. The area we now occupy, the suburbs, used to be an undeveloped desert just like this one, but, she said, we have to actually *be* in the real desert like this to appreciate it. A course in desert ecology is especially important for our students because, she continued, they need to develop a "sense of community with their land."

Flo was writing her PhD thesis at UCLA at the time, and her talk of trying to find new methods of teaching her standard biology classes piqued my interest because I was also straining at the leash under the prescribed methods of teaching my English classes. As she drove, Flo continued her musings about her "wishful thinking" methods of teaching biology. She said she hoped to bring her biology majors out to the desert on a field trip some day for a few days if she could manage to get permission from her department chair. A thought occurred to both of us almost simultaneously as she talked: why can't the two of us work on our own department chairs to combine their resources and bring our two groups, the biology and creative writing students, out to the desert together? Because our college forces our students into separate buildings, the science and the humanities buildings, they never have an opportunity to interact with students in other disciplines as Flo and I were doing.

Our conversations in the following weeks revolved around the idea of offering our students field trips called "Desert Experience for Biologists, Poets, and Writers." We talked about expanding to other wilderness areas—the islands, the mountains, and the forests—and calling the course "Wilderness Experience for Biologists, Poets, and Writers." Writing the proposal and planning a curriculum for the course was fairly easy, but we needed approval for funding and acceptance of the interdisciplinary concept itself (one administrator complained that it was such an odd pairing "the computer wouldn't understand"). It would take a couple of years before the interdisciplinary field trips became a reality.

On our first venture with our students, we fully expected them to exchange impressions of the desert from different perspectives and discover their assigned roles in their newly formed community. We learned, however, on our first disastrous trip that it was not enough to subject the students to desert ecology lectures and then throw them together expecting them to share their experiences with each other. On that first trip, the two groups of students did not come together naturally as we had expected. The biology students were there to observe the desert animals in their natural environment. They felt their biological studies and knowledge of the ecosystem in the desert were "useful to humanity," while the poets were "flakes" whose skills had no practical use at all. The creative writing students felt that the biologists did not understand anything beyond observable facts and their lack of imagination made them incapable of appreciating "beauty for beauty's sake." Flo and I talked up a storm. We tried icebreaker games, had campfire cookouts, and encouraged the students to talk about their experiences of the day in small groups. Nothing worked—although in the end, most of the students reported in their final evaluation papers that they had a "good time" and "learned a lot."

I was more upset about what happened than Flo. She felt that our basic idea was a good one; that this was simply an unfortunate mix of students; and that with another group of students and different dynamics, things would fall into place as we had planned. I, however, felt I needed to prepare my students mentally for their trip because, for some of them, "the biology of the desert" was a completely new idea and they were as awestruck as I was in the beginning. Obviously, we needed to do more than give instructions about camping needs and the rules of conduct in the desert to both groups, as we had done for our first orientation sessions. At those initial joint meetings, we had given students a list of items to pack: the proper type of equipment, clothes, and adequate supplies of food and water. We explained that the ecosystem in the desert was extremely fragile and must be left as untouched as possible. That meant that they had to wrap all garbage and carry it back home with them. Most importantly, they must respect the land and all living things in it. We said nothing about respecting other human beings who might have different goals in life! I tried to think of the most effective way to prepare my students without telling them outright what to expect and what to experience.

I assigned excerpts from *Desert Solitaire* by Edward Abbey and *The Voice of the Desert* by Joseph Krutch, the two books on desert ecology that were accessible to me at the time. I photocopied a few poems about the desert and desert animals that I could find. Among them were Robert Frost's "Desert Places," Shelley's "Ozymandias," D. H. Lawrence's "Bats," and Emily Dickinson's "A narrow fellow in the grass." These poems appeared often in the anthologies I normally used in my literature courses, but it struck me for the first time as I reread them that they were mostly negative images of the desert as "empty spaces" (Frost) or revulsion on the part of the speaker for creatures that are often found in the desert (Dickinson's "zero at the bone"). In the past, because of my prejudices against the desert acquired during World War II, I never questioned these metaphors. (Only Shelly expressed the awesome power of the desert, or nature, to reclaim its own against the arrogance of the powerful Egyptian King Ramses II, whom the poet referred to as Ozymandias.) These poems became talking points for me to encourage my students to write about their impressions of the desert places with fresh eyes.

I then realized the importance of posing some general philosophical questions to both groups of students, in addition to giving them the nuts and bolts of what they needed for camping in the desert. We compiled a list of questions for discussion: Who is to say who has the "right" kind of relationship to nature? What is the "value" of the desert? When we write about the desert and the flora/fauna in it, are we, in a sense, "using" them for our own purposes? When, during the course of these discussions, students started to bring into the classroom related articles and poems they had found from their own readings, we felt gratified that we were getting through to some of them at last. It would take a few more trips, a few more years, for us to compile a proper bibliography of readings and collect an adequate set of slides for orientation sessions. Gradually, the social atmosphere during subsequent trips improved, and things "fell into place," as Flo had predicted.

In personal terms, these semiannual field trips to the Providence Mountains State Recreation Area and the Joshua Tree National Monument that spanned several years had a profound effect on me—more, I believe, than on any of my students. My reintroduction to the desert came at a time when I was more than ready to incorporate new ideas into my system of thought and gave me a language to speak openly about the way I related to my environment.

It validated my previous efforts in my approach to teaching that had come about almost by chance. I had been learning "on the job" and was quietly trying to make changes on my own in both my composition and literature classes.

The transformation had already begun a few years before my introduction to the California desert. I had met feminist poets and writers in San Francisco whose voices urgently called for inclusiveness and diversity in all institutions. Their writings spoke to me with an immediacy that very few writings had done before. Among them was Alta, an energetic feminist poet, who founded the country's first feminist publishing house, The Shameless Hussy Press, in 1969. Alta became the publisher of my first book of poems. Before the publication of my book, she scheduled prepublication readings in the Bay Area for me at women's conferences, women's health centers, and lesbian bars. The women's movement was making historical and social changes all around me.

By 1980, each additional new knowledge about the desert resonated for me, a slow bloomer who became "awake" late in life. By that time, I had already processed my own identity and introduced myself as an Asian American feminist poet at readings. After the publication of my book, I was often asked at readings and panel discussions in which I participated how I self-identified. Was I a woman first or an Asian American first? Where did my loyalties lie? Was I an Asian or an American? What were my priorities? Was I for human rights or women's rights?

The trips into the desert made me realize that these differences are imposed by the mainstream culture and that I should not be intimidated by them. Like the desert, I will simply be myself. The desert would stubbornly return to her own natural self if left alone for a period of time, even after being transformed into a grand city by means of modern technology. I identified with the desert, for she appeared to be, like me, a female personality emerging out of obscurity. I identified with the desert because I was always a bookish person, socially inept and shy. I saw that the desert's seeming inertness and silence did not mean there was no activity there. Many of her animals and plants are nocturnal and can be seen only at night with a flashlight. They reveal themselves on their own terms. Some flowers bloom in long intervals, such as the Joshua tree, bearing flowers every seven years. Compiling a collection of slides of desert animals and plants to show to our students took several years of watchful patience, day and night, on our part. I saw that the most unassuming-looking flowers burst into astonishing multicolored blooms when examined closely under a microscope (Flo always brought one on our outings). I recounted this new appreciation for the desert in a poem, "Desert Under Glass," published some years later in *Desert Run: Poems and Stories*:

> Look at the buckwheat
> magnified
> the biologist
> coaxes my myopic eye
> over glass
> a dusty round desert flower
> with a humble household name
> blooms
> a cluster of brilliant
> or chide-like shapes and colors
> the buckwheat
> growing on a crust
> of unmasked earth
> can be seen
> by one
> steady
> inward
> eye.

I saw for myself how the animals and plants quietly shared limited resources. I admired the desert's stubborn insistence on retaining her essential character in spite of human intrusions into her territory. I came to understand and accept the volatile weather conditions in the desert—the extreme heat and cold, the sudden rains, the violent windstorms—as part of nature's cycles. (One morning after howling winds kept us awake all night, one of my students remarked good-naturedly, "My, was she temperamental last night.")

Only after some understanding of the desert areas did the literal use of the desert for discarding toxic waste, testing atom bombs, and building prisons become repugnant to me. I became aware of environmental justice movements and their advocates.

Having been introduced to the small publishers' world by Alta, I discovered an iconoclastic work, newly published by a small press: *Green Paradise Lost* by feminist theologian and environmentalist Elizabeth Dodson Gray. In this work, the author traces our present ecological crisis back to the Judeo-Christian worldview. Gray makes us examine the deep-rooted causes of our biases towards others unlike ourselves and the dire consequences of our attitudes. She writes that man has interpreted the Biblical text in hierarchical terms, giving humans dominion over all of nature. My students and I studied her cosmological pyramid, where God is at the apex; below God come men; below men come women; below women come children, animals, and plants; and "below them all is the ground of nature itself" (3). Our hierarchical thinking, she believes, gives us permission to exploit those who rank below us as "the Other . . . the Other as another culture . . . below me . . . less powerful" (20). Through these discussions, my students began to find new ways of expressing their observations of desert life beyond the physical descriptions of the land and its inhabitants. Some of the students found new areas of interest outside our prescribed agenda, such as the discovery of the original inhabitants in the desert. They said they had heard that American Indians were the original inhabitants of California, but when they were physically in the desert, they "sensed the presence" of the Chemehuevi Indians in the southeast area of the Mojave Desert. The quality of my students' work improved, for they plunged into writing more intuitively and with a geater sense of history.

The success in initiating a course that did not fit into the regular curriculum at the time changed the way that I saw my role both in the college where I taught and in the community. Cultural adaptation had always been an accepted role in my upbringing. My parents, although they came to settle and raise a family of American children as early as the 1920s, always felt like sojourners and acted as though they were guests who were expected to behave themselves. During my childhood, they always impressed on me that as an alien Japanese ineligible for citizenship in this country, I must defer to my "hosts" at all times. These desert trips gave me courage to introduce to my department my own ideas about teaching as well as new approaches that I had read about in academic journals. I also was encouraged to move out of the academic circles to take some of my programs into the community. When Flo and I were asked to participate in the cultural arts extension series being offered by the Women's Building in Los Angeles, we immediately accepted. We offered a weekend field trip called "Wilderness Experience for Women" for women artists, photographers, poets, writers, and nature lovers.

This group, older than our undergraduate students, had never had any kind of camping experience before this trip and needed more guidance. Some were more fearful than our students, who plunged into the experience with more abandon than we often wanted. At the Kelso Dunes, my exuberant college students spent most of their time jumping and sliding on the hot sand to create the "great boom" they had read about. The women, on the other hand, were content to sit quietly and take in the scenery, the smooth and voluptuous mounds of sand. We sat and reflected on how they resembled the shapes of women's bodies: from the front, the breasts and abdomen; from the back, the buttocks, the waist, and shoulder blades. No wonder, one of the women exclaimed, we call this Mother Nature! These women were also more productive. I was inspired by them to finish my own collection of desert poems and published them in *Desert Run: Poems and Stories.*

By this time, the desert had permeated my thinking so completely that I often used a desert metaphor to argue a point in unexpected places. At one of the board meetings of Amnesty International USA, I proposed that we create a committee on cultural diversity. When a director asked, "What does that mean?" I found myself suggesting that he should study desert ecology. I explained just as I had done many times before to our students that diversity was not only enriching but also necessary for our survival. With a new feminist consciousness, I began to see the connections between my writing and my peace and human rights work. I had joined Amnesty International in the 1960s to write letters on behalf of an Iranian poet whose poems were interpreted by his government as criticism of the Shah of Iran and who was imprisoned and tortured. I then learned that many writers, poets, educators, and religious leaders, as well as human rights workers, suffered the same fate throughout the world. Amnesty International is a worldwide organization with the specific mandate to work "impartially for immediate release of prisoners of conscience; fair and prompt trials for all political prisoners; and the end to torture and executions." Amnesty's position is that we bear responsibility for the plight of others because those who are being exploited by their own tyrannical governments or find themselves in oppressive social situations can neither defend themselves nor expect others to jeopardize their own lives by coming to their rescue. I was often reminded that the quiet desert also needs advocates from destructive forces that would slowly encroach on its territory in the name of urban development. The separate parts of my life—my own writing, my teaching, my active involvement in women's, peace, and humanrights movements—were finally coming together into an integrated whole.

Most rewarding was my greater appreciation for the research that my husband was doing in his retirement at the time. After twenty-five years of working for large corporations as a research chemist, he had decided to return to his old interest in art and write a book about the close relationship between the scientific and artistic minds. He became very interested in our "desert experiment." He suggested that I assign Snow's *The Two Cultures* when I spoke to him about the breakdown of communication between our two groups of students during our first desert trip. He said that the controversy over Snow's work showed that lack of communication between the arts and sciences is nothing new. I persuaded my husband to give talks to our students at our orientation sessions, because his extensive knowledge of both the sciences and the arts were pertinent to what we were planning for our presentation. As a scientist who had had a successful career in industry and as a talented artist who had exhibited his watercolor paintings at museums in the past, he commanded a measure of respect from both the science and creative writing students.

I am no longer a sojourner here in California. Although I have lived in this country since I was three-and-a-half years old (I became eligible for citizenship only after the passage of the McCarran-Walter Act in 1952),[3] I am now adapted to the rhythms of the desert and my adopted country and have become an inhabitant. I retired from full-time teaching years ago but have not retired entirely from teaching or living. In my own backyard, there are a mixture of many types of flora and fauna, from the jungle to the desert, and here a single action must have many, many effects ecologically. Most of what I presently do consciously involves a multicultural perspective, for a single action in multicultural terms does not move in one direction. As an Asian American woman writer and teacher, I know that what I do and write has multiple cultural implications among women, among Asian Americans, among Asian cultures, and among other areas of the communities I live in. The eloquent environmentalist Terry Tempest Williams, in pleading for the right of the wilderness to exist, writes that every individual is a member of a community of interdependent parts. She carries with her the legacy of another early advocate of the wilderness who, she writes, "inspired us to see that in the richness of biological systems all heartbeats are held as one unified pulse in a diversified world" (175). In these unbearably troubling times for millions of people all over the world, this may sound too simplistic, but it is a goal towards which we must work and struggle.

> The desert is the lungs of the world.
> This land of sudden lizards and nappy ants
> is only useful when not used[4]

Notes

1. My colleague, Florence McAlary, earned her PhD in biology from UCLA in 1985. She taught biology at Cypress College from 1966 to 1989. She is presently an independent researcher at Friday Harbor Laboratory, University of Washington.
2. "Desert Storm," "Desert Under Glass," and "Desert Run" from Mitsuye Yamada, *Camp Notes and Other Writings*. Copyright © 1991 by Mitsuye Yamada. Reprinted by permission of Rutgers University Press.
3. The McCarran-Walter Immigration and Nationality Act of 1952 made it possible for Asian immigrants to become naturalized citizens for the first time in the history of this country. Until then, my parents, who had been living in the U.S. for over forty years, and I were resident aliens.
4. Excerpt from the title poem, "Desert Run," in *Desert Run: Poems and Stories*.

Bibliography

Abbey, Edward. *Desert Solitaire: A Season in the Wilderness*. New York: McGraw, 1968.

Alta. *Momma: A Start on All Untold Stories*. New York: Times Change, 1974.

Gray, Elizabeth Dodson. *Green Paradise Lost*. Wellesley: Roundtable, 1979.

Krutch, David. *The Desert Year*. New York: Sloane, 1954.

———. *The Voice of the Desert*. New York: Sloane, 1951.

Snow, C. P. *The Two Cultures*. Cambridge: Cambridge UP, 1993.

Wand, David Hsin-Fu, ed. *Asian-American Heritage: An Anthology of Prose and Poetry.* New York: Washington Square, 1974.

Williams, Terry Tempest. *Red: Passion and Patience in the Desert.* New York: Random, 2001.

Yamada, Mitsuye. *Camp Notes and Other Poems.* Oakland: Shameless Hussy, 1976.

———. *Camp Notes and Other Writings.* New Brunswick, N.J.: Rutgers University Press, 1998.

———. *Desert Run: Poems and Stories.* New York: Kitchen Table/Women of Color, 1988.

10
A More Fortunate Destiny

Jayne Brim Box

I work as a conservation biologist. In 1994, I found a single individual of an endangered species. It was a freshwater mussel. On the same bright summer day I found it, I killed it. No others have been found in the last decade, although I have spent hundreds of hours looking for more. Last year, while standing in the shower, I had a revelation, or more accurately, a sickening realization. What if I had snuffed out the last individual of an entire species?

This realization led to an ugly session of self-confrontation. Was I a traitor to the saint whose name I adopted at confirmation, St. Francis of Assisi? Will it ever be possible to look, without shame, at one of those bumper stickers that asks, "What Would Jesus Do?," knowing that I might have opened up two spots on the worldwide ark? When I attended national mollusk conservation society meetings, was I really an interloper, standing around with my colleagues drinking beer and bemoaning the plight of our "little buddies," the freshwater mussels, knowing that one of the species we discussed, the Suwannee moccasinshell, was last seen by me and put into a jar of ninety-five percent ethanol? And worst of all, that specimen was subsequently lost in a geneticist's freezer in South Carolina; so not only had I killed the last specimen ever seen, but that the poor creature's DNA was never unraveled in hopes of preventing its extinction.

The day we found the Suwannee moccasinshell I didn't even realize it at first. We were testing out some sampling techniques for mussels. Four of us plucked mussels from the bottom of a stream and put them into mesh bags, suspended in the water column. At the end of the day, I identified the catch, counted them, and returned the mussels to the stream. Unnoticed in a pile of small, black, common *Elliptio* was a *Medionidus walkeri*, a Suwannee moccasin-shell. I held the small yellow shell with green rays in my palm. It looked only vaguely like a moccasin. We took some photographs of it. My field crew asked me what I was going to do with it. Pickle it, of course, I answered, without hesitation. The sacrifice of this animal in order to find its DNA sequence seemed like a small price. If we knew genetically that it was in fact a "good" species, we could argue that perhaps it should be listed federally as an endangered species. Besides, I told my crew if this is the only one left, it's functionally extinct anyway. Secretly I knew that if I did a "proper" survey of the entire river, I'd find more.

Freshwater mussels are the most endangered group of animals in the United States. Historically, more mussel species occurred in the southern states than any other area of the world. They are extremely sensitive animals, and we refer to them as our "aquatic canaries in a coal mine," meaning that if a river is altered or polluted badly enough, it's likely they'll be among the first animals to disappear.

Their quirky life history doesn't help them. Because mussels live in freshwater and don't have fins or legs, they need help getting upstream to disperse. If they didn't disperse, mussels could go only where the flow takes them—downstream—and eventually they'd all end up back at the sea.

Over millions of years, mussels have, very cleverly, figured out that fish can swim upstream and have also figured out how their young can hitch a ride. Thousands of tiny young mussels, called glochidia, are held in the mother mussel's gills. Sometimes when we collect mussels, we can see these larval mussels stuffed in the mother's gill chambers like so many little white sausages. When the glochidia are old enough to attach to host fish, the mother mussel will spit them out, and, if things go right, some will find a ride.

Mussels won't use just any fish to spread their young around. Certain mussels use only certain fish, and usually the proper hosts are limited to a few fish species. If a glochidium accidentally snaps shut on the gills of an inappropriate fish host, the fish will slough off the glochidium, killing it. But mussels don't have eyes, so to enhance their chances of attracting the "right" host fish, they use fishing lures. The lures can be parts of their body (e.g., modified tissue along the shell) that look like small fish, insects, or other prey items the mother mussel waves to attract fish. When a fish comes close to the mussel to investigate, the mother mussel may shoot out a cloud of glochidia and infect the fish. Some mussel species use another tactic; before releasing their glochidia into the water column, they swaddle the glochidia in disguises that mimic insect larvae, larval fish, or even minnows. The fake or lure minnows are filled with thousands of young mussels that are smaller than pinheads. To complete the disguise, the minnow lure is attached to the mother mussel by a mucus fishing line that, like the string of a kite, causes the mussel lure to weave and dip through the water column as gracefully as a real minnow. Most of the mussel lures that biologists know about have been discovered only in the last twenty years or so.

Once, we filmed, while snorkeling, a mother mussel releasing her artificial glochidia-filled lure into a spring-fed creek. When we took a break and looked around the creek banks, two local fishermen had joined us. A mother mussel fishing underwater and two human fellows fishing above the water. Unfortunately, freshwater mussels aren't visionaries, because oftentimes their host fish are imperiled too, a sad testimony to the state of the nation's freshwater.

My affection for members of the genus *Medionidus* was cemented when I once spied a female luring in a fish host. Scuba diving in a creek years ago in Georgia, I was looking for a different species of *Medionidus.* The little mussel I found looked as if it was dislodged from the substrate, lying on its back. I was getting ready to place it gently back in the sand, when I noticed it was full of glochidia and flapping its mantle margins. It was doing this on purpose, I realized, to lure in a fish host. I watched as a small, inquisitive darter swam to this mussel and bit at it. I saw tiny opaque glochidia floating in the water column, the ones that didn't make it into the darter's mouth and attach to its gills.

It is difficult to explain how that episode made me feel so connected to one tiny little mussel on the bottom of a creek. Maybe it was the silence of scuba diving, the feeling of being in outer space, in my own world. Maybe it was ego, because I was one of the first people at the time who had witnessed, firsthand, that behavior. But the juxtaposition of that knowledge and the knowledge that I may have killed the last member of its cousin species, the Suwannee moccasinshell, made me feel caught in some twisted biological Greek tragedy. I wanted to relinquish my role in that play. I wanted to find another Suwannee moccasinshell.

I have been searching for years now, returning again and again to the New River, a tributary of the Suwannee River. It is an aquatic biologist's delight to work in this river system. The spring-fed tributaries of the Suwannee sometimes run crystal clear, and it is easy to spot fish, frogs, turtles, and alligators both above and below the water. The Suwannee River is home to a wide array of unique aquatic organisms, from five-foot-long gulf sturgeon to rare orchids and the animal I was preoccupied with finding—the Suwannee moccasinshell. This mussel species is found only in the Suwannee River system and nowhere else in the world. If we couldn't find it there, there was no place else to look.

In the spring of 1994, my coworker Andre and I spent weeks on the New River looking for the Suwannee moccasinshell. On one of our first trips, Andre and I ran into the local landowner who lived next to the New River. His name was Mr. Tomlinson, and he was eighty-three years old. We stood in his front yard, near his pond, and got acquainted. We told him about our work and why we were looking for these mussels. He said some other researchers from the University of Florida had been out in the river recently, looking for reptiles. He said they found a hundred-pound alligator snapping turtle that they estimated was at least one hundred years old. He also said a friend of his called him a few months back, at 6:00 a.m., and said, "Go look and see what has crawled out of your pond." Mr. Tomlinson said he went up to the road and saw a giant rat. He called the sheriff's department and told them to come out to his farm because "there was a monster out there." It turned out to be a 240-pound capybara roadkill. Native to South America, capybaras, the world's largest rodents, continue to gain a toehold in the southern states, like so many other exotic species.

There was something surreal about the juxtaposition of a big, fat, exotic "rat" ambling into the river system and the prehistoric, statuesque alligator snapper, itself a species of special concern in Florida. Two giants—and here we were, looking for a mussel that was about an inch long and weighed less than an ounce. Ultimately, would capybara, Brazilian peppers, Asian clams, snakeheads, carp, and swamp eels—all exotics—replace the alligator snapper and Suwannee moccasinshell, I wondered. Most alarming, would the whole state, a peninsula, fill up, as a glass fills with water, with the entity that has caused the most modern extinctions, the Anglo Saxon? I am one of the latter and, although the one thousand people a day who poured into Florida in the 1990s may have contributed to habitat destruction through their careless use of freshwater, overzealous building of strip malls and roads, and deforestation, was I the only one of those thousands who actually picked up a rare animal and purposely killed it? It gave me little comfort to think of the signs I saw in gas station windows in west Florida that said, "Get your woodpecker stuffed here," a reflection of how some of the locals felt about the red cockaded woodpecker being listed as federally endangered. Most of them were probably not really serious about going out and actually killing a woodpecker. But I had killed that moccasinshell, and it was hard to throw stones.

It's difficult to convey the affinity that you develop with an animal that has no head and only one foot. Mussels are not cute and cuddly, but they do have charisma. How else could you explain the eclectic mix of people—lawyers, publishers, astronomers, mail carriers—who spend time and money to collect and name these animals? Robert Louis Stevenson once wrote, "It is perhaps a more fortunate destiny to have a taste for collecting shells than to be born a millionaire" (17). In some ways, because so little is known about freshwater mussels, they allow the biologists who work on them today to traverse the same frontier the earlier naturalists explored. Every person working with freshwater mollusks can potentially make a significant contribution to the field. In addition, mussels come in every shape and size: some weigh five pounds, some five grams; some have spines, some have ridges; some are purple, yellow, or striped. They're as beautiful as their counterparts who come from the sea. I certainly believe the legend that the Romans invaded the British Isles to obtain pearls from freshwater mussels.

Two weeks ago, I read an article titled "The Global Decline of Nonmarine Mollusks." It suggested that nonmarine mollusks are perhaps the world's most endangered group of animals and that "a staggering forty-two percent of the 693 recorded extinctions of all animal species since the year 1500 are mollusks." It also said that "their extinctions go largely unnoticed by the general public, most biologists[,] and many conservation agencies," which focus their resources and energy on more charismatic vertebrate species (Lydeard 322).

This article troubled me. Not so much because it reported that the world's most endangered group of animals were nonmarine mollusks. That I knew. What troubled me was that their extinction went "largely unnoticed" by my supposed comrades—other biologists and conservation agencies. That bothered me. The latter I held to a higher standard because, rightly or wrongly, I expected "them" to know, to understand the extinction phrase I had twisted from Shakespeare, which was, "What is extinction, but another name for death?" When death is mixed with injustice, cruelty, systematic pogroms, and ethnic cleansing, and sometimes just exceedingly bad luck, trauma is evoked. Was it possible that somehow I was "traumatized" by bearing witness to a systematic "species cleansing"? Why did it feel inappropriate to rail against the death of a species, a species whose embodiment I last held in the palm of my hand? What has happened to me, our culture, and our species that made it seem ridiculous to evoke Auden's funeral blues for a freshwater mussel? Is it inappropriate to feel *this*—

> The stars are not wanted now; put out every one,
> Pack up the moon and dismantle the sun,
> Pour away the ocean and sweep up the wood;
> For nothing now can ever come to any good.

—for an animal that is less than two inches long and weighs less than an ounce? Well, it can be argued that I really don't *love* the Suwannee moccasinshell. Not in the traditional sense of the human use of the word love but perhaps in a more spiritual sense. That is, in the sense of holy monkeys or holy rats, sustained by humans, living in temples in northwest India. Is my own belief in divinity so tied to these creatures that they have come to represent, for me, the embodiment of everything I was taught as a youngster—to help and protect the weak, the unaccounted for, the voiceless?

Years ago, in South Carolina, I worked on small fish species that, when rivers flooded, ventured out onto the floodplains of swamps to reproduce and eat. These were not the largemouth or striped bass that received funding. Again, no one seemed to care about these small fish that apparently had no economic value. As my husband's grandfather, a former sharecropper/cowboy in Texas, once asked me about mussels, "What good are they?"

I wanted to tell him that mussels are like the lungs or, more appropriately, the gills of our river systems. That they, as filter feeders, can remove thousands of tons of solid wastes a year from our rivers. That, like any lungs living in a body with a pack-a-day habit, they're hurting from the daily exposure to toxic soups.

Instead I answered, "I guess they're not good for much."

"That's what I figured," nodded the eighty-nine-year-old.

In some ways I resent that we biologists who study freshwater mussels have to couch our species in terms that make them economically or culturally palatable. Often we pique people's interest by saying, "Well, mussels are resistant to tumors. But they live on the bottom of filthy rivers. Maybe there's something, some enzyme or chemical that makes them resistant to tumors. Maybe we should keep them around so we can look into that."

My colleague Christine called in late 2001 to ask me to help her look for the endangered Altamaha spinymussel. The glorious Altamaha River is home to six endemic mussel species. A few years ago, while reading *Ecology of a Cracker Childhood*, I secretly hoped, in the scene where Ray stepped out of her boat and onto an Altamaha sandbar, that she stepped on an Altamaha spinymussel or lance. Not out of malice, of course, but out of mussel kinship. I have stepped on both spinymussels and lances—the latter a long, pointed mussel that sits, point up, in the sand. Ray missed both.

On my trip with Christine, spinymussels were so scarce that when the water was murky, we both swept the sands with our fingers and toes, hoping to hit one of their inch-long spines. Halfway through our trip I swam into a discarded fishing line, wrapped around a tree stump, still fishing. The rusty hook at the end of the line rooted into my foot. We pulled it out with a pair of pliers. I was overdue for a tetanus shot, so the next day Christine took me to the local health clinic. The waiting room was filled with coughing people, and I joked with Christine that she'd better get out of there before she got sick. She left. I stayed. Later that day, we went back out to the Altamaha to do some more scuba diving and resume the search for our little buddies.

At the end of our Georgia trip, I was tired. So tired, I repeatedly told Christine, that I thought this must be what rock stars felt like when they checked themselves into the hospital for exhaustion. We laughed. I got on a plane in Atlanta, slept the whole way to Salt Lake City, and, when we landed, rushed off the plane to vomit in the nearest bathroom. That's strange, I thought, and forgot about it.

A nasty head cold accompanied me back to Utah. Nothing unusual for mid-November, but it wouldn't go away. On Thanksgiving I walked our dog but remember feeling extremely fatigued. A few days later, I woke with a screaming earache. The pain was excruciating. For some reason my ear acted like a cheap, distorting speaker, amplifying each heartbeat. I called my doctor's office, and the nurse said to try a decongestant. I did, but it didn't help. Right before 5:00 p.m. I called back and told the same nurse the decongestant hadn't helped. She said I could get an appointment with my doctor the next day. I took it. That night my husband, Paul, insisted I go to the emergency room. I did, but, when we got there, I balked. Emergency rooms were for people having heart attacks. I had an earache. I convinced him to take me home without seeing a doctor. Sleep was impossible because it was too painful to lie down. Sitting in the dark, in a stiff-backed chair, I listened to my own version of Poe's "The Tell-Tale Heart." At 5:00 a.m., I decided to write some e-mails. One ended with

> *I guess Paul called you or something. Now it's been 24 hours of this stupid earache. The pain really is excruciating. Paul tried to bring me to the emergency room last night, but I balked when we got there. So now I've been up all night wondering why I just didn't frigging see the doctor . . . . I've got to go; I think my eardrum just burst.*

Weeks passed. My eardrum healed; I didn't. Something else was going on. Suspecting I might have some type of inner ear problem, my doctor suggested I try to stay in bed for three days without moving. With two small children in the house, Paul and I knew this was impossible, so I went and stayed at a friend's. Remaining immobile turned out to be an extraordinarily difficult task. One night, when my friend was out at a Christmas party, I went to the fridge and got a beer. In hindsight not a very smart idea, because I was taking Valium for the nausea and, I think, painkillers, although I don't remember actually being in pain. On her refrigerator were tiny little enamel magnets with words on them. I stared at them and started rearranging them. Using the tiny magnets, I wrote the fragments of a poem that later summed up this bizarre, intoxicated three days of "rest":

> Two months of illness
> walking pneumonia, ruptured eardrum
> hole in my inner ear, undiagnosed

Motion sickness
nausea and lost weight
vicodin, valium and percocet

I had outpatient surgery five days before Christmas but stayed in the hospital two nights. When I went home, my doctor told me not to lift anything heavier than a dinner plate so that I didn't blow out the patch he had put over the hole in my inner ear. My cats and kids all weigh more than dinner plates. I thought to myself, this will be hard.

Recently my colleague John let the mussel world know he was sick. John spent his whole career snorkeling in the rivers and streams of North and South Carolina. John told us that he had been diagnosed with MPO ANCA—an autoimmune disease that essentially destroys the kidneys. John wrote, "Experiencing acute renal failure is not fun. Without expert screening, diagnosis, and AGGRESSIVE treatment, death or worse is ensured."

Lucky for John, he lives near the research triangle and did receive expert care and was slowly recovering. But his doctors also told him that he would never be able to survey "polluted" waters again. John wrote, "Until I'm told otherwise, I firmly believe that surveying in extremely polluted waters this past fall pushed my immune system over the edge."

Slowly, other biologists responded to John's announcement and cautions. One rather colorful biologist from Tennessee wrote,

> *Thanks John, I passed your message on to our WRD folks in Nashville. I hope you get to feeling better. Not the same without ol' grizz out there. I have experienced being burned a couple of times from chemicals in the water that got into my wetsuit during mussel surveys. My skin was scalded from head to foot! In Arkansas during P. capax surveys, obviously some chemical got in our dive booties that literally fried the skin off our feet. We had a name for it "fire foot." With all the junk being dumped in our rivers humans should be included as "Species At Risk." Take care John and look forward to seeing you soon.—Steve*

Humans as a Species at Risk. Because they are potentially imperiled by ecological changes (caused by themselves) and cultural pressures. Or any number of factors. What better place to be at the forefront of imperilment than in the water? What tighter and straighter nexus is there for a human being to become endangered than by sloshing around in effluents that peel the skin off the unarmored human body, in a slurry of microorganisms that penetrate the membranes of the nose and mouth, lodge there, make a home there, and do their damage unseen, flowing through the fluids of a human body until they lodge somewhere and slowly kill the host they had not evolved to parasitize?

In 2003, I received a call from my former boss, who asked if I would consider returning to Florida for a month or so to search for endangered mussels. I jumped at the chance to spend time on the Suwannee River, the same one Stephen Foster had written about. It was wonderful to be back in the river that I knew so well. On the first morning, we tooled down the river in our boat, and I watched as alligators and turtles basked on logs, fish jumped, and herons and egrets lazily flew in front of our boat. The limestone banks of the Suwannee were gray and moss covered or shiny black in the sun. Everything looked, and was, primordial. I thought to myself, this is feeding my soul, this is where I should be; everything is as it should be. That morning I was confident we would find more Suwannee moccasinshells and that I would be released from the guilt associated with my dirty little conservation secret.

On that last trip I took to the Suwannee River, a coworker found, on the dry bottom of a tributary stream that feeds into the Suwannee, a Coke bottle from 1919. We both quickly realized the bottle may have sat there, intact, only because the stream had never dried up before. We walked, in our wetsuits, in a stream channel that had dried up because of too little water, too much irrigation, too little rain. We walked under boat decks perched ten feet above the stream bottom. We walked next to boats sitting cockeyed on gravel and sand. We walked past empty mussel shells that were scattered on the bottom of the stream, like books that had been thrown down, breaking their spines. We walked along a dried streambed, looking for federally "protected" endangered species that *need* water. And as we walked along that parched streambed at midday, I recited a familiar mantra, made from a snippet of poem that I heard only once, ten years earlier, on the radio. All I remembered of the poem was the phrase "not having the power to break people in two, but wanting all of this to happen to you." Although I realized it seemed absurd to compare what was happening to my "little buddies" to a poem about cruelty and genocide, it didn't stop that poem's broken line from running through my head, while at my feet a stream should have been running but wasn't. I wanted the general public, conservation agencies, and other biologists to know these animals had been broken in two.

One of the biologists who responded to John's e-mail mused about the possible vectors that caused John's illness. He wrote,

> *Mycobacterium? Not the usual human tuberculosis, but one of the other species that normally infects cold-blooded animals. These can cause persistent dermal infections in humans (aquarists sometimes get this) and in fish & herps they slowly destroy kidneys, spleen, & other organs. Not sure whether they've ever been reported in internal organs in mammals, but might be worth investigating if your doctors haven't already.*

Mycobacterium? Mycoplasma? That was the type of infection that my first doctor in the emergency room said I suffered from, based on the blisters he saw on my eardrum after it ruptured. Was it possible that whatever had caused my inner ear fistula wasn't from some infection from a local health department but from something, an organism, in the water we had been working in? The thought had never occurred to me.

During the month in 2003 I spent looking for more Suwannee moccasinshells, I was confident we would find some. We didn't. Last Friday, the day after Earth Day, while standing in my kitchen in Utah, I heard on the radio that the government was loosening wetland regulations in the upper Suwannee River, in part, if put most cynically, to allow additional phosphate mining in the headwaters. If there are any Suwannee moccasinshells left out there, this certainly doesn't bode well for them. And because we never found another specimen, the species was never listed as federally endangered. How many species out there go from being plucked from a site, maybe decades or centuries ago, described in the literature, and then forgotten, until their status is revised to

"X"—Extinct? And what does it mean? I suppose we all hope it's close to meaningless. But I believe that it is as impossible to predict which extinction will affect us most directly, given how poorly we understand the interconnectedness of life, as it is to predict which drop of water, born in the headwaters of the Suwannee River, will make its way downstream to the Gulf of Mexico.

When I first started working on freshwater mussels, I never envisioned at some point I would feel like I belonged in a special club with them. Other members of the club include John, Steve, and my former boss, Jim, who recently contracted a nasty staph infection after scraping his knee while working in the Suwannee River. Six hundred species of animals, all extinct, are also honorary members of this club. When I talked to a friend, who works for an environmental organization in the Bay Area and attended the conference on global warming in Kyoto, about this "club," she simply said, "downwinders." And if we are not downwinders in the traditional sense, maybe we are downwinders in the cultural sense—victimized by too many dyes, toxins, and hormones in our food, air, and water. Who could say? What if John or Steve or anyone else who works in rivers and lakes is at risk due not to cultural pressures but to cultural choices? The problem with being the guinea pig is that while you *are* the guinea pig, there are no answers, no results. The next generation, or generation after that, of guinea pigs probably won't be subjected to the same types of tests, contaminants. The next generation of guinea pigs won't be standing in trenches in Nevada (at least intentionally) facing an atomic blast, their faces grotesquely flattened by the shockwave. But there will be a next generation of guinea pigs and many more after that. Unfortunately, these modern generations of guinea pigs never get to be the control group.

I have an unreasonable dislike of clubs. Especially onerous are clubs that exclude potential members based on criteria that are just plain stupid. But the club that John, Jim, Steve, the Suwannee moccasinshell, and I belong to may be acceptable, in the most twisted sense of the word, because its macabre membership is open to everyone. No geographic, watershed, or species restrictions apply. I would like to take the charter of this club and break it in two. But only after that next Suwannee moccasinshell is found.

Bibliography

Auden, W. H. "Funeral Blues." *Poetry X*. Ed. Jough Dempsey. 16 June 2003 <http://poetry.poetryx.com/poems/40/>.

Lydeard, Charles, Robert H. Cowie, Winston F. Ponder, Arthur E. Bogan, Philippe Bouchet, Stephanie A. Clark, Kevin S. Cummings, Terrence J. Frest, Oliver Gargominy, Dai G. Herbert, Robert Hershler, Kathryn E. Perez, Barry Roth, Mary Seddon, Ellen E. Strong, and Fred G. Thompson. "The Global Decline of Nonmarine Mollusks." *BioScience* (Apr., 2004): 321–30.

Poe, Edgar Allen. *The Portable Edgar Allen Poe*. New York: Penguin, 1977.

Ray, Janisse. *Ecology of a Cracker Childhood*. Minneapolis: Milkweed, 1999.

Stevenson, Robert Louis. *Lay Morals and Other Papers*. London: Chatto, 1911.

11
Imagined Vietnams

Charles Waugh

Recently, I gave a reading on campus of some travel writing about my time spent living in Hanoi, Vietnam. Several of my students in attendance, upon hearing of a place of which they knew very little, approached afterwards and asked the simple question I hear most often about my work, from students and colleagues both: "Of all things, why Vietnam?"

By nature I'm an easily rankled person, a disappointed optimist, I suppose—probably because I (however naively) believe in justice and, as George Packer has recently written, the twentieth century didn't see much of it and probably because tied to that belief is another one, namely, that the world could be a whole lot better place if each individual just lived up to his or her own ethics (25). But thankfully I'm married to a woman who has tact to spare and who's helping me to see the advantage of developing some of my own, so I've learned to manage to fight down my initial response—which, in an indignant voice, goes something like "Our country killed four-and-a-half-million people there, gave cancer and birth defects to half a million more by spraying them with dioxin, inflicted grinding poverty on the survivors with a twenty-year embargo, and you ask me why I'm interested?"—and remember that they can in all good conscience ask that question because, aside from a few academics like myself, a few veterans still living in the past, a few business people interested in cracking open a new market, and a few politicians seeking to discredit the personality or politics of another, no one really wants to rake up the mud of the quagmire again.

I suppose that's because so much was said already, so much innocence lost, and so much of the divisiveness of our society today is often traced to that tragic, brutal time when our presence in Vietnam dismantled American civil society. Those who lived through it themselves feel they've already dealt with it, as veterans, as former peace advocates, as the "silent majority" who watched it on TV. Those who weren't born yet may have talked about Vietnam in a history class, but most high schools divide American history into antebellum and postbellum periods, and by the time they get through Reconstruction, World War I, the Depression, World War II, and the beginnings of the Cold War, they have little time to delve deeply into America's war in Southeast Asia. This was true of my own experience with high school history and seems to be the general case among my students as well. In a Literature of War class I taught last year, only five out of twenty-five college seniors had read anything about Vietnam before, and the only one who had heard of the My Lai massacre was a nontraditional student in her fifties who had spent the war years sitting in and dropping out. The present state of international affairs certainly doesn't make the situation any better, since our occupation of Iraq does indeed compel the attention of those who care about world politics but leaves little time to consider—and is only rarely and superficially put into the context of—our presence in Vietnam. For most people today, Vietnam is not just old hat; it's ancient history.

And so I realize I must be thankful that at least these young people standing before me are interested. They want to know not only why I care about Vietnam, but why they should care too, and they've just given me the opportunity to tell them. Deep in my gut, I knot up that vitriolic part of myself that would have been irrepressible in my twenties, keep my indignation in check, and I answer honestly and tactfully, "A lot of people suffered and died there, and I think it's important to ask ourselves why."

Answering that question—Why?—has been a long process and still demands a great deal of my energies, but getting to the point of asking it wasn't easy either. In fact, much of what passed for knowledge about Vietnam, the cultural representations I was inundated with as a youth, stood in the way of its articulation. My adolescence was the age of America's Vietnam era reconstruction, the heyday for Hollywood films about the war. Because of my age, I received, consumed, and accepted these films without critical thought. As the country coped with the humiliation of losing the war, as the military struggled to regain its prestige, as veterans found their way from being pariahs to prodigal sons, the American film industry not only captured their redemption, it helped engineer it. *The Deer Hunter, Apocalypse Now, First Blood, Missing in Action, Rambo, Heartbreak Ridge, Red Dawn, Platoon, Hamburger Hill, Full Metal Jacket, Good Morning, Vietnam,* and *Born on the Fourth of July,* all released during my most impressionable years, played a formative role in how I thought of Vietnam: as a dense jungle, a dangerous place, a place of betrayal; as a setting for tests of American character and endurance.[1] But more than anything else, it was the place that had ruined a generation of men, cheated them of their rightful place in American society, humiliated them and made them less than the proud men they were supposed to be. Thus, for me, as for many Americans, Vietnam existed exclusively in the context of these American crises of identity, as the setting for these stories about American character. In fact, in the movie that might be Hollywood's greatest cultural impact of the late twentieth century, Vietnam was completely internalized by the main character, maintaining it as an important place for the character's development, yet denying it any real representation whatsoever. *First Blood*'s John Rambo doesn't lose his prestige in Vietnam; rather, his experiences there endow him with the superhuman survival qualities the film celebrates. The war is what causes his own society to treat him as an outcast, and thus the real message is that Vietnam is so horrific it no longer needs to be represented as a place at all. Instead it's something the hero carries with him, like a disease that has infected him, and thus the country, turning it on itself.

When I was sixteen, I visited the newly erected Vietnam Veterans Memorial in Washington, D.C., colloquially known as the Wall. I had no context to put the experience of visiting the Wall into, other than the films I'd seen, and so I had no way of knowing then that a wall listing the Vietnamese dead would have to be a cliff, seventy-seven times the height. It didn't even occur to me that there should be a Vietnamese wall; after all, the war in Vietnam was really about us, not them; they were just the inscrutable, black-clad enemy, angry and fierce. Even so, I had a hard time relating to the list of names or to the sense of loss and destroyed lives that the movies depicted. My uncle had served in the war, but he had never talked to me about it and seemed okay, not at all like the men in the films. He was a bank manager. Despite this apparent contradiction, I accepted what the film industry had been projecting for the last ten years: that the real crime of Vietnam was that it made America turn on itself, that we could redeem ourselves entirely by willing it so, and that this memorial was meant to be a small part of making good on society's restitution.

Thanks to an exciting and energetic teacher, at twenty I began to study the war in depth, along with the subsidiary wars in Cambodia and Laos, and it was then that images of the real Southeast Asia burned something up for good inside of me and made me realize I could never again see the world in the same way. I read for the first time about the massive bombings of Laos and Cambodia and saw children's crayon drawings of the first airplanes they'd ever seen, dropping the bombs that killed their families. I read the secret Rand study of the American efforts in Laos, in which "a wealth of useful lessons [were] embedded" (most notably the kind of CIA and Special Forces tactics that have been refined and put to use in Afghanistan and Iraq), all of which was made more poignant by the fact that Laos was merely a "secondary theater," ravaged entirely because of the war in Vietnam (Blaufarb 89). At twenty-one I read about My Lai for the first time, read accounts of little girls explaining how they'd seen their younger sisters raped and killed, read how William Calley grabbed a wounded baby by the heel who had crawled away from an irrigation ditch full of dead bodies, tossed it back to the pile and shot it dead. Equally disturbing, I read how some Americans turned Calley into a hero and how quickly he was returned to public life. I saw Eddie Adams's famous photograph of Saigon Chief of Police Nguyen Ngoc Loan shooting his bound prisoner in the head and Nick Ut's equally famous picture of nine-year-old Phan Thi Kim Phuc screaming, running from the napalm blasts that scorched her unclothed body. I saw a film called *Vietnam: After the Fire* about the massive ecological devastation of the war, saw huge tracts of dead mangroves and jungles, saw large glass jars containing severely deformed fetuses in formaldehyde, their double heads, twisted faces, misshapen limbs all attributed to their parents' exposure to Agent Orange. And finally came the question the films of my youth refused to articulate: Why? Why did this happen? How did this get turned into the movies I'd seen? How could we, how did we, come to this?

Vietnam became a place of hidden crimes, and, like Faulkner's Yoknapatawpha County, it was the location of every sort of human suffering and depredation, kept from the mainstream's sight by physical distance and cultural alienation. But more than that, it seemed that our own government, through hubris and hypocrisy, and our culture, through short memories and an all-consuming desire for pleasurable entertainment, were keeping the lid on Vietnam, making it difficult for Americans to learn the truth for themselves, difficult for even the best stories by the best authors—the O'Briens, the Wrights, the Browns—to make any substantial impact. Vietnam was, as far as I could tell, the setting for the darkest chapter of American history, and somehow the cultural force of America rolled on, as if that place and those crimes never existed. The guilt American society as a whole should have experienced for having committed such heinous crimes had been shifted entirely to the guilt it experienced for not treating its returning soldiers as heroes, even though the whole point of the best of the books and movies from the war was that there were no heroes. I began to realize that the will to forget, the twisting of truth, and the insistence on pride were all screens whose common, primary characteristic was an intentionally maintained ignorance about Vietnam as a place itself. If Vietnam wasn't a real, independent, and self-substantial place and if that place had nothing to do with the American character, then its people and their suffering would not have to be confronted. The economic embargo initiated after the fall of Saigon was very much a part of this willed ignorance. If there is no commerce, there is no connection, no news, no tourists, no reports from the field, no knowledge whatsoever that the place still exists. For twenty years, America held a hand before its eyes every time it looked to Southeast Asia, saying "I don't see you"—long enough to imagine, supposedly, that no one would remember what really happened there or, better yet, that people would remember only what Hollywood had projected onto the screen.

And because of that censure, because of those intentional misrepresentations, I realized that as a place Vietnam still wasn't real to me, despite my initial studies. In contrast, I'd never been to France or England, yet evidence of the existential validity of those places was all around me, all the time, in the fiction I read, in the films I saw, in the language I spoke. But Vietnam continued to exist only in my imagination, potentially as repressed nationalistic guilt, clearly intensified by the fact that very few of my fellow citizens seemed to feel it at all, and then only as a shadow cast by the American occupation, a dark place where crimes had been committed and whose people were simply the victims of our incredible violence.

At twenty-four, these realizations forced me to begin to study the history of America's role in Vietnam, focusing most intently on the formative years of the two countries' relationship, when American advisors first arrived to assist the French fighting to retain their colony and then in the 1950s and early 60s, when Americans engineered the partitioning of the country and installed Ngo Dinh Diem as president of South Vietnam. It would have been easy to continue to see Vietnam simply as a setting for American action, the place in which those advisors enacted their faith in American exceptionalism. The top CIA advisor in Saigon, Edward Lansdale, regularly read to the president from Thomas Paine's *Common Sense*, as if establishing American-style democracy was just that easy, a matter of simple, rational thinking. The Michigan State University Vietnam Public Administration Project advisors were just as confident, at first, that training in American public administration methods could transform South Vietnam into a viable American-style democracy. They expanded the reading lists from *Common Sense* to selections from John Dewey, Ralph Waldo Emerson, and *Reader's Digest*.

But unlike the American nation builders, I decided that it was important to learn something about Vietnam itself, to understand it finally, as best I could, as a place in its own right, without putting it into the context of American interests. I studied the language and culture from Vietnamese teachers and was befriended by Vietnamese graduate students who invited me over for dinner and helped me practice the language. I read histories of the country translated from the Vietnamese. In my imagination I began finally to see a picture of a place that might actually correspond to the people who lived there and whose culture had developed from it. And even though that picture was just as imaginary, I knew it had to be more real, had to be closer to a true sense of the place, if only because the range of values associated with it had grown dramatically. It could still be a dangerous place, with dense jungles and the possibility of betrayal, but it was also a place where there were ten different names for rain and hundreds for shades of green. It became a place where mountains had once been the home of gods, or a dragon's spine, or even just the force in tandem with the sea that helped a culture develop its sense of self, and it was no longer a place where the hills were named by their height in meters or the arduousness of the terrain represented by the lines of a topographical map. Foods and rituals and people became bound up in that imaginary place: aspirations and fears, times for giving gifts and harvesting crops, customs and folklore, stories about what is important about Vietnam as a country and who the Vietnamese are as a people.

These stories had a profound effect on me. In one, for example, two brothers are very close. When the older brother marries, the younger is initially happy for him but later saddened by the inevitable distance that comes between them. In his sadness, he wanders through the forest and sits by a river, lamenting what he regards as the loss of his brother. His sadness transforms him into a limestone boulder. The older brother, who was torn by his love for his wife and the love for his brother, eventually goes to look for his lost sibling. By the river, he sits on a limestone boulder and laments his loss. His sadness transforms him into an areca palm. The wife misses her husband and brother-in-law. She goes to look for them and stops at the limestone boulder, shaded by the areca tree, and laments her loss. Her sadness transforms her into a betel nut tree. Together, the limestone, the areca palm, and the betel nut were presented to the king when he visited the area, and the story so moved him that he proclaimed that the traditional preparation of the betel nut would forever be a part of marriage ceremonies, as a reminder of the need for balance in filial piety and amorous love. Betel is still a part of marriage ceremonies and is still chewed by many people in Vietnam today. The story's depth of love and suffering and divided loyalties cannot be lost on anyone aware of Vietnam's troubled history, and a variety of its metaphorical applications certainly were not lost on me. In my imagination the place became rich with emotion, bound with my own sense of love and honor and duty.

When the opportunity arose for me to live in Hanoi, I didn't hesitate. Professor Rob Proudfoot invited me to join the University of Oregon Vietnam National University Sister University Project, of which he was the director, and I was honored to accept. Rob had been teaching in, and developing cultural ties with, Vietnam since 1993, when he became the first visiting professor from the United States to teach in Vietnam since the war. While there, we worked with the Vietnam Women's Union Museum, met with teachers from Vietnam National University and the University of Hanoi, and made trips to cultural centers such as Kiep Bac, Con Son, and Co Loa. I also worked for a business newspaper, trying as best I could to make sense of how the new wave of Westerners, heralding the miracle of international development, compared to the American nation builders of the 1950s and 60s. To my amazement, much of the rhetoric had been recycled, at times sounding word for word like the same advice.

But the place was finally real. Almost immediately, I began to realize that the readings I'd done had given me a sense of the shape of Vietnamese culture but none of the individual details. I realized that without living there, what I was trying to understand was akin to understanding America by reading Paul Bunyan stories but never eating a McDonald's hamburger or knowing English but never seeing it flash across the screens at Times Square. There in Hanoi, I was finally beginning to feel the texture of Vietnamese life, coming to learn what this place was, and allowing its charm to become a part of me.

In some ways, Hanoi reminded me of Eugene, Oregon, where I'd been living the last two years. Both are green cities, with wide avenues lined by huge trees, and there's a vibrant street life, with cafés on the sidewalks and people everywhere. In the late fall came the rains, which also seemed like home.

But in other ways it couldn't be more different. Nothing could have prepared me for the brilliant green of the rice paddies outside of town under a bright August sky. It feels as though you can actually sense the rice gathering in the rays of the sun, absorbing all that incredible tropical solar energy and then releasing it again in a bright, yellowy green, as if it were the only color that ever existed. Nor could I have predicted how much I would marvel at the waves of two-wheeled traffic surging through the streets, some of the bikes piled six or seven feet high and just as wide with wicker baskets or hatstands or bamboo cages full of pigs or dogs or chickens. Nearly a thousand years have been captured in Hanoi's architecture, which ranges from the Temple of Literature at Van Mieu, erected in 1072 CE, to the mix of hulking, old colonial administration buildings, more recent Soviet-style buildings, and tall and narrow apartment buildings with French windows and balconies with wrought-iron railings. Just as surprising, though I should have expected them, were the new glass and steel structures of globalization, clustering, for the most part, at the edges of town.

I lived in the Ministry of Education guesthouse, an architecturally mixed building—a hybrid of French colonial and 1960s Soviet functional styles—where Vietnamese teachers and school groups normally stay when they come to the capital on cultural field trips. There was no air conditioning in my room or airtight windows sealing me away from the city, so in my mind a Vietnamese morning will always be tied to the sound of street vendors hawking sticky rice and, later, woven mats and fruits and baskets and plastic bowls and steamed rolls and just about everything else. And afternoons to the roll of rain on the tile roof of the university buildings across the alley, dripping into the puddles below. Nights to the melodious drunken pronouncements of the snack shop owner next door winding his way home through the alley; and cool days to the smell of deliciously strong coffee wafting up from the guesthouse café.

The way of life to which these sounds and smells belonged had nothing to do with America. They were the sounds and smells that have been Vietnam for centuries. That life has always been one of hardship, but it has also been one of great camaraderie and friendship. Joining friends at an outdoor café for a drink or some tasty treat after a long day or hustling to sell a last piece of fruit or to get out from under the rain have always been a part of Vietnamese life. And though those things by themselves aren't so very different from my American experience, the texture of them is different. The food is different, sure, but more important is the emphasis on the social sense of togetherness. The Vietnamese even have a special verb for it, *nhau*, that includes eating, drinking, and chatting with friends and is predominantly used for afternoon get-togethers. Americans do those things too, but certainly not with enough regularity and social importance to develop a verb for it. Perhaps more important, the margin of success in these endeavors seemed much narrower— the girl who didn't sell all her produce wasn't working an hourly wage. And maybe that was just it: all over were signs of a dignified people struggling to live happily, without the profligate and gaudy trappings of success flaunted all around them all the time. There is a sense that these people have earned every cent they've got the hard way, without hundreds of years of institutionalized subsidies and the oppression of others. The signs of their deep humanity, resilience, thrift, and innovation were everywhere.

For a while, it seemed every person I encountered was engaged in some way in this dignified struggle to get ahead, to take part in the economic expansion made possible by the government's renovation policy, *Doi Moi*. For the most part, it seemed these were burdens taken in good spirits; after all, everyone had been much poorer during the years of the American embargo, and despite the incredible burden the war had placed on several generations, there seemed to be a general willingness to forget the past, to move on, and to take advantage of the international wealth coming into the city. "Why dwell on the painful past," it seemed most people thought, "when the future's so bright?" Everywhere I went I found gracious and friendly shopkeepers, café owners, and gallery curators. Even the university intellectuals I met were keen on the possibilities the new economy seemed to hold. But just as I was beginning to be persuaded that this era of hope really did have something for everyone, I discovered the exception to the rule.

On a sunny day in November, I was shopping for books. I left a store to visit the next one up the street and nearly ran over a young man lying on the sidewalk. He was on one hip, propping himself up with one hand while supplicating me with the other. His fingers were stumped and twisted, some joined together, his feet gnarled at the ends of useless legs. He spoke to me, but his words weren't right; they were soft and indistinct, unintelligible. But I knew what he wanted. And more important, I recognized the telltale signs of exposure to dioxin, since many of the children I'd seen interviewed in *Vietnam: After the Fire* shared these problems. Here, in one human being, was the physical presence of the war that was otherwise so much removed from every other experience I'd had in Hanoi. Here was the only real reminder that even though Vietnam won the war, the United States was continuing to inflict casualties. Here was one person whose future didn't look bright and who could as likely forget the past as he could ignore the telltale signs of it on his body. The U.S. government wouldn't talk about it, let alone take responsibility, even though the Veterans Administration listed nine Agent Orange–related illnesses qualifying exposed U.S. vets to special dispensation and the manufacturers of Agent Orange (Dow and Monsanto, mainly, among others) had already paid a large settlement to those same vets. No amount of *Doi Moi* was going to make things better for this young man. I took all the loose bills from my pocket and laid them into his hand. There might have been ten or twenty thousand dong there—about a dollar and a half. I have regretted not dropping my entire wallet into his lap ever since.

Later, when I inquired into what kind of health care he might be getting, a Vietnamese colleague from the newspaper explained that the Friendship Village took what care they could of the worst dioxin poisoning cases, but otherwise the guy from the street would be left to the same predicament in which the rest of the populace found themselves: with the advent of a market economy and with international money finally flowing, the first informal "reform" was the socialist system of health care. Of course, it still existed in theory. Anyone could go to the hospital and expect to see a doctor after a day or two. But there might not be any treatment available, no tests or surgery or medications, unless the patient could pay the doctor an off-the-record bonus. The new international money dispersed itself into the economy only in the slowest, trickle-down fashion. Government officials might receive a little extra from international companies wishing to expedite the permitting process, and tourist shop owners might be getting a little more here and there, but it would take a long time for those dollars to see their way into the hands of the typical Hanoian, and they might not ever get outside the city.

And thus Vietnam became for me not only a place of great charm and beauty but also one of deep responsibility. Seeing that man suffer—and knowing that my government not only inflicted that life upon him but also that it is the leading agent in the globalization process that values commodity production and access to labor markets over the subsidization of the health care system that might otherwise offer him some comfort—made me realize that even the questions that had gotten me into all this in the first place weren't the right questions to be asking. Now I wanted to know, How can I help?

Recognizing first what Vietnam, the place, really was and second that it was changing rapidly wasn't difficult. My own hometown back in Ohio hardly resembles the place I grew up. What was difficult was conceptualizing the degree to which Vietnam was changing, and the pace of that change was an exponential factor faster than anything I'd ever seen. Essentially closed off from the world for decades, wearing the blinders of a forty-year-old struggle for independence before that, then reemerging on the world scene only to be confronted by the Spice Girls, Super Nintendo, the IMF, and legions of transnational corporations was enough to make me wonder how many of the typical Vietnamese had any idea what they were in for. But who was I to tell them what to do? I certainly wouldn't (even if I had the power to do so) deny them the right to embrace some aspects of Western materialism after so many years of being deprived of even basic necessities. And I have no intention of trying to "preserve" some antique, desperately poor identity just for the sake of what I find charming.

And yet, as Fredric Jameson writes of the role of the Western imagination in globalization, I couldn't help but feel that there must be as many paths to development, indeed, as many definitions of what developed might mean, as there are nations in the world. But, as citizens of the nation leading this globalizing process, and thus the people most capable of improving its domineering nature, it really is up to us whether to embrace and celebrate difference, allowing nations like Vietnam to determine their own paths to development, or to allow it to be crushed by the monolithic, free-trading, Western democratic vision that the U.S.-dominated World Bank and International Monetary Fund tend to espouse. It's up to us, says Jameson, to imagine a better way. In order to do that, I decided, Americans must first be able to imagine that a place like Vietnam exists without its American character-building content, and to do that, they have to know what that place is really like. Beyond that, it seemed desperately important that the United States take some responsibility for the worst of its actions or, at the very least, take a special interest in providing for a people it had wronged. The trick then, ironically, was to reach out to American hearts and minds.

Which is where I am today, teaching and writing whenever I can about a place far from here, Vietnam, with the hope that my efforts will change this place, the United States, so that the first place can decide for itself what it wants to be. It's a complicated arrangement, I know. I'm aware that each time I represent Vietnam, it is in some way a misrepresentation. But I am also aware of, as Linda Alcoff has suggested, what's at stake in these (mis)representations. The image of the young man with his dioxin-related ailments continues to motivate me, to make me remember that more depends on my success than my own career. I see the smiling faces of the friends I made in Vietnam, so sure of the brightness of their futures, of the improvement of the world they live in, and I think how likely Hanoi's air will soon resemble the smog of Bangkok unless some other way is envisioned. I remember the charm of the mixed architecture, the traditions represented by places like Van Mieu, and the beauty of the tree-lined streets, and I worry that with each new international high-rise that goes up, those qualities become more endangered than ever. If I can capture that initial beauty, if I can make the charm of Vietnam come across on the page, if I can reach out to my nation of story-hungry citizens and fire their imaginations, then maybe I can make them see it's a place worth reconsidering.

I write to counter what Vietnam means to so many Americans, to provide a different picture than the one created by Hollywood or even the one created in the stellar works of America's veteran authors. I write about a place experiencing global change at warp speed, a place that emerged from forty years of armed conflict into a world at the height of the postmodern moment, on the cusp of the next great technological leap of globalization. I write about a culture rich with traditions meeting with postmodern unmoorings—about a silky texture of life being wrapped in polyester. I write to make Vietnamese people real with real problems and legitimate concerns, bent on finding their own way in the world, to an American audience who, for the most part, has seen them only as black pajama–clad barbarians whom we could've beaten if we had just been allowed to by Congress. I write to remind Americans that even though they may have forgotten the Vietnamese, the Vietnamese do indeed still exist and are still suffering because of us. I write to make that place as real as I possibly can and to demonstrate how this place in which we live is irrevocably bound to that one, tied together by our choice to go there and do what we did, forever linked by common experience and responsibilities.

When I teach, I try whenever I can to assign Vietnamese literature, to create in my students' minds the fabric of life there. In my literature of war course, I have them read many of the same books and see many of the same films that had such a profound impact on me as an undergraduate, making them aware of the horrible, lingering effects of the war and of the need for action. In my travel writing workshops and courses on theories of globalization, inevitably the examples that I use to talk about representing the other, or creating a sense of place, or examining the effects of World Bank or IMF policies on local cultures are Vietnamese examples. Whether these examples create that place for my students I'm not sure, but I think it does them good to begin to think about Vietnam as having a special place in my interests and in the world. If nothing else, it brings them to that same simple question that my students posed after hearing me read the travel writing—"Why Vietnam?"—and creates in them the potential for finding out more, arouses their sense of justice, and motivates some of them to do something to make things right. After all, these are the sorts of things that began to make Vietnam mean something to me, fifteen years ago.

Notes

1. *Heartbreak Ridge* and *Red Dawn* are not films about Vietnam, but veterans of Vietnam play important roles in both of them, contributing to the notion that the men who were outcasts would in time become heroes. The time between these films was compressed even further for me, since I was not old enough to see *The Deer Hunter* or *Apocalypse Now* in the theater and saw them on video in 1986 after seeing *Platoon*.

Bibliography

Alcoff, Linda. "The Problem of Speaking for Others." *Cultural Critique* (Winter 1991–92): 5–32.
Apocalypse Now. Dir. Francis Ford Coppola. United Artists, 1979.
Blaufarb, Douglas. *Organizing and Managing Unconventional War in Laos, 1962–1970*. 1972. Christiansburg, VA: Dalley, 1989.
Born on the Fourth of July. Dir. Oliver Stone. Universal, 1989.
Brown, Larry. *Dirty Work*. New York: Vintage, 1990.
The Deer Hunter. Dir. Michael Cimino. Universal, 1978.
First Blood. Dir. Ted Kotcheff. Orion, 1982.
Full Metal Jacket. Dir. Stanley Kubrick. Warner Bros., 1987.
Good Morning, Vietnam. Dir. Barry Levinson. Buena Vista, 1987.
Hamburger Hill. Dir. John Irvin. Paramount, 1987.
Heartbreak Ridge. Dir. Clint Eastwood. Warner Bros., 1986.
Jameson, Fredric. "Notes on Globalization as a Philosophical Issue." *The Cultures of Globalization*. Ed. Fredric Jameson and Masao Miyashi. Raleigh: Duke UP, 1998.
Missing in Action. Dir. Joseph Zito. Cannon, 1984.
O'Brien, Tim. *Going After Cacciato*. New York: Delta, 1978.
———. *If I Die in a Combat Zone*. New York: Delacorte, 1973.
———. *The Things They Carried*. New York: Houghton, 1990.
Packer, George. "Comment: Trials." *New Yorker* 5 Jan. 2005: 25.
Paine, Thomas. *Common Sense*. Philadelphia: Bradford, 1776.
Platoon. Dir. Oliver Stone. Orion, 1986.
Rambo. Dir. George Cosmatos. Tristar, 1985.
Red Dawn. Dir. John Milius. MGM/UA, 1984.
Vietnam: After the Fire. Dir. J. Edward Milner. Cinema Guild, 1988.
Wright, Stephen. *Meditations in Green*. New York: Scribners, 1983.

IV
Everywhere

12

Teaching on Stolen Ground

Deborah A. Miranda

This essay is a mosaic of my thoughts and experiences as an American Indian at the beginning of her fourth year as a professor. I dedicate the whole made from these shards to the memory of Gloria Anzaldúa, who taught—and still teaches—so many of us how to survive and thrive in the Borderlands with courage, compassion, and sensual delight for the energy of being alive.

It happens every year. This time one of my blond, blue-eyed male first-year students stomps into my classroom, saying to the group at large, "I'm changing my ethnicity to Native American so I can get free college tuition. They don't have to prove anything, just check 'Indian' on the form, and it's a free ride all the way." As a Native American professor with $50,000 in student loans, who teaches in a university that—like all universities in North and South America—is built on Indian land, this student's statement makes me a little crazy. This is where I teach from: an occupied country. My university resides on land stolen from local indigenous peoples—but we rarely talk about that reality in our classrooms or question how that theft continues to impact our daily lives as U.S. citizens.[1] In this essay, I'll attempt to re-create my pedagogical and gut responses to this academia-wide state of affairs—responses, not necessarily "solutions." My purpose is not to write a "how to" guide; instead, I want to communicate, as honestly as possible, the tensions and negotiations that happen among my body, place, and the academy.[2]

Reality Check 101

My students come to me, for the most part, conditioned and educated by our culture to think of this land as always already "American." As the mother of two children nearing the end of their public school educations, I can attest to the rampant and "unintentional" racism, particularly anti-Indian sentiment, present in curriculums from preschool through high school—so I'm not surprised by the lack of information, and the presence of misinformation, that undergraduates bring to the academy. Manifest Destiny is alive and well and living inside our children.[3] In the case of the student quoted at the top of this essay, my first thought was, "Do you have any idea what that 'free' education cost? In land, in lives, in health, in emotional well-being, in wealth?" What came out of my mouth was, "Have you ever heard of the Medicine Creek Treaty?" No one had. So we learned.

First, the official version: we read a typical report such as that found under "Medicine Creek Treaty" at HistoryLink.org (the online encyclopedia of Washington State history):

> *The Treaty of Medicine Creek was signed on December 26, 1854, at a meeting at Medicine Creek in present-day Thurston County. Sixty-two leaders of major Western Washington tribes, including the Nisqually and Puyallup, signed the treaty with Territorial Governor Isaac Stevens (1818–1862). The tribes ceded most of their lands in exchange for $32,500, designated reservations, and the permanent right of access to traditional hunting and fishing grounds.*

The bands and tribes signing the treaty were the Nisqually, Puyallup, Steilacoom, Squaxin, S'Homamish, Ste-chass, T'Peek-sin, Squi-aitl, and Sahheh-mamish. Yes, some of these Indians still exist as tribal entities, some still have reservation lands, and some of the original "signers" of the treaty received *some* of the money they were promised (hunting and fishing rights remain contested to this day). Why persist in labeling the land as stolen? Looking further, my students sought out alternative sources such as Thomas Bjorgen and Morris Uebelacker, who point out in their 2001 report (commissioned by Washington State and the treaty tribes), "Determination of the Southern Boundary of the Medicine Creek Treaty Ceded Area," that exchanging 2.5 million acres for $35,000, undesirable lands, and hunting/fishing rights that were and are constantly disputed is not what most would call a fair deal. In particular, the pressure that the tribes were under at that time (a state of war and invasion) made resisting this treaty seem unwise to tribes that had already lost thousands of lives to disease, racial violence, and malnutrition. According to David M. Buerge, "The twenty-thousand-odd aboriginal inhabitants who were assumed to be in rapid decline were given a brutal choice: they would adapt to white society or they could disappear" (73). Thirty-five thousand dollars, students noted, wouldn't go very far among 20,000 Indians. Then my students discovered that the tribes present at the signing were not even actual representatives of their people; Bjorgen and Uebelacker's report reveals that "rather, Governor Stevens united various bands and villages into larger tribal entities for purposes of reaching agreement to the Treaty" (2). Basically, Stevens gathered up as many people from local tribes as he could find and literally *appointed* them chiefs and headmen with the "authority" to sign away these lands on a treaty.

And finally, my students realized, these appointed Indians were not honestly apprised of the vast amount of land they were being asked to sign over. Again, Bjorgen and Uebelacker provided key information: not only was the treaty written in English, which none of the tribal "representatives" could read or speak; it was translated for them not into their own languages but the Chinook trade jargon—a system consisting of about six hundred words and signs, none of them designed to convey an exchange of this magnitude. Bjorgen and Uebelacker conclude,

> *It is quite possible that some had in mind that they were ceding or giving up only the immediate areas around their winter villages, as well as customary hunting and berrying grounds in or near the drainage in which they lived. If so . . . the government representatives likely intended a larger ceded area than did the representatives of the Tribes. (6)*

When students assume that land was "given up" in exchange for promises of money and future benefits such as health care or education, I want them to understand the depth of that land's meaning. I want them to have some knowledge of the desperation, fear, and anger that went into making such a decision or accepting such an exchange. I want my students to at least begin to realize that when someone says "place" to an Indian, there is an immediate and visceral response in that Indian person: place means land, story, culture, history, memory. Place means relationship between self and land. Between human spirit and earth energy. Place means more than that: it means knowing there *is and must be* such a relationship between self and land. In order to even begin to grasp Native concepts about land and identity found in Native literatures, students need the grounded, tactile realization that it's happening right now, beneath their feet.

A Metaphor in the Master's House

Recently the Clackamas tribe in Oregon filed a claim for a sixteen-ton meteorite under the Native American Graves Protection and Repatriation Act. The meteorite, the Clackamas explain, had been a sacred entity, embodying three sacred realms—sky, earth, and water—and, for thousands of years, Clackamas youths were sent on vigils to the meteorite to await messages from the spirit world. Other tribes in the area also made pilgrimages to the meteorite, and the rainwater that collected in the craters of the monolith was prized for its holiness and healing powers.

"Discovered" by a part-time miner in 1902 (on Clackamas land previously appropriated by an iron company), the meteor was quickly moved from its ancient site and began a journey through the hands of various entrepreneurs. Starting out at twenty-five cents a look in the miner's barn, the meteorite eventually sold for $20,000 and was then donated to a New York museum, where it has been ever since. In fact, the meteorite is the main attraction in the newly rebuilt Museum of Natural History planetarium in New York, a remodeling that has complicated the repatriation of the object for many reasons. Money and investment in the new building (the Rose Center for Earth and Space) as a showcase for the meteorite is, of course, one factor; however, an Associated Press article by John Jurgensen in the *Seattle Post-Intelligencer* points out other less tangible difficulties:

> Ann Canty, a museum spokeswoman . . . made clear that it would not be easy to move the meteorite from the planetarium. . . . "Because the meteorite is so massive, parts of the facility had to essentially be built around it," Canty said. The meteorite . . . was moved with a

> large crane when [the old] building was dismantled in 1997. Two years before the new center was finished, contractors installed three structural piles—60-foot tubes driven into the ground—just to support it.

Enter the metaphor: a gigantic meteorite, the ultimate stolen Indian religious artifact, housed in a non-native, scientific, Western-oriented planetarium that has been built around the object in such a way as to require nearly complete destruction of that building in order to return the object to its Indian "owners" (whether the Clackamas tribe claims to actually "own" the object is yet another topic).

In unpacking this metaphor, students quickly see that removing the meteorite means not only removing many successive walls within the building, as well as the exterior wall; the sixteen-ton object can actually rest nowhere else but on the precise section of floor constructed to support it. This means that pulling the meteorite across other floors or resting a crane on any other flooring would also destroy those floors or require substantial and expensive subfloor support construction. The same article reported that when asked if the meteorite could be moved, Todd Schliemann, one of the architects who worked on the Rose Center, said, "We could find a way, but we would have to disassemble a large portion of the building. It's a permanent fixture. It landed there, and there it will stay." One has to admire the simplicity of Schliemann's stand: the meteorite's presence within the planetarium is a done deal; it happened, get over it.

In fact, Schliemann makes more of a point than he realizes. Removing the meteorite from this building goes beyond questions of what is "right," "religious," or even "possible." The costs of moving such a huge object cross-country are now further inflated by the costs of basically ripping open a new building, repairing the building, and then rebuilding the building *without* its former centerpiece as a draw for paying visitors. In a sense, the purpose of the building would no longer exist, and the building itself would be superfluous.

The Willamette Meteorite serves as a massive metaphor for the colonization of the land and peoples of North America. Like both land and people, the meteorite was "discovered" and immediately appropriated—engulfed, fenced, contained, claimed—for the financial benefit of the colonizer; like many native peoples, holy relics, or places, the meteorite has a history and purpose that predates colonization but that is denied by the dominant culture. And yet, at the same time, the dominant culture has become dependent upon the meteorite's presence to provide an economic and mythological profit. By remaining *where* and *how* the dominant culture has relocated it, the meteorite's presence as an *owned object* allows the structure of the dominant culture to remain standing and operating in its capitalist economy, disconnected from the very land it rests on.[4]

I often return to the Willamette Meteorite as an example of the intricacies of long-term colonization. Like mixed-bloods, the Native and the Colonizer are intermeshed in so many ways that black-and-white solutions—such as outright repatriation of an object or the land—are no longer easy and, sometimes, are not even the best solution. This is why the academy, placed where it is, has a responsibility to help facilitate new solutions that accept and incorporate, rather than deny, history. This is also why my presence on campus is all too often a thorn in the side of academic tradition.

Teaching on stolen land affects everything about my relationships with students, colleagues, administrators, and other staff. It often sets me apart and reveals a distinct rupture between my position as a professor, a member of "those with power," and my position as an Indian woman, a member of "the conquered." When we discuss the weather, local hikes, plants, place names, historical events, literacy, literature, feminism, theory, vegetarianism, animal rights, *Moby-Dick*, or *The Bean Trees*, my position as an indigenous person pervades my perspective. When students mention the beautiful mountain visible from my campus, they call it "Mount Rainier." I inform them that the local Salishan Indian word is "Tahoma." When colleagues mention a hike out at gorgeous Pt. Defiance over the weekend, I think of the Puyallup tribe, who lost that beautiful land in the fraudulent Medicine Creek Treaty. When my students talk about going to Lakewood to shop or see a movie, I know from local Indians that the flat, prairielike land used to be a natural gathering place for potlatches, celebrations, and trade—before "contact." I argue with environmentalists about sacred land use, tangle with vegetarians over animal rights, caution religion professors about "experiencing" Native culture at a weekend "sweat lodge." All around me as I walk through the academy, place speaks in ways that non-Native ears can't hear or often don't want to hear. For me, and for other Indian academics, teaching in a university is about more than educating, more than self-representation, more than Equal Opportunity. Every day, we go about the work of repatriation. We take back our land and our *right* to that land—and by this I mean both literally and spiritually—from within the very institutions that taught generations the art of theft, of erasure, and crafted the mythology of America. We do this in many, many ways but, most importantly, with our bodies. Sherman Alexie (Spokane/Coeur d'Alene), speaking in an interview with the *Honolulu Star Bulletin* reporter Cynthia Oi, said of a non-native writer, "When you finish writing about Indians, you get up from your typewriter and you're still white. When I finish, I have to go out and buy groceries, as an Indian." I consider simply showing up at the university every day in my Indian body to be a large portion of this repatriation effort. After all, it wasn't easy getting my indigenous body into the academy in the first place.

Reality Check 102

Native Americans currently make up less than two percent of the total population in the United States, yet we have the highest rates of suicide, poverty, illiteracy, and incarceration in prisons of *any* ethnic or cultural group in the U.S., including all other "minorities."[5] So if Natives are eligible for a "free ride" through the university system and if a college degree guarantees some kind of financial security, what's the problem?

First, I ask my students if what they've learned so far about Indians and the U.S. government honestly supports the idea that a "free ride" through college for every single Indian person is somehow a guarantee. As Devon Mihesuah explains in *American Indians: Stereotypes and Realities*, this is simply a myth that is perpetuated by misinformed and perhaps racist rhetoric. Secondly, my students find the publication *American Indians and Alaska Natives in Postsecondary Education* from the U.S. government to be very handy. Available online, you can also receive a free copy of it, in bound form, simply by filling out a request form at their website. Among the conclusions the U.S. Department of Education has drawn for 1994 (the most recent survey) are these:

> Total number of PhDs earned in the U.S. by U.S. Citizens: 27,105
>
> American Indian/Alaska Native degree recipients for PhDs: 134—less than .5 percent of all PhDs

Total number of MAs earned in the U.S. by U.S. Citizens: 385,419

AI/AN degree recipients for MAs: 1,697—about .4 percent of all MAs

Total number of BAs earned in the U.S. by U.S. Citizens: 1,165,973

AI/AN degree recipients for BAs: 6,189—slightly more than .5 percent of all BAs

As you may suppose from the low numbers of Native PhDs, Native faculty at U.S. institutions of higher learning are also rare: in the Fall of 1993, in four-year universities, there were 1,218 Native professors with tenure, 474 on tenure track, and 371 adjuncts teaching part-time or full-time on year-to-year contracts. In addition, the report notes that since an earlier study in 1975, tenure-track Native professors had fallen by 10 percent in 1993, while nontenured (adjunct, visiting, guest positions) Native PhDs increased. Long-term employment possibilities (read health benefits, tuition breaks for children, job security, career advancement) for Native PhD scholars actually *fell* during the height of Affirmative Action policy! (Note to self: remember to ask the next student who complains about Indians getting a free ride through college, "And how many Native teachers/professors/doctors/lawyers have you had in your lifetime? How many do you see at this institution?")

Buffalo Poop, Buffalo Poop! Buffalo Poop All Over This Land!

I wish I had written that, but I didn't; I found it on a bumper sticker at a Native business selling bison meat. I loved that bumper sticker at first sight; it speaks volumes to me of invasion, colonization, survival, fertility, indigenous resistance, and the deep, abiding relationship with homeland that resonates within Indian people even five hundred years after the invasion. To me, this bumper sticker is a pungent reminder to both Native and non-native that everything under our feet is part of a rich, purposeful cycle; that everywhere we step, we walk on indigenous soil, land springing up out of a revered animal's excrement. Holy shit, indeed. This bumper sticker exhorts us to acknowledge and celebrate that older and honest history; it's about knowing and seeing, accepting and reveling in origins. I teach on stolen land; my students learn on stolen land. What is there for us to know from this, beyond statistics and thought experiments designed to teach or at least introduce compassion?

Excerpt from an Indigenous Teaching Journal

Indians in the academy perform daily acts of repatriation and healing. Our presence in this place, in these places, on these lands constitutes a ceremony for recovery. When Gloria Anzaldúa writes in a poem from her book *Borderlands/La Frontera: The New Mestiza*, "This land was Mexican once, / was Indian always, / and is. / And will be again," the hairs on the back of my neck stand up (3). Yet the population and culture of the North American continent have been changed forever, and few Indians imagine a time when all the white people get back in their boats and "go home." This is, truly, the heart of the repatriation work ahead of us: How do I teach American Literature in the academy in ways that don't drive me insane, that don't perpetuate a mythology of conquest and Manifest Destiny, and that allow the land upon which I teach to speak through me? How do I teach what I know? *Can* I teach what I know?

As if she knew I would ask these questions one day, Linda Hogan, Chickasaw poet and novelist, writes,

> [I]t is not so easy. There are no roads through, no paths known, no maps or directions. . . . Who knows where to step, how to find wholeness? It's not that we have lost the old ways and intelligences, but that we are lost from them. . . . [A]ll the elements of ourselves and our world are more than can be held in words alone; there is something else beyond our knowing. (14–16)

It is important that I understand Linda Hogan's caution that some kinds of knowledge, some forms of information or direction cannot be captured in words or taught using words—even, if we are blessed enough to still speak them, the most sacred words of our native language. There is a knowing that *cannot be held in words alone.*

So, I have to ask myself, are there some things we can't teach? Or, to put it another way: are there things we can't learn? There are times when it feels like that—not only with "normal" topics like math or composition, but also with keenly felt abstracts like racism, oppression, justice. As a female, queer writer of color, as an Indian academic, I want to argue that intangibles (or as Hogan calls them, *intelligences*) are in fact inherent in all of us, perhaps just deeply hidden or needing the right language to bring out. Literature—poetry, fiction, narrative nonfiction, personal essay, mixed-genre, and bent boundaries—is that language for me. Maybe melody can't be "carried" or "conveyed" from one being to another—just scooped up like a sack of flour and given to someone else—because that knowing is, somehow, already within. Hogan also says that "[the old ways] are always here, patient, waiting for our return to their beauty, their integrity, their reverence for life" (14–15). What if these knowledges, *always here*, can be *evoked* from one being to another—in a moment of resonance?

When tuning a drum, you lean down with your face right over the drumhead and hum the note you want the drum to hold, while adjusting the sinews on the back or bottom or sides of the drum (depending on construction) that tighten or loosen the drumhead accordingly. I learned this not as a young Indian girl in traditional training, but as a junior high student who bucked her counselor's advice to take typing or accounting and followed, instead, a powerful yearning toward tympani and snare (where tradition is lacking, perhaps the body remembers). I have since discovered that it's the same for any drum, though, whether symphonic or native, machine- or handmade. Tuning a drum is a whole-body effort—foot, leg, diaphragm, lungs, breath, lips, hands—because you must stand with your feet firmly planted, knees bent a little to keep the body's energy open, humming and simultaneously tapping the drumhead with a stick or finger. And as you hum out into the drum, tap the drumhead, and pull or release the drumhead ever so slightly, the drum searches for the note. And when everything coalesces—the pressure of the drumhead, the humming in your mouth, the angle and punctuation of a strike—the drum sings the note back to you. Then your whole body, starting with your head (and teeth!), continuing down to the very soles of your feet, is enveloped in the totality of *rightness*; the note sings its way back up your spine and out through your molars and connects with the drum's note. Then, it's complete. Then, you *know*.

Writing, the art of literature, is like tuning a drum: a whole-body experience. I can't leave my body behind when I read and write; not the flesh-and-blood body I really have, nor that body's "Indian" identity that my audience and I have been culturally trained to see and respond to. So I work with what I bring. When I write about being a child of color in a white world, when I write about sexual abuse, the intergenerational violence that a Native American father passes on to his children, or what it's like to fall madly in love with another Indian woman, I can't simply insert information and understanding into my reader's minds. As a teacher, I can't open my student's minds and drop in a magic computer chip that will explain the intricacies of Native literatures. But I can, I hope, *evoke* a resonance within them: through a multisensory, multimedia approach that includes Native poetry, literature, song, film, live readings, storytelling, visual/performance art, and, of course, awareness of place and local tribal connections to that place. These are my tools, with which I "invite" (rather than "strike," a distinction I make thanks to Thich Nhat Hanh's caution about sounding a meditation bell) the heartdrum of students and with which I keep searching for the note that will resound for each one, offering the practice of a whole-body discipline that will, one day, allow what it is that I know—and more, maybe, that I don't know—to find a pathway from my heart to the heart of a student. I'm not really passing on what I know, of course; I am passing on a key to a door, a window, a glimpse of something beyond what they've known. Maybe it's compassion, tenderness, or a larger way of seeing our complexities as human animals. I know that other writers, artists, and musicians do this for me, even when I am at my angriest and most resistant.

Fine-Tuning the Mind: Teaching Resonance

Immersion in Native arts is not the only way to open those hearts, however. *Re*-teaching American and European literatures is also a tool for repatriation. I've often thought that the captivity narratives of early contact (in which whites were taken captive by Indians, enduring all sorts of humiliations, traumas, and "savagery") have continued into contemporary American literature, with a twist: the Indian is taken captive by the white man via plot, symbol, and construction. So when I teach *Moby-Dick*, for example, we spend quite a bit of time on passages like the following, in which Melville examines the indigenous Queequeg's body, especially his tattoos.

> And this tattooing had been the work of a departed prophet and seer of his island, who, by those hieroglyphic marks, had written out of his body a complete theory of the heavens and the earth, and a mystical

> *treatise on the art of attaining truth; so that Queequeg in his own proper person was a riddle to unfold; a wondrous work in one volume; but whose mysteries not even himself could read, though his own live heart beat against them; and these mysteries were therefore destined in the end to moulder away with the living parchment whereon they were inscribed, and so be unsolved to the last. (455)*

Much as Europeans judged the North American continent "unused" by its indigenous inhabitants, then, Queequeg's resources ("intelligences") are wasted on him; he cannot read the markings or the maps his own body carries. Queequeg's skin also bears his "mark"— ∞ —the symbol for infinity. It is, in fact, the only mark he knows how to make and signifies his name on his whaling contract. Infinity is literally written on Queequeg's skin. Poor guy! He's a walking indigenous institution of learning; thus, his body becomes the site of a great conflict: the battle for North America. Queequeg is, as Ishmael says, "a wondrous work in one volume," and if Ishmael can possess that knowledge, he has the essential qualifications for possessing the land. We can, as others have, call this a homoerotic text, but to give the passage *only* that reading avoids the American concept of Manifest Destiny—with which Melville's culture and psyche (and our own contemporary identities) are imbued. Instead, I ask my students to read the text hidden within the text: those wonderfully symbolic tattoos. It is not simply a question of possession, but of *how, why,* and with *what intent* Ishmael possesses indigenous knowledge.

When the *Pequod* sinks with everyone aboard but Ishmael, Ishmael survives by clinging to Queequeg's empty coffin, the same container to which Queequeg had spent days "transferring" all of his tantalizing tattoos by carving each design into the wood. Queequeg's "skin" saves Ishmael from drowning in a wilderness of waves. This coffin-turned-lifeboat sets Ishmael upon dry land, reborn in the skin of the "new" Native American. To the end, Queequeg continues to serve, his skin a container and receptacle for Ishmael's new life. Queequeg has been taken captive; he has been invaded, colonized, and appropriated from the inside out. Like the Willamette Meteorite, like the North American continent, all spiritual and culture meaning has been stripped from Queequeg's "resources"; all that remains is the utilitarian shell.

Meanwhile, Back at the Meteorite

Why is it important for my students to be able to read *Moby-Dick* and other American texts through an indigenous lens? Does it mean I hate Melville? Does it mean early European-American literature is racist? Back to the Meteorite! Albert Memmi asserts that the process of genocide is not purely a physical one; genocide depends upon, in fact, the appropriation of the identity of the colonized by the colonizer. Misinterpretations and misrepresentations of Native culture, religion, character, and worldview for consumption by the nonindigenous are the crucial elements in such a genocidal agenda. What Memmi emphasizes is not the *repression* of the indigenous cultures involved, but the *repackaging* of those cultures as a way to "capture" the indigenous into the dominant culture and keep it there, separate and contained. Elizabeth Cook-Lynn, speaking of works by Wallace Stegner, which "terminate" the American Indian presence on the North American continent via literary moves very similar to the ones I've explored here, puts Memmi's thoughts into a Native American context this way:

> [T]he Stegner phenomenon of [white] exclusivity in literature and history . . . takes over, colonizes, invades the reality of human experience in North America to the extent that the concepts of indigenousness and aboriginality are quite misdefined and ultimately misunderstood by the reading public. When that happens, the American Indian's literary, historical, and cultural presence in America is repeatedly falsified or denied. (38)

Cook-Lynn acknowledges that "the business of claiming indigenousness and inventing supportive mythology is an activity of the human imagination," one that both Native Americans *and* the colonizer can legitimately engage in as part of the storytelling process. The problem, however, is that because of the oppression of voice experienced by Indians and the tremendous privilege of voice experienced by white Americans, there is little opportunity to challenge this repackaging. What should be a dialogue between peoples is too often a false history that "forever excludes Indians from participation in the community of contemporary human thought" (37). The negation of place is closely linked to the negation of indigenous bodies, knowledge, and human rights; if you can deny or distort ideas about Indian bodies or culture, you make it much easier to rationalize or justify the theft of land from a population deemed savage, incompetent, or vanished.

We are back to the idea of those "free" Indian educations again, aren't we? Literacy entered this continent as a weapon against Native peoples, attacking the core of Native existence through treaties and erasure of Native languages: the connection and claim to Homeland. Thus when, as in the Meteorite metaphor earlier, it seems that the American House is constructed and dependent on the appropriation of Indian spirituality and land, Indian resistance in the form of repatriative texts and Native readings of American Literature cannot be judged simply as complaining, politically correct theory or as a scholarly refutation that deserves equal time. Indigenous "criticism" of misrepresentations of Indians by non-Indians is nothing less than self-defense, as Indians resist being taken captive and made into a collection for study—like the Willamette Meteorite, like Queequeg's very body—and having American history and mythology built around our captive identities.

Audre Lorde wrote, "The Master's tools will never tear down the Master's house" (112). But perhaps Lorde did not realize that in the case of American Indians, it is not tools filched by the natives that the Master should be concerned with, but rather what *the Master* has stolen that is captive in his own house. The native-constructed metaphor is resistance incarnate, plotting repatriation from within the Master's own walls. This Indian is thinking, *You steal the land, build a country on a stolen foundation, construct a cage around it. All that you have—your possessions, your ethics, your history—depends on keeping this land captive. Your cage must grow still more complex: you must construct more restraints. Literature that serves as steel bars, schools that serve as locks, textbooks that are prison guards. What keys are available to us to dismantle this perpetually tightening confinement?*

The Location of "Indian"

Most Native American literature teachers, both Native and non-native, will tell you that they also teach U.S. history, law, anthropology, psychology, spiritual belief systems, indigenous ideas about gender, and even medical information (such as early forms of germ warfare) in order to cover texts like, say, *Mean Spirit* by Linda Hogan, *Ceremony* by Leslie Marmon Silko, or poetry by Luci Tapahonso, Joy Harjo, or Chrystos. But there's something else Native professors have to do: teach our lives, our bodies, as texts and documents and evidence of a crime. Our bodies become the site, the *place*, of conflict in ways that no white professor can ever know. This can be disturbing and invasive, as well as exhilarating, empowering, and freeing.

For me—Indian, woman, professor, United Statesian—teaching in the academy is one of the most complicated acts of my life. It is complicated because of who I am, where the university is located, the history of that location with my ancestors' lives, and, by virtue of that history, my own daily life. I have had my ethnic identity challenged by students and faculty. I have had my motives challenged. I have been accused of "reverse racism." My authority and my credentials have been questioned by students who insist I do not have the ability to properly instruct or grade them. I have been told that I present an unbalanced and untruthful agenda. The lack of respect accorded to me by students (and sometimes faculty and staff) is hard for my white colleagues to understand. Many days, I think of Paula Gunn Allen (Laguna/Sioux) telling me in conversation about her abortive attempt to tell an allegorical story of being held hostage in one's own backyard. She couldn't write it, she says; it was too heartbreaking.

Allen's words highlight my fear of who I'll turn into, living within this context of struggle. Will I become hard, competitive, mean-spirited, defensive? Beaten, cowed, ashamed? A professor known for her anger, her intrusive ethnicity, her insistence on complication? Will my mostly white colleagues regard me with suspicion, pity, "tolerance," ridicule? Can I continue following my heart as a poet? Will my poetry have any guts, any tenderness? Will frustration destroy all that's good in me? Will my grief and anger leave me wordless, useless?

So far in this essay about Indians, place, and the academy, I've written about theft, murder, miseducation, racism, intolerance, fear, and the small daily violences of teaching in a university. If I sound angry to some readers, let me reassure you that your impression is correct. If you are asking, *where's the lyric beauty in this essay? Where are the fragrant wild meadows at dawn, the deer pausing at the foot of a mountain, the sign of bear on a tree trunk? Where is the red clay, the healing spring bubbling up, the holy burial grounds of ancestors? Where is the Indianness in this essay?*—look closer. It's all here. Because I cannot separate my identity from the land, this is how my relationship to place and the academy plays out. Every day. Every hour. Every lecture. Every time I step foot on a university campus, all that beauty—and all that violence—is there, and I am the mouth that testifies. This essay, like the invitation of a drumstick to a drumhead, asks you to listen. In her powerful essay, "The Uses of Anger," Audre Lorde writes that "anger is full of information and energy" (127), stressing that the crucial difference between anger and hatred is the intended outcome: anger seeks to communicate, while hatred wants only to destroy. I've tried to use my anger wisely, but it is anger nonetheless, and I do not apologize for it. I am more Indian in the academy than anywhere else in the world. Indianness is accentuated for Indian academics because we teach within our homeland, yet in enemy territory. Repatriation is at the core of our teaching, our hours of advising, the classes we guest teach for colleagues, the papers we grade, our articles, our poetry, our presence. It's in our love poetry. It's in our anger. But it's not just revenge, taking back, in order to *own*. It's a reclamation of the right to engage in a creative, thinking, compassionate, sustainable world. When I communicate my anger about injustice to my students, they are often angry in turn—at me, for waking them up, at their American educations for keeping them uninformed or misinformed, at themselves for never questioning the history or stereotypes they'd been fed. The question I hear most often, "Why didn't anyone ever tell us about this?" asked with anguish and real regret. Then, right on the heels of that question, comes the cry, "What else do I not know?" Then I know that my students have transformed themselves into critical thinkers and have begun the long journey towards reestablishing their own relationship with place and with justice. Suddenly, they locate themselves on the planet, and *they have questions.*

What's it like to be the hostage, held captive in your own backyard? What's it like to be the sacred relic encased in a museum cage? What's it like to be hollowed out, a shell of your sacred self, a divine text used and discarded? Chrystos, Menominee poet and artist, responds to this kind of indigenous trauma in her poem, "Leaf behind My Ear." When a woman asks her, *How do you have hope to go on?* the poet replies,

> I can't answer that question I've carried with me
> except to say I'm alive I'm loved
> there's work to do (128)

This work of repatriation in the academy is not about victimization or blame games. It's about the acknowledgment and resolution of real and tangible crimes so that a future truly is worth living. That's what I want to tell you. The people and the land are one. As long as the land is held captive by lies and ignorant "owners," so am I. So are we all. Take a deep breath. Smell that fragrant, fierce, fertile buffalo poop beneath your feet. Let it teach you your place in this world.

Notes

1. I taught at Pacific Lutheran University in Washington state immediately preceding the writing of this essay and now teach on Monacan land at Washington and Lee University in Virginia—where many of the same issues about land and heritage must be negotiated, especially in a state where not one of the eight Indian tribes still existing have "received" Federal Recognition.
2. Like many American Indians, I grew up using the word "Indian" to self-identify; this term is widely used among tribes in the United States (as a quick look at Native literatures will reveal). "Native American" is a term recently invented for use in the academy but is misleading since it can also be used to refer to any person born in North or South America. "Indigenous" and "Native," "First Nations," or "First Peoples" are common terms as well, often used interchangeably by American Indians. In this essay, I use many of these terms for rhetorical variety, but especially "Indian," as it is used most often by my American Indian peers and colleagues.
3. Excellent, concrete descriptions of the miseducation Americans receive about American Indians may be found in James Loewen's *Lies My Teacher Told Me: Everything Your American History Textbook Got Wrong* (specifically, United States public school systems); Robert F. Berkhofer's *The White Man's Indian: Images of the American Indian from Columbus to the Present* (specifically, American culture); and *The American Indian Quarterly* Special Issue "Native Experiences in the Ivory Tower" (edited by Devon Mihesuah). Mihesuah's *So You Want to Write about American Indians? A Guide for Writers, Students, and Scholars* is a helpful beginning text for those wishing to take corrective measures regarding such miseducation.
4. In 2000, the Museum and the Confederated Tribes of the Grande Ronde Community of Oregon signed a historic agreement that "ensures access to the Willamette Meteorite at the museum for religious, historical, and cultural uses while maintaining its continued presence at the museum for scientific and educational purposes" ("Tribe," *Sheridan* [OR] *Sun*).
5. See *Mental Health: A Report of the Surgeon General 1999*, U.S. Dept. of Health and Human Services.

Bibliography

Allen, Paula Gunn. Telephone interview. 8 December 1998.

Anzaldúa, Gloria. *Borderlands/La Frontera: The New Mestiza*. San Francisco: Spinster, 1987.

Beidler, Peter. *A Casebook on Ken Kesey's* One Flew Over the Cuckoo's Nest. Ed. George J. Searles. Albuquerque: U of New Mexico P, 1992.

Berkhofer, Robert F. *The White Man's Indian*. New York: Random, 1978.

Bjorgen, Thomas R., and Morris Uebelacker. "Determination of the Southern Boundary of the Medicine Creek Treaty Ceded Area." 15 March 2006 <http://wdfw.wa.gov/wlm/tribal/medcreekdetermination.pdf>.

Brester, David, and David M. Buerge, eds. *Washingtonians: A Biographical Portrait of the State*. Seattle: Sasquatch, 1988.

Buerge, David M. "Big Little Man: Isaac Stevens (1818–1861)." Brester and Buerge. 73–95.

Chrystos. *Dream On*. Vancouver: Press Gang, 1991.

Cook-Lynn, Elizabeth. *Why I Can't Read Wallace Stegner and Other Essays: A Tribal Voice*. Madison: U of Wisconsin P, 1996.

Crain, Caleb. "Lovers of Human Flesh: Cannibalism and Homosexuality in Melville's Novels." *American Literature* 66.1 (March 1994): 25–53.

Hanh, Thich Nhat. Address. Plum Village, France. 16 July, 1997.

Harjo, Joy, and Gloria Bird, eds. *Reinventing the Enemy's Language: Contemporary Native Women's Writings of North America*. New York: Norton, 1997.

Hogan, Linda. *The Woman Who Watches Over the World*. New York: Norton, 2002.

Jurgensen, John. "Tribe Claims Planetarium's Meteorite as a Holy Object." *Seattle Post-Intelligencer* 19 February 2000. <http://seattlepi.nwsource.com/local/holy19.shtml>.

Kesey, Ken. *One Flew Over the Cuckoo's Nest*. New York: New American Library, 1962.

Loewen, James W. *Lies My Teacher Told Me: Everything Your American History Textbook Got Wrong*. New York: Simon, 1995.

Lorde, Audre. *Sister Outsider: Essays and Speeches*. Trumansburg, NY: Crossing, 1984.

Melville, Herman. *Moby-Dick*. New York: Penguin, 1961.

Memmi, Albert. *The Colonizer and the Colonized*. Boston: Beacon, 1967.

Mihesuah, Devon. *American Indians: Stereotypes and Realities*. Atlanta: Clarity, 1966.

———, ed. Native Experiences in the Ivory Tower. Spec. issue of *American Indian Quarterly* 27.1, 27.2 (Winter/Spring 2003).

———. *So You Want to Write about American Indians? A Guide for Writers, Students, and Scholars*. Lincoln: U of Nebraska P, 2005.

Monacan Nation. 15 March, 2006 <http://www.monacannation.com/>.

Oi, Cynthia. "Man and Myth: Acclaimed Author Sherman Alexie Aims to Kill the Myths Surrounding Native Americans." *Honolulu Star Bulletin* 18 January 2000. <http://starbulletin.com/2000/01/18/features/index.html>.

"Tribe, Museum OK Deal on Willamette Meteorite." *Sheridan (OR) Sun.* 15 March 2006 <http://www.sheridansun.com/News/2000/0628/Front_Page/01.html>.

United States. U.S. Dept. of Health and Human Services. Office of the Surgeon General. *Mental Health: A Report of the Surgeon General 1999.* 15 March 2006 <http://www.mentalhealth.samhsa.gov/cre/fact4.asp>.

———. U.S. Dept. of Education. *American Indians and Alaska Natives in Postsecondary Education.* 15 March 2006 <http://nces.ed.gov/pubsearch/pubsinfo.asp?pubid=98291>.

13

The Blind Teaching the Blind
The Academic as Naturalist, or Not

Robert Michael Pyle

I had just returned to Logan, Utah, from the Teton Science School in Wyoming's Grand Tetons National Park. Though it was a Sunday in deep midwinter, I had a class to prepare for Monday, so I visited my cold office in the second story of the English department. The campus of Utah State University was deserted; a new storm had left three feet of snow on every surface, and more flakes were falling, like cabbage whites gone crazy in a cauliflower world. A different flicker of movement called my eyes away from the student manuscript claiming my attention. In a leaf-stripped hawthorn outside my window, a great flock of cedar waxwings had appeared. For the next hour, until the early darkness blotted both the snowfall and the birds, I got nothing done. Nothing, but to watch the silky gray waxwings grab haws with their sharp bills and swallow them, their bloody-waxen pinfeathers out-redding the fruits and their yellow tail tips flashing. How those masked and crested wonders made it through the Wasatch winter amazed me, but at least I knew how they would make it through the night.

There have been dozens of campuses in my life. Every one has been a distinct, physical, inhabited place, rich in encounters such as that with the waxwings. It is my condition that I need to situate myself and take account of the citizenry of any place I inhabit, however briefly—the airs, scents, colors, seasons, substrates, waters, plants, and animals. Most of all, what matters to me in a workplace is the ability to walk and to be surprised by what I find. I maintain that an acute visceral attention to the literal places where I work as a transient academic has made me who I am as a scholar and teacher and has dramatically enhanced life for me and for my students. Furthermore, much in my writing and study depends directly upon the living details of these places. I doubt, however, that many campus denizens—even place-conscious scholars—pay this kind of attention to their professional surroundings. In fact, in my experience, it seems that most of my colleagues have been almost oblivious to that which makes the academical enterprise not only tolerable, but often delightful, for me.

My physical introduction to colleges came as a youth at Colorado campuses for visits to see my coed sister in Greeley, for an aunt-inspired speed-reading class at the University of Denver, and for track meets at Boulder and Fort Collins. I liked the ersatz "olde" buildings and the parklike settings, whether for the crispy Norway maple leaves underfoot in autumn or the air redolent of hopa crab blossoms on May nights. These visits set the pattern for a near-infinitude of campus explorations to come.

When I left dry Colorado for the moist and verdant University of Washington as a beginning undergraduate, I dived into site survey and discovery with a passionate thirst for new landscapes, plants, and weathers. My daily prowls of the Seattle campus, its marsh and arboretum, over seven years, were part self-education in the stuff of place and part displacement activity. Deeply wishing to be studying ornithology instead of physical chemistry, I failed the latter while indulging the former and spotting one hundred species of birds on campus in one hundred days: #99 was a black-sterned gadwall in Gadwall Cove, #100 a Bullock's oriole, brilliant orange above it. I came to know virtually every corner and thicket of the large campus and what could be found there in each season. This devotion both saved and radicalized me. Harry W. Higman and Earl J. Larrison's book *Union Bay: The Life of a City Marsh* showed me what these habitats were like before the university leased them to the city for a landfill; my own explorations showed me what was left and committed me to helping to save it.

In clear danger of flunking out altogether, I found academic salvation by making up a sixties-style curriculum based largely on the natural history I found around me, with the assistance of a remarkable group of professors hanging on before the purge of the naturalists in a modern biology department became complete. And when the campus wetlands, already compromised by a dump, were threatened with paving over, I led a band of students, faculty, and staff on a march to save them. While others took over the administration building and demanded peace and justice, we took over the marsh and landfill, demanding topsoil and trees (Pyle, "Union Bay"). Our actions as student conservationists went far beyond campus, and we protested the Vietnam War as well. But the Union Bay Life-after-Death Plant-In colored all that followed in my life as an activist. And when, after Nixon's Cambodian invasion, thousands of students faced off against hundreds of riot police, I sought the infinite sanity of the evening grosbeaks thronging the elms in front of old Denny Hall.

Coming to know my college precincts so well made graduate school in the East both exciting and intimidating in its utter novelty. New Haven is an old industrial city, but the traprock ridges known as East and West Rocks loomed within easy reach of the Yale School of Forestry and Environmental Studies, and Atlantic shores lapped close to campus. The mature groves of hardwoods that graced the older colleges and cemeteries not only introduced me to the resplendent eastern autumn without having to go farther afield in New England but also stood ready to receive the warbler waves when they appeared in April and May. Ailanthus trees along railroad cuttings were hung with Cynthia moth cocoons like Christmas balls (Pyle, "Silkmoth"). Architecture and natural history merged as I took to seeking out the academic owls of Yale—stone carvings, wooden effigies, copper weathervanes—tallying in three years more than seventy-five "species."

Self-consciously Oxbridgean Yale was bracketed by the real thing, as I spent several years in and near Cambridge as a Fulbright Scholar and postdoctoral consultant. Wicken Fen, where Darwin collected beetles while skipping classes, was some distance from campus. But the college Backs, spattered with celandine and crocuses in early spring, opened onto the River Cam (or Granta)—whose towpath could take you into fen, field, or forest, not to mention pub. I found ways to walk from my digs to my lab, three miles, entirely on footpaths, never on a road. I knew what nettle patch was most likely to offer up small tortoiseshells coming out of hibernation and which water meadows echoed with the rising and falling skylarks. Another season, I lived a block from Virginia Woolf's one-time residence in Newnham, in a lane ending at a nature reserve known as Owlstone Close, where tawny owls really did wail at night. Blue tits and English robins haunted Little St. Mary's, and swifts zipped open the ancient air between the Cavendish Laboratory and the Free Press Public House. It wasn't the Selborne of Gilbert White, but much of England's familiar natural history could be found in and around Cambridge's colleges.

Since then, as an independent scholar, I have been the guest of scores of academies. Most frequently, Evergreen State, with its deep woods and long shoreline on southernmost Puget Sound; the urban enclave of Portland State; and the erstwhile department store magnate's estate of Lewis and Clark College, where poet William Stafford once had the right to glean fruit from campus trees written into his contract. I have watched a red vole skitter among gardens at the University of Saarbrücken; confirmed global warming by giant mauve pasqueflowers blooming in April at the University of Alaska in Fairbanks, where I'd been promised dogsledding and found bare-chested frisbee throwers instead; and marveled at a lemon-and-heliotrope imperial moth hanging beneath a midnight archway in College Park, Maryland. At Thomas Jefferson's "academical village," the University of Virginia, I've watched pairs of cardinals (a big deal to a western birder) courting among old pines and a weathered and crocketed spire imported from Oxford in one of the many walled gardens. At a little college on Florida's west coast, wood storks stalked the lawn, while across the state, alligators cruised campus waters at the University of Florida in Gainesville. Recently, walking the shore path along Lake Mendota at the University of Wisconsin in Madison, I reveled in the chartreuse explosions of fireflies (another biggie for westerners) in the campus bosque called Muir Woods after the esteemed naturalist and alumnus. One lampyrid beetle, plucked from a spiderweb, flashed on and off in my hand for half an hour. I can't think of a college or university I have visited without taking home some such sharp image of its living placehood.

Since I have never assumed a full-time faculty position for long, I have not (since Washington) had to contend with the daily reality of a particular academic locus for year on year, day in, day out. As an itinerant don, I have not had to face committees and quotidian life and the strains they impose. No doubt this has made it easier for me to view every appointment as a longer or shorter field trip.

Even so, I fully believe that, had I satisfied my original objective of a long-term professorship, I would have treated whatever campus on which I went to ground in exactly the same manner: as a habitat, to be known more and more intimately for all it offered in the way of teaching, placement, and pleasure. If anything, such a relationship with one's place of employment ought to provide a balm for the more tedious and difficult demands of the profession.

The closest I've come was as a visiting professor of creative writing at Utah State in Logan, the place of the waxwings in the snow. I designed and taught undergraduate and graduate courses in environmental writing for spring semester, 2002. This furnished the opportunity to get to know a particular academy's locality in greater detail than those I might call upon for an afternoon or a week. Normally a habitué of rainforest that does have its seasons but that drips between them almost insensibly, I was struck by my first opportunity since childhood to experience a Rocky Mountain winter and its abrupt morphing into full-blown spring. It seemed that one week I was snowshoeing in the Wellsville Mountains west of town, the next hiking among balsamroot blooming in the Wasatch foothills to the east. The campus itself had suffered major disruption for new steam tunnels and was in any case fairly manicured. But one side of its hill dropped directly into the mouth of semi-wild Logan Canyon, and another fell away toward town through a squirrel-haunted arboretum. Pollination biologists and botanists in other departments steered me toward rare plants, such as the magenta MacGuire's primrose, which bloomed in Logan Canyon when the naturalized violets spread their mauvy carpet across every unsprayed lawn in town. Two of my students were good naturalists active in Audubon, and together we found the best local wetlands for waterfowl. Most of the others, though from small Mormon towns and farms, were not much oriented toward the voluntary out-of-doors. But through writing invitations and field trips, I got them out, sharing my discoveries and reminding them of things they had forgotten to remember.

But the most vivid memory of emplacement I took away from Utah State had to do with an alien invasion of the English department. Actually, the invaders were native; the students, staff, and faculty who noticed their invasion were the aliens. At least since the late Pleistocene, bright fire-engine-red-and-black insects known as box elder bugs (*Leptocoris trivittatis*) have frequented the canyons of the Rockies. They lay their eggs in the bark of box elder trees (*Acer negundo*), a kind of maple, in the early spring. By fall, millions of adult box elder bugs descend from the mountains seeking shelter in caves and hollow trees at lower elevations. When people erect big, heated buildings—the kind that campuses commonly consist of—within box elder bug range, they should not be surprised when the bugs treat them as caves. Yet people repeatedly express shock and indignation when their domiciles and workplaces are chosen for winter quarters by thousands of bright little bugs. And this was the case at Utah State, the winter I arrived.

I'd been enjoying the box elder bugs all term, as they clustered in corners over the ineffectual radiator in my office. As the days began to warm, they flew about the hallways like bright little ingots, seeking egress. Occasionally, I witnessed common varieties of entomophobia or mild irritation as b.e.b.'s flew into someone's careful coif or circled someone else's spectacles. But the first I knew that anyone was seriously disturbed by them was when a memo came around announcing that an exterminating firm had been engaged to spray the English building, as well as Old Main and the library. Apparently, some students and staff had become much distressed by the abundance of b.e.b.'s, especially in the computer room, where they congregated in special abundance, sometimes damaging the hardware, other times dissuading users from even coming in.

I was disturbed by the bad biology of the plan, as well as the decision to subject workers to toxins without their assent or knowledge of the agents to be used. Especially worrisome was the company's assurance that they would monitor for the bugs a month after application—by which date the insects would naturally have dispersed in any case! Between the opportunism of the exterminator and the entomological naiveté of everyone else, a bad situation had developed. Fortunately, many members of the faculty were incensed about the planned poisoning of their workplace for dubious reasons. As I wrote in a return memo, vacuums would do the job just fine where numbers of bugs constituted a real problem, and the bugs would soon evacuate the premises regardless of what we did—and, it was important to note, be back again next fall. The only way to prevent the annual influx would be to air-seal the building or to eradicate box elder trees from the canyons. Furthermore, the bugs were fascinating and quite beautiful, observed closely. Live with them, I advised my colleagues; even enjoy them.

Vacuum them if you must. At least that spring, we forestalled the spray. But I was sure the issue would arise again, after I was long gone. At least my colleagues would be better informed next time. The whole episode illustrated the disconnection many people feel with regard to their nonhuman neighbors, a trait that too often distances academic employees from their workplaces.

As a matter of fact, many academies go to lengths to eradicate or damp down the experience of the more-than-human on campus. For example, sprays are not limited to controlling unwanted residents in college buildings. Too many campuses suffer heavy exposure to chemicals applied to their lawns and gardens. Driven by some administrator's floraphobic dictate that greenswards be pure bluegrass monocultures, grounds and facilities crews regularly spray the grass with herbicides and insecticides. When the snow melted and the grass greened in Logan, I was distressed to see work-study students employed to broadcast toxins here and there, completely free from protective equipment. I have also watched kids in shorts and sandals spraying herbicides at Albertson College in Idaho. This scene is repeated annually at many colleges and universities across the country. Recently, I witnessed with incredulity as an agricultural rig suited for a Midwest cornfield, with ten nozzles on a boom, sprayed the very swards where students routinely bask, nap, study, and make out at the University of Maryland. At the same time, soccer and softball camps were in progress. The little yellow warning flags were invisible over most of the expansive lawns. Many of the most commonly used biocides have been linked to lymphomas and an array of reproductive ills, and growing numbers of chemically sensitive people react badly to any sprays (Wargo). How sad to think that the blandishments of going barefoot may lead to bodily harm for trusting scholars. Not to mention to boring lawns that might otherwise host an attractive and interesting array of clovers, veronicas, violets, English daisies, native grasses, and their attendant pollinators.

I reserve special disdain for another, nearly ubiquitous abomination on the campus scene: the leaf blower. Is it not ironic that the very ideal of collegiate tranquillity, the much-vaunted and beloved Grove of Academe, where the din and fumes of the hurly-burly mercantile world are left behind in favor of the serene life of the mind, is the very place where one can almost be assured of hearing damnable leaf blowers every autumn? Many is the lovely campus where

I have experienced the shriek of two-stroke gasoline engines shattering the contemplative calm, never worse than one perfect afternoon at Lewis and Clark College in Portland, Oregon. Couched as a labor issue by landscape foremen who call the shots, the displacement of the soft sough of rakes by earsplitting and calm-wrecking leaf blowers and weed eaters can be considered at worst nothing less than a certain sign of the decline of the academy in a deeply philistine land. At best, poisons and machines serve to further disemplace campus residents of ours and other species.

Not that academicians need any further disincentives. In my experience, few campus habitués—whether students, staff, or faculty—attend to the actual place of their college homes with much care. Even those who live much out-of-doors tend to flee the campus as soon as possible for the trails, beaches, kayak waters, and climbing rocks far away. This is perfectly understandable, when the less exciting campus claims so much of their time already. But while they must be present, I maintain, there is no reason not to be more attentive to their surroundings.

I have known a few academics who exercised mindfulness toward their workplace. Not surprisingly, some of these were the relictual naturalists with whom I studied as an undergraduate in Seattle. The great botanist Arthur Kruckeberg, still situated at Washington after half a century, knows its every tree and shrub; he—along with Estella Leopold, another botany professor and daughter of Aldo Leopold—once chained himself to a special South African tree at risk from a paving project. Kruckeberg's friend and late colleague, mammalogist and ornithologist Frank Richardson, taught me how the eastern gray and fox squirrels partitioned their adopted homes of the campus and arboretum. But one of the keenest such devotions was evidenced by a philosophy professor, John Chambless. When a resident of old, postwar faculty housing beside the landfill, he crossed the remnant marsh on foot daily to get to classes, bird-watching all the while. He became an astute birder, often presenting his introductory philosophy course in terms of local ornithological experiences and metaphors. This made Plato, Berkeley, and Descartes much more memorable for me, and I suspect for others, too.

Likewise, my mentor at Yale, Charles Remington, always knew what was happening outside his rooms in lab and museum. Sometimes, inside and outside merged seamlessly. I recall him lecturing on wasps of the genus *Vespula* one spring day when, as if on call, a big queen yellow jacket flew in the open window. "Yes, just like that one," he said with a flourish. "Thank you very much." The wasp took one turn around the room and flew out again the way it had come in. That lesson was not forgotten (Pyle, *Walking*).

It is not surprising that some the academics who have most closely noticed their surroundings have been literary writers. Writer/biologists such as E. O. Wilson, Bernd Heinrich, Lynn Margulis, May Berenbaum, and Vincent Dethier quite naturally sprinkle their texts with observations from their home institutions as well as from distant settings (for example, Wilson). The genre of academically based fiction is also rich in examples. Vladimir Nabokov, still smarting from leaving the wilds of St. Petersburg's hinterlands, paid little attention to Cambridge while there, apart from boating, dating, and playing soccer (Boyd and Pyle). But his mordant and hilarious parody of a confused émigré professor, *Pnin*, deftly catches details of the campuses where he taught in this country, especially Cornell. In one scene, he even gives himself a cameo role, when Pnin disturbs a puddle-club of celestial blue butterflies: "'Pity Vladimir Vladimirovich is not here,' remarked Chateau. 'He would have told us all about these enchanting insects'" (128). They were, of course, the famous Karner Blue, now a conservation *cause célèbre*, originally given its scientific name and description by Nabokov. In Jane Smiley's *Moo*, we see the ag campus in intimate detail between an obsolete horticulturist character and a protagonist pig whose lone mad dash finally gains it brief freedom. Jon Hassler's several novels set in a small college in the upper Midwest dwell upon the physical setting with such loving depth that there is no perceptible separation between people, building, river, and geological substrate (e.g., *The Dean's List*). David Lodge's collegiate comedies, while hardly natural history, closely observe the airy Californian and red-brick English universities he loves to contrast. And in an inspired touch, his novel *Small World* apotheosizes the Two Cultures by placing the arts at one end of an expansive, new greenfield university, the sciences at the other, their planned bridging abandoned due to budget cuts that leave the intervening miles a wilderness both real and metaphorical.

The antithesis of Lodge's bicameral campus is Nabokov's High Ridge: "Does there not exist," he asks, "a high ridge where the mountainside of 'scientific' knowledge meets the opposite slope of 'artistic' imagination?" (Pyle, *Walking*). A recent academic job of mine was posited directly on the existence of such a meeting place. The

65,000-acre H. J. Andrews Experimental Forest, a joint enterprise of the Willamette National Forest and Oregon State University, has advanced our knowledge of Cascade Range forests and streams for more than half a century through a program known as Long-Term Ecological Research. A recent initiative of the U.S. Forest Service and the Spring Creek Project of the OSU Department of Philosophy, spearheaded by ecologist Fred Swanson and writer/philosopher Kathleen Dean Moore, launched a parallel program to be known as Long-Term Ecological Reflection. One of the first efforts I know of anywhere to attempt a left brain/right brain bridge based on place, the ecological reflection scheme is precisely an exercise in placing the academy. I was fortunate to be appointed to the first residency for this enlightened notion, subtitled "the Continuum Project" (Pyle, "Long Haul"). Subsequent residents have included Pattiann Rogers and ecocritic Scott Slovic.

As I drafted these thoughts while physically situated among deep wilderness, surrounded by massive Douglas firs and Pacific yews slung with boas of lichens and moss, I realized that I was taking part in literally bringing the academy to the wild. I found that my habit of peering closely into each of my successive domains had prepared me to extend my view beyond the actual H. J. Andrews campus and into the old-growth territory beyond. Of course, as an ecologist and a writer, I had an advantage over one whose biology was less embedded. On the other hand, the experience of a scientific naif, while less informed, might be more revealing for its freshness of view. What one *would* need for such an experience to be successful is the inherent or cultivated habit of close observation of external detail—for it is the details that make the place, whether or not one possesses names or facts to attach to them.

As stimulating as the H. J. Andrews immersion might be, it would be a grave mistake to imagine that genuine emplacement requires wildness in the strict sense. Fortunate is the nature lover situated at Williams or Middlebury colleges, backing up to the Green Mountains of Vermont as they do. Yet when I visited Columbia University last spring, in its hyperurban Manhattan setting, I saw that it not only possesses its own green space, but that it abuts the close of the Cathedral of St. John the Divine, which runs into relatively bucolic Morningside Park, which further connects to Central Park, where I had watched hermit thrushes, white-crowned sparrows, and brown creepers that very March morning.

Nor are we talking strictly about native species. Ornamentals, cultivars, weeds, and the animal life they support all add to the diversity of any scene. Because most campuses are wildly mixed montages resembling no particular ecosystem to be found in the wild does not make them any less arresting to the eye and the mind. In fact, gardening, if not applied as a sort of ethnic cleansing against all things uninvited, may actually increase the overall diversity of a site over what one might find in that region and season in a more "natural" setting.

True placement should always lead one *out*, beyond the pale of the ivory tower, into the profane precincts beyond, crossing ecotones and back again like every other creature. We are, after all, the only species (and this may be the one thing that truly differentiates humanity from other beings) that has forsaken its animal vigilance and ecological adeptness for comfort and security, such as it is.

So, how to get some of that back? By being a better naturalist, day by day, regardless of one's academic discipline. This is not a matter of becoming a dedicated birder or botanist, carrying around a Roger Tory Peterson as an inseparable text (though that can't be a bad thing, for any scholar interested in place). Rather, it is an openness toward gradual acquaintance, a willingness to get to know neighbors outside our species, let alone our departments. Most of all, it is an active resistance to that anti-intellectual, anticommunitarian quality that John Fowles has beautifully described as "contempt in ignorance." I am again and again taken aback by otherwise bright people who, in their lack of familiarity with the so-called natural world, exhibit actual contempt for it or for those who pay it much attention. In his novel *Daniel Martin* (1973), a Fowles character tellingly asks, "Why isn't it enough that I just love it here? That I don't want to know all the names and the frightfully scientific words." The title character answers, "Because you shouldn't justify contempt in ignorance. In anything" (350).That gets it just right.

To place yourself in your academy, nothing serves better than walking. Walking, in the Thoreauvian sense from his essay by that name (Thoreau), means sauntering with few expectations other than being surprised—not dashing madly to class while shouting into a cell phone or trying to remember if you brought your lecture notes or what's for dinner. It means dedicating otherwise unchallenged time to perambulation of your immediate environs, again and again, through the changing seasons, and then, following up on some of the questions that invariably arise. What *were* those huge pigeons in the deodar cedars? Are these madhouse squirrels native or introduced? Those mushrooms behind the greenhouse—were they palatable, poisonous, or psychoactive? This kind of looking and asking can lead not only to extradepartmental conversation, but to the occasional lyric impulse or connective insight.

I take special pleasure in long night walks on campuses, when sounds and smells are especially vivid and human bustle almost absent. On my lengthy noctivagation of UW Madison one recent summer, I watched Boston ivy ruffle in the breeze on the side of the carillon tower as if it were green waves, just before the bells rang eleven. College-gothic shadows, bits of stained glass, greenhouse palms, and premating primates all showed as they never would have by day, and a lean, feral black cat spotted not far from a small cottontail at graze predicted either a short food chain or a close call. I readily admit to a nocturnal advantage as a large male animal. Even so, company, if not overly loquacious, does not necessarily spoil such dark rambles. They may also be indulged on wheels, in fact more and more so on our post-ADA campuses.

In the end, placing the academy means, to me, paying true attention to one's academic surrounds. I am both saddened and disturbed by how few seem to do so. Strangely, I have known few less versed in natural history than some of those who style themselves "deep ecologists." Doubtless these thinkers lead splendid seminars, but most could no more lead an informed nature walk in their own home precincts than they could survive a month in the wild. Likewise, many ecocritics, ecofeminists, ecophilosophers, and environmental historians of my acquaintance tend to neglect their own backyards. I have known professors of place-based disciplines, not to mention molecular biologists, who couldn't name five native plants or animals outside their offices.

I do not intend this charge as an indictment as much as an invitation. Of course, our jobs seldom demand or reward intimacy with the grounds outside Old Main, nor have we any call to go forth into the wilderness naked (as former University of Washington professor of anthropology Monty West once did in order to perceive the plight of the unequipped aboriginal; he survived, barely) (Pyle, *Bigfoot*). What, then, *is* lost through the failure to attend? *Just this: anyone who is concerned with the literature or meaning of place, yet who ignores the physical and living details of the very place where she or he works is forsaking a vast reservoir of inspiration, grounding, instruction, authority, tranquillity, consolation, physical and intellectual stimulation, spiritual succor, fun, and sometimes ecstasy, but above all, interest in the real world.* When you care about your own place, what you have to say about place in general is certain to mean, and matter, much more. If my experience is any measure, getting to know the campus *sensu stricto* can dramatically affect one's teaching, research, writing, engagement, and well-being.

Finally, I do not think it out of order to suggest that intellectual workers whose subjects of study impinge on place (and I can scarcely imagine a field that does not) bear a certain responsibility to know something about the locality where they live, study, and teach. The aunts of Frank Lloyd Wright interviewed prospective teachers for their Hillside Home School based on their knowledge of the local flora and fauna (Chase). While we are unlikely to return to such an Arcady, there is something in that view of pedagogic qualification that still rings true. Would it be too much to ask of our academics that they make an effort to know their nonhuman neighbors, as well as their colleagues and students? For me, doing so has been nothing but a pleasure. And when I arrived in Missoula not long ago for an appointment at the University of Montana and found a bill tacked to a telephone post a block from my apartment urging everyone to be watchful for the local black bear, I knew I was in for another adventure in placement.

One recent year, I had cause to return repeatedly to the University of Washington during a successful course of chemotherapy for my wife, Thea. These occasions gave me the opportunity to revisit many of the crannies and corners I'd known so well some thirty years ago. Picking my way among new buildings since sprung up in the rich fertilizer of Gates and Allen cash, I sought the old haunts. The skyline and footprints of university buildings had grown radically, becoming more an academical city than village. Unaltered habitats had equally shrunk, one of my favorite bird groves having disappeared beneath the new law school, for example. But I found that much remained—from attenuated madrona patch to revivified herb garden. The route of the then-railroad—now the many-mile Burke-Gilman Trail girdling Seattle's midsection—took me round the campus when it was painted by autumn. In winter rain I found the immense graduate reading room of Suzallo Library, though recently earthquake-proofed, still one of the finest rooms I know, and the mauve stained-glass chipmunk still guarded a small stairway nearby. Come spring, I circumnavigated the shore of Portage Bay, from Montlake Bridge to University Bridge, past marsh and freeway, past houseboat and dorm, past salmon-spawning pool and birch grove, past Fisheries and Oceanography and Early Childhood Development. Coots and spotted sandpipers still frequented bay and beach, marsh wrens the cattail patch, and Anna's hummingbird rose to the peak of his molten-throated courtship arc. As I returned to the hospital through the early dusk, the powerful seashore stink of *Cornus mas* and the thick sweet scent of *Daphne odora* displaced the diesel fumes of the day.

Bibliography

Boyd, Brian, and Robert Michael Pyle, eds. *Nabokov's Butterflies: Unpublished and Uncollected Writings*. Boston: Beacon, 2000.

Chase, Mary Ellen. *A Goodly Fellowship*. New York: Macmillan, 1959.

Fowles, John. *Daniel Martin*. Boston: Little, 1973.

Hassler, Jon. *The Dean's List*. New York: Ballantine, 1998.

Higman, Harry W., and Earl J. Larrison. *Union Bay: The Life of a City Marsh*. Seattle: U of Washington P, 1951.

Lodge, David. *Small World*. London: Secker, 1998.

Nabokov, Vladimir. *Pnin*. Garden City, NY: Doubleday, 1957.

Pyle, Robert Michael. "The Long Haul." *Orion* 23.5 (Sept.–Oct. 2004): 70–71.

———. "Silkmoth of the Railroad Yards." *Natural History* 84.5 (May 1975): 44–51.

———. "Union Bay: A Life-after-Death Plant-In." *Ecotactics: The Sierra Club Handbook for Environmental Activists*. Ed. John G. Mitchell and Constance L. Stallings. New York: Pocket, 1970.

———. *Walking the High Ridge: Life as Field Trip*. Minneapolis: Milkweed, 2000.

———. *Where Bigfoot Walks: Crossing the Dark Divide*. Boston: Houghton, 1995.

Smiley, Jane. *Moo*. New York: Knopf, 1995.

Stafford, Kim. *Early Morning: Remembering My Father*. St. Paul: Grey Wolf, 2002.

Thoreau, Henry David. *Walking*. 1862. Boston: Beacon, 1991.

Wargo, John. *Our Children's Toxic Legacy*. New Haven: Yale UP, 1998.

White, Gilbert. *The Illustrated Natural History of Selborne*. 1789. London: Thames, 2004.

Wilson, Edward O. *Naturalist*. Washington, DC: Island, 1994.

14

Where Are You From?

Lee Torda

Where are you from? Since beginning graduate work, first in Maine and then in North Carolina, this was the singular question I answered over and over. And it should have been entirely expected: if you choose to live an academic life, you are subject to a fickle job market and, thus, to a certain amount of moving around. In the academic life, the assumption is relocation. Few of us work and live in the place we grew up in. We can and often do end up anywhere. It is the individual who must decide if she can stand the anywhere she finds herself in.

The question, with each year that I spend in some new place, resonates differently and with such a complexity I find it hard to bear. I am flummoxed at how to respond, though it should be such a simple answer to such a simple question: *where are you from?*

I.

I am from Cleveland, Ohio. How do I explain the way this news is received in the Northeast, my current academic home? There is that delicious scene in *The Philadelphia Story* where Katharine Hepburn as Tracy Lord asks Ruth Hussey's reporter character where she is from (South Bend). Hepburn replies, "South Bend. That's west of here isn't it?" To which Hussey answers, "Yes. But we occasionally get the breezes." It is the same, much the same, when I tell a Bostonian in particular or New Englander in general that I am from Cleveland. Sometimes a music aficionado will ask me if I know the difference between Cleveland and the *Titanic*. It's an old joke. There is never need of an answer (Cleveland has a better orchestra). I politely laugh along. Some ask if Lake Erie is still burning. But the worst reaction is the Tracy Lord reaction: *that's west of here, isn't it?*

My favorite drive into the city of Cleveland is over the Hope Memorial Bridge, where the major highways, I-71 North and I-90 East, converge. The bridge used to be named the Lorain-Carnegie, after Andrew Carnegie, the steel mogul, but when Bob Hope died, it was reborn the Hope Memorial. I can't think what says Cleveland better than punch lines and dead steel. As you whiz over the arc of the bridge, the Cuyahoga River runs below you. You will know it, if not by name, then certainly by reputation: the river that burned (it was never Erie). A mishmash of warehouses dot the shores. The new Justice Center juts out precariously. Then the unimpressive skyscrapers—the BP Building, the Ameritech Building. They still hold the names of companies that no longer have their headquarters there. The Terminal Tower stands alone as the glorious thing that it is—a throwback to an earlier time when Cleveland and her terminal were not lost in a sea of taller buildings in bigger cities.

Then the city herself dips down to greet the lake. There Cleveland sits, hunkered down almost, as if she were bracing herself against the cold wind off Erie, like a passerby in February on the corner of Ninth Avenue and St. Clair. The new Rock Hall, with bold architecture by I. M. Pei, and the new football stadium and the new science center rise up out beyond the downtown proper, right along the shore of the lake. You can't see them from the bridge, though. Back where I am, careening over the bridge, I-90 East rushes down by Jacobs Field, where the Indians play. The buildings surrounding the baseball stadium here are brick and old and low. Then you shoot out past all of that, past Public Square and the old, moldering department stores, the Halles and the downtown Mays, all gone now. You'll come to dead man's curve, a sharp, hard right angle: you've reached the lake, the Port of Cleveland, a lovely, hideous, sprawling, working port. Now, when I am coming to or going from Cleveland—all I ever do, now that it is not my home—I shout from my car, "Hello to the lake!" or "Good-bye to the lake!" depending on the direction I'm traveling in.

I did not always have such affection for my hometown.

I'm not even from Cleveland proper. I'm from Parma. If Cleveland is the Cleveland of the country, Parma is the Cleveland of Cleveland. There are jokes about Polish people, white socks, polka bands, and pink flamingos. I don't know or understand the origin of these jokes entirely, but it has to do with a certain suburban sensibility and a large Slavic population. It could be that there *are* a lot houses in my neighborhood that sport more than one plastic pink flamingo on their lawn. And there are a lot of Eastern Europeans who settled in Cleveland and moved, in the 1970s, in the full throng of white flight, to places like Parma. There was work to be had then in the Ford plant and the GM plant, steady union jobs. At my grade school, St. Columbkille (an Irish saint, a sort of cut-rate version of St. Patrick, if you ask me), on international day, the largest numbers of students identified themselves as Polish, Italian, and, a distant third, Irish.

    I wish I could offer a story more entertaining and less cliché than to say that it was my lifelong dream to escape Cleveland in general and Parma in particular and that academia, of course, was my ticket out. But unfortunately, I can offer you no other explanation for either the course of my life or the nostalgia I seem steeped in as I tell the story of it. I grew up hating the very fact that I was from Cleveland, had big, heady ideas of making a name for myself someplace else, and set myself on some sort of a course that would more or less get me there. As a girl, this consisted mainly of reading about places and lives other than my own and developing a scowl to register the great distaste I had for home. I read about some other, better place, where I imagined that men wore tweed and women smelled like rosewater—*Little Women*, *Anne of Green Gables*, the *Little House* books, and even *Gone with the Wind*. Of course, pioneer life on the prairie hardly involved tweed or rosewater, but I didn't know what rosewater was, really, and I did not see tweed, a natural fiber, until my midteens; but as a professor of mine in my PhD program once said, you may not know exactly the name for what it is you are looking for, but you know you still want the Oriental rug.

    As a little girl at St. Columbkille, we would go as a class on field trips to the West Side Market, one of the oldest continuous open air markets in the entire country. We would bring home exotic fruit—like cantaloupes—to our mothers. We'd grimace at the blood sausage, and we'd squeal with fascination and repulsion at the cases of sweetbreads and cow's tongue and everything else we wouldn't eat. It was widely known in Cleveland that if you were looking for some spice your grandmother used in the Old Country that the Market was the place you would find it. The Market is located near Fulton road, where my mother grew up, the Old Neighborhood. The Market was and is a place full of the foreign and the familiar for me, safe and extraordinary all at once.

    In terms of the relationship between the city and the suburb, my students in Massachusetts are a lot like me. They do not live in Boston proper but in the many towns that have sprung up on the south shore of Massachusetts along the major highways of 128 and 24. They remind me a great deal of myself in some ways, but they don't seem to want to leave. When I ask my students why not, even for a little while, they offer me a range of answers: family, mostly, is the number one answer, but also they just *like it here.* They want to stay.

It could be the ocean. The ocean is a powerful draw on the soul to stay in a place. A lot of my students come from the Cape. They grow up with the wide ocean in their eyes, and perhaps they think, what bigger place could there be to go? The ocean could be for my students the equivalent of what the Market was for me—both the wide world and the comforts of home. But it must not be the perfect equivalent because I still wanted to leave.

For me, the way out of Cleveland was on the very highway that holds my favorite views of the city. Of all the highways in my life, I-90 East has taken me the farthest the most often. It first took me to the University of Maine for my Masters. And, now, it is the road that connects where I live in Massachusetts to where I was born and raised. Ninety snakes through the city of Cleveland and on out. To points North. Away and away. Tempting me all my life at each tight turn to go where I don't belong. And, finally, I went.

II.

In Maine, where you don't think anyone lives, let alone Jews, I found an unlikely enclave of Orthodox Jews via the friendship of a less Orthodox one. I came to be the Litwacks' babysitter more or less for the entire time I lived in Maine. I watched their three children over long weekends, the gentile keeping them from turning on lights or carrying things on the Sabbath. After pickled herring, we would sit on the front porch and play spit and war and hearts. The neighbors, the Pidulskis (I went to school with Catholic Pidulskis in Cleveland), would let me into their house on Friday and Saturday evening to begin and end the Sabbath on those weekends I babysat.

When I was a kid, I wanted to be Jewish. I was ready to cast off my entire Italian, swarming family and take on a new life. In no small part, I know my interest had to do with the fact that the Jewish neighborhoods of Cleveland were all on the East Side. As I was from the all- white, all working-class West Side, this held great appeal to me. The art museum and the best shopping malls were all on the East Side with the Jews. And there I was, west of there, with a lake in between. It did not seem to me that we got the breezes at all.

I didn't really learn much about being Jewish from the Pidulskis and the Litwacks in the general way I would have wanted to when I was younger and searching for something other than my own experience to help me decide on an identity. I did learn some things about the rigors of orthodoxy, about meat plates and dairy plates—things that I would have been fascinated to know as a child the way my own Protestant friends were fascinated by my rosary. Mostly, I learned about these particular families because they let me into their homes.

I learned about where they came from (Long Island). I learned about who their children were, what they did, which ones settled close to home and which ones had relocated and where. The Pidulskis were also founding and powerful members of their synagogue, and so I learned something about how this particular Orthodox community came to be. I learned about how the founding families had raised the money to build the synagogue and the school. It was a pioneer's story, really: most of the people who started the community were from cities like New York or Boston but decided that they didn't like the closeness of cities they were born in and moved north to the more sparsely populated, less predictable state of Maine.

Bill, the father of the Litwack family, felt suffocated in Long Island with his politically conservative family, fled to Minnesota, where he married his wife, Jane, a Lutheran, then moved back to Maine, where they both became Orthodox and raised their family in an Orthodox house. I found in his story the familiar: his move from the East Coast out of his parents' home to the Midwest (via Nova Scotia, mind you) nearly tripled my journey in length, only in reverse. What always surprised me is that Bill had settled so permanently where he landed, both geographically and spiritually.

As I moved around in my academic life, I never lost an affinity for Jewish neighborhoods. In North Carolina I lived a block from one of the only synagogues in a three-city area. I wondered if this was coincidence. I don't think so. All the images of Jews I encountered and all of the real Jews that I encountered were so good at setting up shop wherever it was that they landed.

I could have lived anywhere in Boston. I could have lived with the Irish in the city, because they are everywhere. I could have lived in the North End, where the Italians settled and felt at home, but I didn't because I couldn't afford it now that gentrification has made the neighborhood fashionable. I could have lived with the academic elite in Cambridge, but I couldn't afford that either, and, besides, I get tired of being around academics all the time. You can't take a step without tripping over a PhD in Boston, Massachusetts. I could have lived in Bridgewater, where my college is, thirty miles south of Boston, equidistant from the Cape and the city. But I moved to Brighton (like the beach)—to be precise, to the very borderline of Brighton and Brookline. I can't keep track of the temples—Orthodox, Reformed, Sephardic, Conservative—I run past every day. Biblically and historically, Jews have been forced to settle again and again among the inhospitable. I envy this ability to make a home where no home is offered. Perhaps I thought that proximity would be enough to teach me the same lesson.

III.

In Vincente Minnelli's *An American in Paris*, Gene Kelly is always dancing and singing for and with Parisians. Kelly entertains French children and café-goers with his routines. The Parisians, every one of them, stand around smiling at Kelly the way you might smile at your kid at a school recital. That they were patronizing is the only thing French about these movie Parisians—it is the only thing French about the entire movie. I don't care how much residual World War II gratitude towards Americans was floating around Paris in 1951. I don't care how great Gene Kelly dances: no Parisian would be so happy to have some American dancing all over his or her cafés. I envy Kelly's character, Jerry, and his easy entry into this world that is not his own. I have not found it so easy myself. But that's why Jerry's story is a movie—and a musical at that—and mine, well, mine is not.

Sometimes I have this perverse fantasy that all of Boston will fall at my feet. That I'll run with some in-crowd and know the place as well as I know how to get to my Aunt Phil's house. Where—this is a piece in part about Boston, and I can't have at it without saying it at least once—*everyone will know my name*. There is no singing and dancing in my fantasy. Usually it has something to do with speaking at Harvard or marrying into the Red Sox. But, unlike Gene Kelly's Parisians, Bostonians will have nothing to do with my song and dance.

Another one of my Boston fantasies is that I run the Boston Marathon. To run it, you have to buy a spot or place your way in with a remarkable time at another official feeder race. Boston is the only race you have to qualify for, which is in large part the reason for much of the allure and hype for the event. And, too, it is wreck of a course, designed to make you earn every inch of it. It is to me another example of how unwelcoming a place Boston can feel. I ran my first marathon back in Ohio, surrounded by the people I love, by Ohioans and other midwesterners and many, many slow, honest, determined people.

But back to my fantasy: in this scenario, I make my way into the race the hard way, by running faster than I've ever run before at some other marathon. I run a good race in Boston, and, crossing the finish line, thumb my nose at all those Yankees and keep on running.

But, here's the thing, the part I just don't understand: *I don't run back to Cleveland.* At this point the fantasy splinters in myriad directions. Sometimes I move to New York and become a book editor. Sometimes I move to New York and become a writer. Sometimes I move to Europe—to London or Paris or Rome. I have no idea what I would do to make a living in those fantasies, but that is the cool blessing of fantasy: I don't have to know. In one version, I must have become independently wealthy just prior to the start of the fantasy because I don't work at all; I just travel from one remarkable place to another.

I have been trying to get myself someplace new for the better part of my life, but, having got there, what do I seem to want to do? Get someplace new all over again—and again and again and again.

The summer I trained for the Ohio marathon, I learned that the allure of the race was, for me anyway, the training. It was not the race itself. To train for a marathon you have to run every day for varying distances at varying speeds. Some days I had very swift, powerful runs. Other days, I trudged miserably, and there was, I confess, the occasional fall. But, no matter what, I was always moving, like a shark through water (I've heard they die if they stop). For that summer, I seemed always to be in constant motion, faster and stronger as the summer progressed. And I was, if not blissfully happy, remarkably content.

But the physical sensation of all that running around I remember so very keenly is only a half of the equation, I think. The summer I trained I worked out different routes all over the city—three miles, five, ten, twenty. Having run twenty miles' worth of Boston, I understood the layout of the city so much better. I could drive it better and walk it better. I found favorite places to get coffee, breakfast, Mexican food, stationary, bagels, *saag paneer,* and sushi. I know that such a thing as having favorites doesn't make a city a home; there is much more to it than that, but it certainly created a rather convincing illusion for me that Boston was becoming mine. I didn't dance in the streets of Paris; I ran by Fenway Park.

In contrast to my itch for motion and moving, there is also this yen of mine to feel, simultaneously, entirely at home. In all of my other-city fantasies, foreign and domestic, I am always ensconced in a cozy apartment, always within walking distance of many local favorites—the barriers of economics or language never sully the picture, a longing for family and friends never in evidence. It might as well be a musical, except I can't sing.

I know that it is not that old Cleveland home, specifically, that I am longing for, but the feeling of home, of *a* home. If the question that academics are always asking of each other is *"where are you from?"* the question my family asks of me is *"when are you coming home?"* That is a very good question that I most wholeheartedly wish I had a good answer to, but, when it comes down to it, I simply do not. The best I can offer is this: *whenever I get there.*

IV.

I am endlessly fascinated by the story of my great aunt, Vincenza Sanzano, who took the boat over to this country in 1921. Even more interesting to me, she came at the age of thirty-one. You can live an entire life by the time you are thirty-one, I know, and she left the one she lived behind. I wonder if she imagined the particular kind of new life she was going to start. I certainly would have—I continue to do it even as the particular kind of life I might have is growing easier and easier to predict. According to the manifest of the *Minnekahda,* my great aunt left her hometown of Foggia, catching the boat in nearby Naples. In possession of fifty-one dollars, she paid for her own passage. She is reported to have been headed to 3197 Fulton Road and to her husband, a man by the name of Montanella. That is what the ship's manifest tells me. I know she did, in fact, arrive. Within the year, I also know, she had a son.

When her son was barely four, her husband died, killed like the petty mobster he apparently was. My aunt moved into the parish house of St. Rocco's Church, still to this day standing on Fulton Road, where my parents and all of my aunts and uncles and most of my cousins were married. She kept house for the priests, cooking and cleaning for them, ironing their shirts. She traveled the distance between two continents but never learned to drive a car. She lived into her nineties. The parish house was her home until the very end of her life when she was moved to a nursing home. Her world must have been, it seems to me anyway, breathlessly small. I have a secret hope that she and a handsome priest had a secret and long love affair, spending clandestine nights in a narrow bed, whispering to each other in Italian.

I knew her, like I knew my grandfather, in only the vague, distant way you can know someone so old, someone who has lived only in another language from your own. The only way I knew anything about her was through my Aunt Lee, her translator and ambassador. But my memory of and affection for her are great. When Auntie turned ninety, my Aunt Lee threw her a birthday party at the nursing home. All of the family came. There was cake and ice cream and the smell of the old. The family clamored for some speech after she blew out the token candles on her cake. I don't think any of us expected her to take us up on our request, but, filled with a kind of respect for the moment, she spoke for a long while, softly and in Italian. My Aunt Lee translated for her.

Auntie talked about her life before America, about saying goodbye to her mother (she would never see her again), about the boat over and being quarantined at Ellis Island with tuberculosis, about arriving at her new house to her husband. And then her voice rose with emphasis, surprising even my Aunt Lee, who took a minute to let Auntie finish before she translated: "I am so grateful for this life I've had," Auntie said, "so grateful I've had it to live so long. I thank God that I got to come to this country and to have this life."

When Auntie died, we processed from Ripepi's funeral home on one side of the street back to St. Rocco's on the other side of Fulton, the same small block she had lived in her entire, grateful American life. I am humbled by her satisfaction with a life that, by all accounts, was hard and largely unrewarding. She could have been mightily disappointed, and no one would have blamed her. But she was not.

V.

Several years after I settled in Boston, I went to visit a friend on the opposite coast. We worked together on an article, my first real article, at a rented cottage along a beautiful stretch of the Pacific

Ocean. I was running there in the early evening on a gray day in spring. In the distance I saw what I imagined to be a log, thick, round, and black, washed up on the shore. But something about the size of it made me wonder if it wasn't possibly something else. What else I didn't know, but whatever it was, it unsettled me. I purposefully stared out past the bulge to another point on the beach, trying to ignore that it was even there.

As I neared, though, I couldn't help but finally see that it was a seal that had, presumably, beached itself. I didn't really know because I don't know about things like that, though my students do—another consequence of their having lived their lives by the ocean. I don't understand the mystery or biology of casting yourself up on a shore to a certain death—although, I must admit, the idea of drifting in just the wrong direction at precisely the wrong moment without ever noticing how bad off you are until it is too late rings true enough. Every so often, the evening news will feature the heroic efforts of Cape locals and wildlife experts trying to save the lives of beached whales or dolphins (sharks, as I said, die if they stop and—savvy creatures—seem never reported as beached). These good people, more often than not, fail in their efforts.

The seal I saw on this day didn't look like the sleek, petite pets of childhood visits to zoos and SeaWorld. It was mammoth and ungraceful. I didn't know for sure that it was even dead and wondered for a moment if I should stop to see. But even as I slowed, I knew I wouldn't stop, because what would I have been able to do? I passed the poor, stuck animal and kept on my pace.

When you run or walk along the beach like that, you always turn at some point and come back the way you came. That's just how it is. As I neared this seal on the return trip of my run, an old man, very old and shrunken, was circling the seal. Just as I passed in front of them, the man turned from surveying the body. The old man and I caught each other in our respective glances, and so I broke from my run, reluctantly, and asked him if the seal had beached itself. He said only that the animal had been alive the night before. The old man's answer wasn't an answer to my question, but it was all I got.

There wasn't anything else to do or say. I was itching to be back to my run, regretting the time I had already lost to this talk. I said to the old man that it was a terrible shame, but I knew as the words left me that I didn't mean it. I couldn't muster the sympathy I should have for the poor beast. On some level, I felt empathy, but empathy in this instance did not make me want to do anything other than run from the spot where that animal was going to die. I didn't want to witness in any shape or form such a miserable end. Not waiting for a reaction or a response, not looking again at the seal or the old man, I ran hard and fast the rest of the way back.

I came to be running on this beach because I was writing an article that would help me get tenure back at my New England school. That I could have written the article in my apartment in Brighton is true, but, fortunately for me, my writing partner lived on the other coast and my school was willing to help pay me to go there to work with her. Interestingly, the article we were writing together was about the way our own childhood reading habits inform our current teaching practices. The gist of our argument was that book clubs helped students otherwise unfamiliar with college-level reading and discussion by using the group experience, the community created through the club part of book club to gain more solid footing in the academic landscape (an example—of which there are many—of my own experiences of academic life so obviously informing the experience I try to design for my students).

I read my way out of one life and into another, and now I was writing about that very journey in order to secure that coveted measure of academic security: tenure. And I did get tenure. I am not at such a high-powered institution that getting tenure was as hard as it must be for some of my more auspiciously positioned graduate school friends. At my institution, I did my job as well as I could, and I got tenure.

I am not sure that I understood what this really meant in an academic's life until I was saddled with it myself. The traditional idea of tenure is as a means to secure academic freedom but also, for better or for worse, to secure one an academic home. What such a thing as that *is* I am still trying to answer. It is, of course, your institutional home, the letterhead you send out with possible publications or letters of recommendation. But one imagines, or, at least, I imagined, that an academic home also meant a place where I would develop meaningful personal and professional relationships, where I would develop my own circle of friends and colleagues, where I would build a full, rich *life*.

While tenure is a valuable and wonderful thing to have, there is a chance that I could be burdening this one institution with too much expectation.

Tenured faculty who are happy with their institutional home speak with great reverence for tenure, while less content colleagues tell me how long they've held tenure the way you might tell someone how long you've lived with chronic pain. I personally have thought a great deal about how my institution offered me many service and teaching opportunities that helped me to prove myself worthy of tenure *at this institution.* But my success in these areas would make it markedly harder for me to leave the college and work elsewhere. Having made this observation to a colleague in my department, she threw up her hands in agreement and yelped, "Oh yes. We're stuck."

An academic home should secure every other sort of home, both in the intellectual sense and the literal sense, but that is the thing: getting tenure at a place does not guarantee a desire to stay there. And yet, despite this, we all spend our pretenure years in a hard scramble—a kind of tap dancing not fit for any musical or any movie Parisians—to make sure we are tenurable. And, thus, I was writing in Washington state.

The place where I saw the seal and wrote the article is called Cape Disappointment. It is a quiet vacation spot on the ocean in the Pacific Northwest. I can't think of a stranger thing than such a name for such a place. It was beautiful, a beautiful place for a long run on a cool spring day. There seemed nothing to be disappointed in.

I tried, in my short stay, to locate the history of the name of the region from the few locals I ran into but could not. Left to my own devices, I decided that someone, probably from the landlocked Midwest thought, as I did, that an ocean would be a preferable place to make a home. Perhaps they arrived on a day like the one I ran on, gray and misting, and thought that the flat, gleaming rows of cornfields under cloudless skies were better in the end and went home. Perhaps they arrived on a perfectly fine day and stayed through a storm that took everything they owned out to sea. Perhaps it was nothing so dramatic: maybe this place just wasn't what they expected.

As it turns out, in 1788, a Captain John Meares looked for shelter from a rough sea at a cape located near the mouth of the Columbia River. He found no such shelter and gave the spot the local Indians called *Kah'eese* the English name of Cape Disappointment. Sixty years later, a ship bringing materials to be used in the construction of a lighthouse at the Cape ran aground before reaching land. The crew of the *Oriole* barely escaped with their lives; the cargo was lost. The wreck of the *Oriole* delayed the building of the lighthouse for another two years. When, finally, the work on the lighthouse was nearly completed, it was determined that the upper reaches of the tower were not large enough to accommodate the all-important lantern lens. The entire lighthouse had to be dismantled and the construction begun again.

I have nothing but respect for Captain Meares and all those nameless men who built and rebuilt the lighthouse at Cape Disappointment. I admire Meares—and the crew of the *Oriole*—for taking the journey in the first place, despite the obvious potential for peril. And I admire Meares even more for sizing up the situation that day and without sentiment or melancholy naming the place for what it was—not every place we land holds all the delight we hope it will. And I admire the lighthouse builders, perhaps I admire them most of all, for being brave enough to dismantle what they had made, and, realizing their error, begin again, finally finishing what it was they set out to do in the place they set out to do it in.

Bibliography

An American in Paris. Dir. Vincente Minnelli. Perf. Gene Kelly and Leslie Caron. MGM, 1951.

Gibbs, Jim. *Lighthouses of the Pacific.* Lancaster, PA: Schiffer, 1997.

Gibbs, Jim, and Bert Webber. *Oregon's Seacoast Lighthouses: An Oregon Documentary.* Central Point, OR: Webb Research, 1992.

The Philadelphia Story. Dir. George Cukor. Perf. Katharine Hepburn, James Stewart, and Cary Grant. MGM, 1940.

V
In Between

15
Going Away to Think

Scott Slovic

I find myself constantly impressed with how quickly the sensational world compresses itself into sameness and mundanity, how easily our species etches routine tedium into the structure of every day. Whatever it takes, I think to myself . . . whatever it takes to revivify experience, to bring my mind to life, may well be worth the cost.

Like many people in the world, academics and artists chief among them, I delight in the life of the mind. In my love-hate relationship with the office, I find myself often seduced by the lure of my book-filled lair, knowing deeply the spell that occurs when I enter Frandsen Humanities Room 038, hit the light switch, and then turn on the gleaming white dome of the eMac. It is quite possible to lose entire days staring into the screen of the machine, absorbed in words and ideas, translating life and life's intuitions into text. Even for a scholar fondly devoted to the world beyond the words, the temptation to perch in a semidarkened room staring for many hours at a computer is often overwhelming, seemingly unavoidable. And yet sometimes it seems not to be enough.

I write these words in March 2004, sitting on the porch of my rustic casita in La Manzanilla, Jalisco, Mexico, where I am participating in an Earthwatch program coordinated by my PhD student Jerry Keir, director of the Great Basin Institute. Half a dozen volunteers and university students and a similar number of Guadalajara-based ecologists have come together for the week to discuss "Mexican Mangroves and Wildlife" and to conduct bird and crocodile censuses and studies. I squint into the sun as I write these words, savoring the humid sea breeze. Families walk past on the beach, a hundred feet away. Dogs wrestle for control of flotsam and jetsam. I watch an elderly man bodysurf amid jellyfish and stingrays, oblivious to the painful presence of the creatures that have been washing ashore all day. The sun lowers beyond the tropical sea as afternoon passes into evening, and my squint tightens. The dazzling sun corresponds to my properly bedazzled mind. "You are not in Reno anymore," I tell myself.

In truth, even this extraordinary scene would become ordinary if I lived here all the time, as many do. Jerry Keir points out that the tropics seem to induce such torpor among residents that he anticipates difficulty in accomplishing his conservation objectives. Neither the locals nor the expatriots can be roused easily to activism on behalf of mangrove swamps, threatened crocs, or endangered sea turtles.

But torpor has not yet addled me, reduced me to a condition of unawareness. My flight touched down in Manzanillo just twenty-four hours ago, and when I arrived here at the beachside camp, it was so dark that all remained mysterious until morning. I had no inkling of the glinting Tenacatita Bay, the palm-lined beaches, or the pelicans and terns diving for fish until dawn, when I left the thatched-roof hut and trotted to the surf for my morning run. For me, as an academic, this sort of experience—arriving in a new place at dusk and waking to an astonishing world of unfamiliar beauty—is one of the ultimate pleasures. The question is how does this contribute to "thought," to work? And are these merely the self-satisfied musings of a privileged traveler?

A large, black frigate bird, with its noticeably arced wings and v-shaped tail, flies overhead. There are many of these birds here, circling high above the fracas of the pelicans and gulls. Ornithologist Al Gubanich, who has accompanied me to this week's program, tells me that the frigate birds scavenge and steal to make their living, benefiting from the industry of other birds. I sometimes wonder if academics do much the same thing, hovering over the sweep of reality, allowing others to struggle through life, and then descending to pick up the pieces and offer hazy explanations. The frigate birds of the species.

Several months ago, while speaking at a gathering of nature writers in Australia, I found myself referring to literary critics as the "third wheel" of the literary world: those who provide context and commentary for "texts," while others experience the world directly and render that experience in rich and riveting words. I believe the contextualizing perspective of the scholar is important, and yet, to me, it doesn't quite seem enough. I love the telescoping process of engagement and retreat, conscious living and detached contemplation. The attractions of this rhythm—coming close, going away—may be what induce me to do both personal essays and formal, analytical "scholarly writing," sometimes combining the two in so-called narrative scholarship. Perhaps this rhythm parallels the process of "going away to think" and then coming home to see the familiar anew.

My reflexive comparison of academics and frigate birds is only half sincere. I do think some kinds of academic work are exploitative and self-serving. But I also recognize the idealism and selflessness—the taste for beauty, elegance, and justice—that can drive intellectual work. I take to heart the title of historian Richard White's well-known essay, "'Are You an Environmentalist or Do You Work for a Living?'" Sometimes I rephrase it in my mind: "Are You a Literary Critic or Do You Work for a Living, Do You Contribute Meaningfully to Society?" I do actually believe environmentalists—and literary critics—"work for a living." I suspect Richard White—despite his forceful complaint against self-righteousness, privilege, and arrogance—would agree. And yet I appreciate the warning not to become complacent and self-satisfied, oblivious to the toil and suffering of others, to different ways of knowing and expressing. When I see the elegant frigate birds floating free of the mob below, I find myself wondering how the flock of literary critics serves the rest of its species and, indeed, serves the planet. Travel can shake us free from accepted routine and enable us to use metaphor as a tool of self-examination and critique.

Name one activity your mother would have forbidden you to do. Had it occurred to her, it probably would have been the following. Walk down a dusty, lightless road in rural Mexico next to a mangrove swamp filled with crocodiles. Hop aboard a small metal boat with a local biologist and three friends. And then launch out into the steamy darkness, headlamps on, searching for red beads in the blackness—the signs of floating dinosaurs.

Last night my colleague, Al Gubanich, and I joined Paulino Campos of the conservation group Bosque Tropical on a nighttime crocodile survey in the white mangrove swamp of La Manzanilla.

We clambered over a small wire fence to reach the skiff, shoved off from the fecal-smelling bank into the brackish water, and paddled our way into the middle of the first lagoon. Here and there we saw red dots, like cigarette ends. At about eight-thirty on a cool, March evening, this was not an ideal night for crocodile viewing—but even to be out on a dark body of water in pitch-black night with a single animal of this kind would defy the fiercest warning of one's mother.

We maintained a calm chatter as we drifted further into the swamp, staying in the center of the water to achieve the best possible viewing of each bank. Eventually, Paulino, who'd begun the trip in the rear with an oar in hand, traded places with Rudolfo and used a headlamp to spot "crocs" hiding in the shoreline mangroves. Again and again, he exclaimed, "There's a croc! I see another"—his practiced eyes noticing life where the rest of us observed only empty space. We marveled at the discernment of his experienced eyes in contrast to our novitiate blindness.

Eventually, near the site where local people are contemplating the development of a crocodile farm, Paulino caught sight of a small croc near the bank, leaned forward from the front of the boat, and grabbed the eight-month-old animal in his bare hands as easily as I might have snagged a water lily. We spent twenty minutes measuring and examining the hapless animal. I was struck by the softness of the saurian skin—the twenty-inch juvenile looked as if it was wearing a suit of armor and yet it felt like soft leather. It became motionless, passive, under our attention. Paulino handed the small croc to each of the passengers in turn and snapped digital pictures of us posing with croc and pretending to release it into the saline soup of the lagoon. He said this is what he does even when he captures large crocs on the shore—animals reaching up to two and a half meters in length. He invites local people and tourists to come and touch the animals and pose for pictures with them. This helps them to understand the crocs and to value them rather than think of them as hostile, mysterious monsters lurking in the hidden depths of the mangroves. It's clear that, in his own way, as a conservation biologist, Paulino has thought carefully about the rhetoric of environmental education.

We spent two hours in the boat, pushing ever further into the tightening vice of the mangroves, fighting our way through the jigsaw puzzle of branches. Sometimes the glint our headlights caught was only the reflection of a spider dangling in its web. I wondered what other living creatures were awake and moving in the darkness—snakes, insects, wildcats, birds. Occasionally, the clanking of our oars on the metal boat startled roosting herons, who squawked and flapped loudly aloft, unhappy to be rousted from their night's rest.

We made our way back to the beach where we had begun our evening journey, pleased to have held a small croc and come slightly closer to appreciating its intimidating otherness. Al and I clambered out of the boat while our Mexican companions stayed aboard to return it to its hiding place. We walked back to the camp with our headlamps off, a little less afraid of the dark.

There's something about the process of coming face to face with the exotic, the scary, or the bewildering—of "normalizing the new," so to speak—that emboldens me to breathe in experience more deeply. Floating among the mangrove crocs at night has helped me to open my mind and senses more widely to the experience of La Manzanilla. I suppose my goal is to carry home some of this renewed openness at the end of the week, a state of mind I can direct toward my everyday work and surroundings.

This morning I took a brief walk along the beach before breakfast. A hundred yards from camp, I found a plump red fish lying on the sand. Three days ago, I suspect I would have gingerly kicked it with my sandal, reluctant to infect myself with whatever disease resulted in its beaching. Today I pick it up and marvel at its red skin and its redder-than-red eye. It is a jewel of life, present on the beach as if by magic. Soon it will feed the ever-hungry shorebirds—willets, night herons, turkey vultures. Sometimes it takes an encounter with living jewels on faraway beaches to respark our inquisitiveness about gems and germs of meaning in our ordinary neighborhoods. This reawakening to the daily meanings of our lives, hidden in texts and present in the physical world, is a big part of why I travel. Through my life as a writer and teacher, I wish to pick up and examine the brilliant red fish of reality.

"You stay home," admonishes poet Wendell Berry. "I am at home. Don't come with me" (199). This, of course, is the quandary, the anxiety, of the place-conscious scholar. Should we wish to sustain our species on this planet, we must learn to live more lightly—to use fewer resources and trample less aggressively on this surprisingly delicate globe. Chances are this will be a very difficult lesson for us. We seem programmed to accomplish whatever is in our power, and we have a devil-may-care attitude about the consequences. If we can do something today, we'll do it—tomorrow will take care of itself. Or so we seem to think. This mañana attitude is not limited to any particular culture; it's certainly as true of the mainstream view of conservation in the United States as it is anywhere else.

In his brief poem "Stay Home," Berry pricks my conscience and leads me to consider the virtues of my traveling life and the possible virtues of a more sedentary, home-rooted life. I choose to take the poem as a prompt and point of departure for such meditations, not as an absolute statement of prohibition—a literal condemnation of movement and exploration. I suspect the work was written precisely with people like me in mind—and with *himself* in mind, for Berry, too, is a traveling writer and public speaker. The point is not to push everyone into sudden immobility but to nudge those of us who travel frequently to do so more mindfully, with more awareness of the costs of such a life to ourselves and to the planet.

Environmental activists and scholars sometimes joke that a "bioregionalist" is someone who travels around the country urging other people to stay home. This may not be far from the truth. But most bioregionalists understand that we can all benefit from more engagement and attentiveness to our home places and from the revivifying experience of movement across the earth.

The bathroom in my beachside casita is walled from the sleeping area by vertical rows of slender bamboo poles nailed side by side. There is plenty of room between each pole to peer through the wall into the bedroom and through the front door beyond that, out to the beach and the ever-pounding surf. Standing in the bathroom a few minutes ago, I found myself looking past the upright screen of my laptop to the rows of waves beyond, new waves pouring themselves onto the beach every six or seven seconds, on and on and on. The process is so routine and yet so variable. No two waves are quite alike, and yet the process has occurred uncountable times. Perhaps there is nothing more beautiful in all the world than the simple act of waves falling upon sandy beaches. Perhaps, as well, there is nothing more routine.

I think to myself that the ultimate lesson of this particular journey to tropical Mexico may not be how to savor the exotic. That is a lesson that needs no teaching—a lesson as automatic as breathing. No—the lesson here was present in the waves I heard breaking immediately upon arrival at this dark beachside camp and has been witnessed each day when I awaken to run along the surf and dodge jellyfish and spiny puffers. The lesson of the routinely pounding surf—the utter everydayness of the motion. Water and sand doing what they must do in relation to gravity, wind, and rock. Is this not what we, too, ultimately seek? To know what we must do and then to do it?

Let me see if I can recall my travels of the past year—Spring Break at Zion National Park in southern Utah, a late-March trip to speak at an international symposium on environmental literature in Okinawa, a talk to the senior class of St. Bonaventure University in upstate New York in April, ten days in New England in early June to participate in the biennial meeting of the Association for the Study of Literature and Environment, a week in Mississippi in July for the thirtieth annual Faulkner and Yoknapatawpha Conference, and ten days on Australia's eastern coast in October for the Watermark Nature Writers' Muster, followed immediately by two days at Iowa State University, plus various family trips to Seattle and Washington, D.C., mixed in with the work-related wanderings. Each of these journeys has been delightful and inspiring in different ways. The drain of falling behind with my teaching, writing, and editing responsibilities at home is outweighed by the pleasures of interacting with new and old friends and absorbing various landscapes.

I draw my title for this cluster of informal meditations from Gary Paul Nabhan's 2002 book, *Coming Home to Eat: The Pleasures and Politics of Local Foods*. Although the bulk of his book focuses on the experiment in local eating that he conducted in Tucson, Arizona, in the late 1990s, he actually begins his discussion by telling the story of his trip to see family members in Lebanon and the experience of eating local delicacies with distant relatives in the Bekaa Valley. Traveling to experience other people's local places and cultures and ideas triggered Nabhan's own experiment in local living.

Much the same thing tends to occur as I respond to each of my own journeys. Place is a central component in my academic life, and place, for me, is built from the tension between going away and coming home. I've found that my own working life is fundamentally shaped by my habit of traveling to visit new landscapes and talk with literary and scientific colleagues in order to gain perspective on the meaning of my life at home. My teaching and writing at home are rooted in the specific physical environments of office, house, and nearby mountain trails, and the experience of these places provides a kind of ballast or core of meaning that helps me to appreciate and understand the implications of my travels.

When I travel, I try to wake up each morning and go running. This week, Earthwatch participant Bob Lewis, a semiretired dentist from Seattle, said, "You can take the boy out of Oregon, but you can't take Oregon out of the boy" when he saw me return from an early morning run. These runs are one of the key features of my traveling regimen. I ran competitively for many years in junior high, high school, and for part of college, but now I run simply for fitness and for geography. I experience places most vividly while oxygen deprived, moving steadily through neighborhoods and along trails and beaches. One of the frustrating aspects of being at home is the tendency to become so compulsive about rushing to the office each morning and staying late "to get things done" that meaningful exercise drops by the wayside. And yet using my body helps me to be at home in this body—and being at home in my body enables me to exist more fully in place and to think about the implications of placedness in literature.

 I wake up each morning while traveling and explore the neighborhood, ranging from Naha's winding alleyways in Okinawa to the cornfields skirting Ames, Iowa, to the man-made and natural debris washed up on La Manzanilla's three-mile beach. Not only does this running help to sharpen my attention for the rest of the day, but it gives me a view of the layout of the place—a view unavailable from most meeting rooms. I pay close attention to the shape of the land, the direction of the wind, the feel of the air, the types of trees and birds I see and hear. I feel as if I begin to belong to each place as I pass through it, breathing steadily and knowing it with the strain of my leg muscles.

 I once told an interviewer that many of the ecocritics I know are "muscular scholars," people who enjoy using their bodies on mountains and hiking trails as well as their minds in offices and classrooms. I realize that academics in general are often quite interested in physical fitness, understanding that their mental abilities are linked to the health of their bodies. Growing up, I spent quite a bit of time in the summer running with my father and his colleagues at the University of Oregon, and I have clear memories of the psychologists and biologists and literary scholars gathering in the locker room before noontime runs. But it seems to me that ecocritics are particularly given to this sort of activity and that our actual work is enhanced and deepened by getting outside and testing our strength and frailty against the physical features of the landscape. From early on, as the community of ecocritics began to gather under the auspices of the Association for the Study of Literature and Environment and similar organizations, there has been a tendency to make field trips—and often significant hikes and climbs and river trips—an integral part of our academic culture. I recall, for instance, several days of hectic meetings at Boston University last summer during ASLE's fifth biennial conference, followed by a climb of Mt. Monadnock in New Hampshire with more than a dozen colleagues on the last day of the academic meeting, intellectuals continuing their conversations while huffing up the trail in a chilly June rain.

I lay awake most of last night listening to the explosive smack of waves on the nearby beach, frustrated by the disruption of my rest. At home the sounds of night are almost indiscernible, even when the windows are open during the warmer months. Sometimes we hear doves cooing outside the bedroom window. Here on the beach at La Manzanilla, there is a steady rhythm of shushing water withdrawing into the sea followed by the thwack of a new wave, shush then thwack, shush then thwack. Paulino Campos tells me he loves the sound of the crashing waves here, but to me they are a disruption, even sometimes an annoyance. This is in so many ways a beautiful place—a good place to rest and put my life and work into broader perspective. And yet at the same time there are inconveniences and annoyances—the sleepless nights caused by the thunderous waves outside the casita, the mosquito and sand flea bites, the inability to control my own diet as at home. Travel has its benefits and its banes—not to mention this would be to distort the truth. But even the frustrations can, and perhaps *should*, be savored—even pain, fatigue, and aggravation are interesting dimensions of life.

"*La vida tiene sabor*," says the Coca-Cola billboard we passed en route to Barra de Navidad yesterday afternoon for a few hours of shopping and lounging in the jellyfish-free surf. I savored those words as we drove, quickly forgetting that they come from a corporate advertising campaign. Life has flavor, life has flavor. The words lose their consumer context, and it occurs to me that this is absolutely true—life has, indeed, many flavors. And this is what I try to remember in everything I do, even during the sometimes numbing process of reading freshman papers and discussing familiar pieces of writing with jaded students. Life has flavor, I suggest to my students. Life has flavor, I remind myself.

In the process of traveling to distant beaches to lie awake to the whip-crack of dropping waves and the nasal hum of mosquitoes, I am saying to myself, "*La vida tiene sabor.*"

Life has flavor, and life has risk. One of the risks is complacency and tedium. As I meditate on the sound of the waves, I remember the sea life I find washed ashore each morning, particularly the striking spiny puffer fish, so different from the shells on the Oregon beaches and the stinking alewives on Lake Michigan's shores I've known since childhood. Each morning while running here in La Manzanilla, I've wrenched my back by dodging tattered fish carcasses and still-breathing puffers. Multicolored, covered in inch-long white spines, with striking white bony beaks, these fish of tropical reefs are clearly out of their element lying on the beach. Soon they will be food for insects and birds. After five days of observing them, I take a moment to look them up in a field guide to "reef life" and learn that they are "black-blotched porcupine fish" (*Diodon liturosus*). They are meant to inhabit coastal reefs in the tropical Indo-Pacific. To be honest, I do not know why they've ended their lives on the beach at La Manzanilla. But it occurs to me that they've somehow allowed themselves to drift free from the reefs of home and become complacent in the relatively calm waters of Tenacatita Bay—and then suddenly their benign environment thrashes them violently onto the sandy beach, where they wash, stunned, to their sunny doom.

Our species, too, is prone to complacency, perhaps even more so than most other organisms. We insulate ourselves from risk—Americans are particularly eager to achieve security, to have insurance protecting us from loss of property, loss of health, loss of life. Here in Mexico, the unavailability of true security is all too plain. Floating through the crocodile estuary, I watch schools of tiny fish leap momentarily ahead of the boat, knowing that they will soon feed baby crocs and multitudes of long-beaked fishing birds—herons, egrets, kingfishers, stilts—perched in the nearby trees. Sitting yesterday beneath the cloth umbrella at Barra de Navidad, I reflected upon the many hawkers wandering from one cluster of tourists to the next, selling trinkets, multicolored baskets, and even donuts and cakes. We marveled at the man with the broad basket of chocolate-covered donuts, eager to unload calories to bikini-clad vacationers. A weathered, dark-skinned woman, seemingly beyond her sixties, lugged heavy buckets of arroz con leche and ceviche to prospective customers—no one was buying. "That's a hard way to make a living," someone from our group muttered. "Imagine feeding your family like that," said another. On a day with no sales, one would have no income. There is no security.

But back to the example of the porcupine fish: imagine the significance of a benign environment suddenly turned lethal. This is, perhaps, the core message of environmental literature, science, education, and activism. Many people today can see the future coming. They know what's happening to the planet and to specific, local places. And they wish to get the word out. Sometimes these writers and educators sound like Jeremiah, seeming to issue exaggerated warnings of unrealized catastrophes. More often, their fate is that of Cassandra—a classical story I learned from Alan AtKisson's recent book, *Believing Cassandra*: they can see the future, but they are fated not to be heard, to be believed.

The evening before leaving on this trip to Costa Alegre, Mexico's "Happy Coast," I was hosting visiting author Bill McKibben in Reno. His talk was titled "Global Warming, Genetic Engineering, and Other Questions of Human Scale." He began his lecture with a brief bible lesson, summarizing the book of Job, in which God admonishes Job to remember his small place in the scheme of the universe, for after all only God can determine the tides of the sea and other elemental natural processes. Bill then rehearsed, as he's done hundreds of times in the past decade, the facts and figures of global climate change, convincingly demonstrating the fundamental changes occurring in our planet's atmosphere and down on earth as well, chiefly the result of our releasing so much carbon into the air through the use of fossil fuels. Next, Bill explained the field of "germ-line" genetic engineering, a process by which contemporary scientists have been able to mold (without a great deal of control) the minute genetic codes of life. Bill concluded his lecture by suggesting that, unlike Job, we can now reply to God that we, too, are able to affect the large and small dimensions of nature. We have that power. And yet the consequences of wielding this power may well be to create a planetary environment deeply inhospitable to our own continued existence. It seems, for instance, entirely likely that in the coming decades, there will be a profound shortage of water for drinking and agriculture, and desalination of sea water will not be able to compensate for this shortage. As Bill stated the other evening, these ideas make him sad and worried, and he travels to give lectures in order to make his listeners "sad," too. This elicited a nervous laugh from the full auditorium at the Nevada Museum of Art. Why would a speaker wish to make his audience sad? Could this really be so?

After other questioners were unable to summon an explicit prognostication about the future of life on earth from the speaker, a final questioner struck home by reminding McKibben of his ten-year-old daughter. "What sort of life do you expect for her?" the man asked from the audience. "I'm afraid her life will be very difficult," was the answer. "We are approaching an ecological bottleneck, and it's unclear who will make it through—which species will make it through."

A boy wades into the surf before me, shirtless and in gray shorts, carrying over his left forearm a circular net that he casts into the sea with a quick motion of his right hand. He can see glints of silver in the water that indicate a school of fish. He casts his net, crouches to help it sink into the water just beyond the surf, and waits for the fish to become entangled. Then he gathers a dozen wriggling fish into the folds of the net and wades ashore to his waiting friend, who carries a red plastic grocery bag, laden with their catch. This, too, is a ready metaphor, a literal casting of one's net into the sea of reality, hoping for a worthwhile take. I continue to watch as the young fisherman scans the surface of the bay in search of more fish, much as the flock of pelicans circles down the coast, also seeking nourishment. And here I sit, perched at my yellow wooden table on the porch of a simple casita, shielded from the rising sun by the thatched roof of palm fronds. I scan the view, I watch the neighboring encampment to the left, and I listen to my friends and Earthwatch colleagues under the palapa to my right. I am reminded of my constant daily search for ideas and words, the substance of my own life.

Before me, the sea is placid here on the Happy Coast. The fishing boy has moved on in search of richer waters. There are no tourists. The water has become glassy and reflects the sky's wispy clouds. And then suddenly the next wave crashes ashore, and somewhere along the curves of Tenacatita Bay, porcupine fish and jellies are cast from the benign environment of the bay onto the hostile sand.

I come to this place for a change of scenery, yes, and also for an enlivened perspective on the familiar scenery of home. No matter where I travel on this planet, I can never forget where I normally dwell, the other places I visit, and the fact that the place I inhabit at any given moment is connected fundamentally to the places I've passed through before. My senses are sharpened, my view broadened, my consciousness deepened.

I have gone away from home to think, and now I am ready to return home, still thinking. There will be no crashing waves, no gasping porcupine fish, as I gaze from the windows of home at the snowy foothills of the Sierra. But the waves will pound ashore in my memory, motivating my continued efforts as teacher and writer, until my next journey.

Always the push and pull of home and away—I reflect on the pull of home as I fly back from Manzanillo to Los Angeles and then to Reno. The last few days of this Earthwatch trip have been filled with learning and adventure, and now it's time to return to the eastern slopes of the Sierra, to the quiet mountain nights with no surf pounding nearby, to the dining room table where I work at home (tomorrow will be a day of grading student papers), and to the office lined with thousands of books and networked via phone, fax, and e-mail to the rest of the world. Despite the fact that I have been almost wholly "off-line" during this week on Costa Alegre (apart from one call home to let Susie know all was going well), I have felt in many ways more deeply engaged with the specific concrete details of place than I do in my hurried, abstract life of the mind at home. Yesterday's itinerary began with a six-kilometer kayaking trip on the Rio Cuixmala, including a pineapple and trail mix snack enjoyed on a pristine Pacific beach near the Cuixmala Biosphere Reserve. After loading the eight kayaks back on his trailer, Dave Collins from Immersion Adventures drove a bumpy, dusty back road to the village of Tanacatita, where our bunch of students, professors, trail crew leaders, and retiree volunteers donned fins, masks, and snorkels and spent an hour bobbing in the sea, observing fluorescent tropical fish near the fringing coral reef. While birding from the kayaks, walking along the beach at the mouth of Rio Cuixmala, and gazing downward at the reef life, our only task—my only task—was to be as fully present in these places as possible. To pay attention. To practice the mindful condition I so often speak and write about in my classrooms and my office.

Without such an opportunity to *live* the mental processes I think about abstractly, these processes would eventually cease to happen—and I would cease to believe in them. I fear my work itself would grind to a frustrated halt.

Indeed, following yesterday's trip to Cuixmala and Tanacatita, it was finally my turn to offer a formal presentation to the Earthwatch group. At 4:00, tanned and sweaty after the day's activity, full from the beachside Mexican seafood I'd eaten at our late lunch, I lectured on "Art and Activism: Literature and Environmentalism in the United States and Mexico." I expected the group to fall asleep and feared that my own voice would be drowned out by the pounding surf near the wall-less, thatch-roofed palapa at our La Manzanilla camp. But just the opposite occurred. I introduced my three premises—that words are powerful, that there is a physical world surrounding us of ultimate importance and meaning, and that words are not merely mental toys but also tools of activism. I read and commented on Ofelia Zepeda's "It Is Going to Rain" (emphasizing the idea that poetry emerges from ordinary experience and values attentiveness) and John Daniel's "Ourselves" (showing how careful, intensified use of language elevates the ordinary into the magical, deepening our appreciation, combating complacency). Then I asked crocodile biologist Paulino Campos to read Octavio Paz's "*Viento, Agua, Piedra*" ("Wind, Water, Stone"), University of Guadalajara undergraduate Diana to read Homero Aridjis's "*Ballena Gris*" ("Grey Whale"), and ornothologist Sara Huerta to read Aridjis's "*Poema de Amor en la Cuidad de Mexico*" ("Love Poem in Mexico City"). We talked about Paz's use of poetry as a medium for contemplating profound, timeless concepts of nature's interconnectedness and Aridjis's activist use of poetry to combat air pollution in Mexico City, destruction of gray whale calving waters in the Vizcaino Biosphere Reserve near Baja California, and the logging in Michoacán that threatens Monarch butterfly wintering areas. Despite a day of physical exertion and parching sun, the group was alert and lively. Seventy-seven-year-old Oyvind Frock, one of the Earthwatch volunteers, raised his hand at the end of the session and read a poem he had written during the lecture about the week's experiences in La Manzanilla. The discussion of nature and language and science and Mexico's future was energetic and emotional over dinner.

As my friends made their way one by one to their tents and I prepared to return to the casita and climb under the mosquito netting,

I felt the push and pull of travel and home with new intensity. I regretted the fact that I would be leaving the group the following day to return to my office and classroom, following a morning of birding in Barranca del Choncho, an afternoon adventure capturing and measuring crocodiles, and a sweaty dash to the Manzanillo airport. And yet I realized, too, that I can—that I must—take away from La Manzanilla a commitment to reengage myself with the specificities of Reno. Naturalist Ann Zwinger once wrote that traveling by plane offers her a splendid sense of isolation for writing, and especially *editing*, a sense of being enclosed in a "blessedly impersonal aluminum tube" hurtling through space, undistracted by the daily realities of home (288). I know what Ann means and share this feeling of momentary freedom. And yet as I glance away from my laptop to appreciate the meta-bird's-eye view of the Sea of Cortés en route to Los Angeles, I understand that this freedom is an illusion. The opportunity to "go away to think" is an extraordinary privilege. It is a gift, and with this gift come inevitable responsibilities.

This sense of my work as something more than a way to "pay the bills"—as a way of contributing positively to society and to the planet—preoccupies me every day. Life and work, self-interest and altruism—I have trouble recognizing any distinctions among these processes and attitudes. When I go away to think, I do so with an appetite for joy and an earnest hope to do work that others may find helpful.

Sunday morning, back home in Reno, Nevada. After a run through the neighborhood hills, I pour a cup of coffee and walk down to our rustic backyard with the dogs. A week ago, I would have restlessly toured the yard, looking for projects to do. Today, I look for a plastic chair and find one resembling the shape of those at the La Manzanilla beach camp. I then find a spot in the sun and take a seat for ten minutes, gazing at the mountains, listening intently to bird song. I recognize the coo of the mourning doves, the bubbly cackle of the California quail. I hear chatter from many small birds and feel an urge to grab my field guides from the house and identify birds I've always been content to categorize lazily as what birders call "LBJs" (little brown jobbies).

With my "habit of attention," as Thoreau put it in his journal (351), sharpened at the beaches, mangrove estuaries, and arid hillsides of Jalisco, I settle back into home. And then I come back inside, boot up the computer, and return to work.

Bibliography

Aridjis, Homero. "Grey Whale" and "Love Poem in Mexico City." *Eyes to See Otherwise/Ojos, de otro mirar: Selected Poems*. Trans. and ed. Betty Ferber and George McWhirter. New York: New Directions, 2001. 207, 201.

AtKisson, Alan. *Believing Cassandra: An Optimist Looks at a Pessimist's World*. White River Junction, VT: Chelsea Green, 1999.

Berry, Wendell. "Stay Home." *Collected Poems, 1957–1982*. San Francisco: North Point, 1985. 199.

Daniel, John. "Ourselves." *Common Ground*. Lewiston, ID: Confluence, 1988. 62.

McKibben, Bill. "Global Warming, Genetic Engineering, and Other Questions of Human Scale." Lecture. Nevada Museum of Art, Reno. 12 March 2004.

Nabhan, Gary Paul. *Coming Home to Eat: The Pleasures and Politics of Local Foods*. New York: Norton, 2002.

Paz, Octavio. "Wind, Water, Stone." *A Tree Within*. Trans. Eliot Weinberger. New York: New Directions, 1988. 25.

Thoreau, Henry David. *The Journal of Henry D. Thoreau*. Ed. Bradford Torrey and Francis H. Allen. Vol. 4. Boston: Houghton, 1906.

White, Richard. "'Are You an Environmentalist or Do You Work for a Living?': Work and Nature." *Uncommon Ground: Toward Reinventing Nature*. Ed. William Cronon. New York: Norton, 1995. 171–85.

Zepeda, Ofelia. "It Is Going to Rain." *Jewed 'I-Hoi/Earth Movements*. Tucson: Kore, 1997. 19.

Zwinger, Ann. "What's a Nice Girl like Me Doing in a Place like This?'" *The Nearsighted Naturalist*. Tucson: U of Arizona P, 1998. 281–92.

16

Fronteriza Consciousness
The Site and Language of the Academy and of Life

Norma Elia Cantú

In the Borderlands you are the battleground where enemies are kin to each other.

                                        Gloria Anzaldúa

Geography is destiny. And my destiny has been the geography of the U.S./Mexico borderlands where I was born and raised, where I continue to live. In 1980, I returned to the border to teach at a small public university in Laredo, Texas; in 2000, I moved 150 miles north to San Antonio to teach at a much larger institution where I could work in the budding and innovative doctoral degree in English with a focus on U.S. Latino/a literature. The lessons of life on the border have served me well in the "geography" of academia, for I have always been an outsider and yet I have managed to integrate my academic and social activist roles while also writing scholarly and creative works. As Gloria Anzaldúa with her articulation of the *mestiza* consciousness philosophy and Emma Pérez with her ideas of *sitio y lengua* have taught us, the border is the place where one lives a life in *nepantla,* in the in-between, but also a place where one lives a life of power and of strength, if one survives at all, that is. It is a hard place, a place as hard as the dry *caliche* of the *monte* and as rough as the prickly thorny bushes and plants, from the mesquite to the *huisache* and the cacti, whose colorful blossoms belie the hardy survival capacity of the succulents. To survive life in this terrain, one must develop a *concha*, a thick shell. Driving in the back roads and even on the interstate in South Texas, one often encounters dark brown turtles crossing the road. I sometimes feel that I, too, have to wear a shell like these creatures to survive in the academy, for it is a place that demands that a woman of color live in two worlds, both of which can be as hard as the asphalt of the parking lots and as *aspero* (rough) and hostile as the *monte*—a place that demands that one become as hard and as resilient as the hardy flora and fauna of the region. But the toughness and survival of the turtle must be tempered with the soft underbelly that provides balance. The myriad roles that I must play as a professor, a community activist, a writer and public intellectual all have one common foundation: I am a Chicana from the border. That is what informs my being.

I was born and lived the first twenty-six years of my life on the U.S./Mexico border. After a hiatus of seven years, while I was away in graduate school, I returned, leaving and returning for short stints over the next thirty years. But that formative time, those first twenty-six years, shaped who I am and informs my academic work as well as my writing and indeed all my work as a human being on earth. *Este pedacito de tiempo y este pedacito de tierra*, this small piece of time and small piece of land, where I am destined to live. My mother, a *tejana*, and my dad, a *mejicano*, shared allegiances to the land, the land that the journalist Barbara Renaud González once told me is our last and our first inheritance—who we are. Just as that old platitude goes, it doesn't matter how old you are but how you are old, I think it doesn't matter where you are but how you are where you are. And I have been a *tejana* while in Europe, Madrid, Vietnam, Nebraska, and California. *No importa*, it doesn't really matter, the border is with me; my *tejana*-ness is who I am. That semitropical land of south Texas shaped me as much as the DNA I inherited from my parents, their parents, and the many generations back, *mis antepasados*.

But the cultural education I gained didn't include certain skills and knowledge that the academic world valued and expected. As I navigated the academic waters, first as a student and then as a professor, I found that my borderlands skills and knowledge—the epistemological formation that made my brain think a certain way, made my body react a certain way—often conflicted with what the academic world expected. I understood that to survive I had to confront this conflict; I had to *superarlo,* to overcome it. Anzaldúa's *mestiza* consciousness answers my doubts as to how it is that we trust who we are and how we behave in the world. It is this multifaceted and all-encompassing view of the world that allows the conflicts between the academic world's culture and my own to be resolved. What are some of these conflicts? Most are not apparent and surface in unexpected ways, creating dissonance. The manifestations of this dissonance are also many. The way I am always cold in air-conditioned buildings or anywhere where the weather is colder than sixty degrees. The way I feel the ocean is on the wrong side in California. The way my body relishes warmth and I feel that all is right with the world when I see the Gulf of Mexico to the East or hear the *urracas,* those ever-present black grackles, cawing at dusk. All this is shaped by where I first learned to be in the world, on the border. The wide open flatlands between Laredo and east to Corpus Christi and the Gulf Coast; north to San Antonio and the hill country; and south to Monterrey and the *cerros del Mamulique.* That is home. The geography that shaped me is also what sustains me, what offers me a sense of belonging.

My work. My creative work feels most at home in this terrain where the world conforms to my expectations. It is where my social self is at home, too. My parents taught me to be "*bien educada,*" polite, and to greet everyone. So, I say good morning or good evening to the cleaning staff as well as to the administrators, for not to *saludar,* greet, even strangers, is rude and a sign of disrespect. One is expected to at least smile and nod; the lesson sticks, we must never be so into ourselves as to erase the others around us. So even when I am in large urban cities where passersby walk without even seeing those they bump into, I say excuse me and smile a good morning. Civility begins with something as simple as a greeting. When I lived in Washington, D.C., I worked in a government office that had precious few Latinos, and I recall how comforting it was to have a Puerto Rican coworker notice that I was wearing black and ask if someone had died. Indeed an uncle had died, and I was keeping "*luto,*" although not rigorously, by wearing mostly black for a couple of weeks. No one else noticed or commented on it. My cultural mourning practices were not evident to those who didn't understand the "code," but a Latino who knew it recognized it immediately.

Navigating different sociogeographical terrain is as challenging as survival is for those who dare venture into the physical geography of the borderland. The seasons are different, too, in my land of little rain, a land with few trees in the landscape, yet private gardens resplendent with color—the mimosa, the red hardy hibiscus—gardens exuding aromatic scents of mint, rosemary, and rue, my favorite herbs. But the few trees, *mesquite, huisache, retama,* and, of course, in certain areas the *nogal,* the pecan tree, also mark the land where I was born and where I grew up. The animals that roamed wild have all but disappeared, as Arturo Longoria notes in his aptly titled, *Adios to the Brushland.*

My academic work by luck and by choice has been in this land. Teaching in Laredo from 1980 until 2000 and since then in San Antonio has been an extraordinary gift that life has given me. I am lucky to live and work in the place where I feel at home, where people speak my Spanglish and the smells of *carne asada* cooking in backyards—even in winter—permeates Saturday and Sunday afternoons. I see the bright orange-violet-hued sunsets in Port Aransas or in Laredo or in San Antonio and then scan the night sky for the dippers and Orion and the Pleiades, and I know the sky. I am centered. It is the same sky I have seen for over fifty years. I recognize it. Know it. Own it. It is the same sky my ancestors looked to for guidance, for direction. When my father would intone a prayer to the sliver of a new moon in the dimming light of dusk, I knew it in my heart.

The land has taught me to be aware and to be careful: rattlesnakes, fierce ants, and tarantulas among other creatures, the pests that have taught me caution and patience and to be fearless. Additionally, I rejoice in the sounds of the land: the songs of the *cenzontle* almost year round and on rainy nights in September the croaking frogs, the *canta ranas* that gave our barrio its name. As a child I reveled in the sounds of the wind caressing the *cubreviento* trees in our backyard and the palm trees, the fronds swaying in the wind making a sound unlike any other. The gifts of this fertile land—*nopales, mequite, quelite* that fed the indigenous, the melons and the lush citrus fruit trees (grapefruit, orange, lime, and lemon trees) that sustain the Valley—nurture our economy, even as those who labor in the hot south Texas sun to harvest such fruits become one with the land. My father kept a home garden, a hankering to his own childhood no doubt, when *Mamagrande,* his mother, my grandmother, grew corn, squash, tomatoes, a variety of chiles, and many other foodstuffs that she would then make into meals for her large family, including delicious *dulces de calabaza,* the sugared pumpkin delicacy of late summer and early fall. That garden needed tending and along with the fruit trees—the grapefruit, orange, lemon, and peach trees in our yard—supplied us with fresh and nutritious meals. Even the *nopales*—the prickly pear with its difficult-to-harvest fruit, the *tunas*—and the *pencas* and *tiernitas*, tender and the color of the inside of the kiwi, once "cleaned" of all thorns, provided delicious food.

When I go home to Laredo, I am transported back to those summers of my childhood when we ran around barefoot in the hot sun chasing *lagartijos y camaleones*, whose color would turn from a gray-ecru to a deep green according to where they were, and the fiery red *santa closes*, the "*toritos*" or sand lions that burrowed into the sandy arid dirt under our house. How we loved to play under the frame house, in the cool shade protected from the hot August sun. I must have been about ten when I realized that I could no longer sit comfortably under the house that was built two feet off the ground and that grew as the family grew and my father added first an indoor bathroom, later a kitchen large enough for all of us to sit at a table, and much later two more bedrooms and a "*cuartito de atrás,*" a back room where we stashed stuff—his carpentry materials, Mom's sewing machine—a sort of den and garage all in one. Later it became my youngest brother's room, but we still call it "*el cuarto de atrás.*"

When I am in that childhood home, I hear the church bell ring every morning and evening calling people to mass, an ancient call to prayer, to awareness of being on earth, so far from the school bell or buzzer signaling the end of class. At least that practice has disappeared and classes begin and end without bells or buzzers. And yet, the academy can be a daunting and fearful place. A place of trauma and dissent. I recall my first forays into the business of presenting papers at conferences and feeling out of place as it appeared everyone knew everyone else and "belonged." One particular experience taught me that unlike what I had been taught in education classes, one didn't "present" a paper; one was expected to literally "read" a paper. I had been trained in education to use talking points and to adhere to a more conversational tone. But my academic field of English required reading from a prepared text. It began my lifelong apprehension of presenting at conferences. The traumatic experience of many young scholars as they prepare tenure files is another occasion for stress and trauma. The demands of academic work can be daunting. Aside from teaching and all its multiple demands and aside from presenting and publishing one's research, one is expected to participate actively in university governance and be involved in numerous committees at all levels—department, college, and university—in addition to participating in extracurricular service activities.

But even as the academy can be a fearful and daunting place, it can also be a place of refuge and of sustenance. I choose to make it the latter even when there are circumstances that make it the former. I will not allow a disgruntled student who is perhaps too lazy to do the work for a course to spoil the memory of hundreds of other students who are happy and glad to be in my classes, who can say at the end of the semester, it was tough, but I am glad I did it. I will not allow a capricious colleague who disagrees with me to ruin my trust and good faith in my fellow human beings who work alongside of me and who are doing their best and are products of their own environments. Some of them need to learn from me about fairness, about justice, about civility. What will I gain if I alienate and fight them and establish an adversarial relationship with them? What will my students gain? Of course, this does not mean that I will deny to myself or to others that there are injustices and that there are wrong policies, that there is racism and raging backlash against my feminist positions. No, it means that I will continue to struggle with passion and with whatever means are at my disposal. The locations within the academy are hierarchical and work in such a way as to deflate any positive action. But I will continue to struggle. I work from within. Carrying on the guerrilla work in the academy often means that others think you are a sellout: after all, you are teaching in the very institution that perpetuates the system. But there are ways of changing the system with the masters' tools, to paraphrase Audre Lorde (110). I believe we can use the language, the rules, the very institution to change the oppressive conditions, the injustices. I have seen it happen, not just in the academy where a heretofore-racist college or department is transformed by the presence of one individual with vision and with the courage to proceed and do what needs doing. Even a single faculty member can be a catalyst for change. But at what cost? I have seen too many of my colleagues succumb to illness, their goodwill and good intentions bashed by committees where they are the minority—literally the only woman, the only Chicano or Chicana, the only Black, the only person of color—and have to speak up and then be castigated for doing so. How reassuring when our allies speak up. They sometimes come to the forefront and make it obvious that it is not just because I am in the room that they must think about diversity and about equal treatment and not even because it is the law, after all, but because it is the right thing to do, to treat all human beings with respect. When there is trauma, there is a need for healing. For me, healing always means going home. I am wounded, but I will heal. And the scar will remain as a reminder, as a testament of what has happened, what has injured me. Us.

What shape does the trauma take? It can be as simple as denial of one's presence or ideas. A slight comment made at a committee meeting, such as when one brings up a new idea only to have a curriculum committee question how solid the course would be, or to have one's text selections questioned or one's approach—is it serious enough? Is it theoretical enough? Isn't it just fluff, touchy-feely, to have students work in groups? It isn't high theory if it is grounded in experience. One's scholarship becomes contested terrain as colleagues question the legitimacy of doing cross-cultural work or interdisciplinary studies, that which is at the core of many area studies programs such as Chicano and Chicana Studies or Women's Studies. Or the clash can loom larger as the stakes are higher, such as when these smaller battles affect the larger ones of our tenure and promotion decisions. Our work is invalidated by administrators and colleagues who don't understand or choose not to understand the value of our work out in the world, who do not value the groundbreaking nature of working in these fields, who question our commitment to our classes because we volunteer to do work with community groups. Service-learning courses or innovative pedagogical strategies that are rewarded, albeit not always, when it is a white professor are often suspect when it is a professor of color who proposes or engages in such practices. That is when I become a warrior, when I practice what I preach and I don't give up, don't regret a thing, and proceed with what my heart tells me is what needs to be done. I follow Anzaldúa's charge to do work that matters ("Healing" 102).

My biggest challenges in the academy have come when I have had to deal with budgets and administrative tasks that required skills that I had not picked up in any of my educational settings but which I had learned to perform, albeit in a rudimentary fashion, as an office worker. When I worked as an administrator, first as department chair, then as acting dean, I had to prepare budgets and submit requests for funding projects and the daily operations of the department and the college. Although I was successful, I always felt that I couldn't possibly be doing all that I could. My own working-class background didn't present me with models of how to ask for funding, especially when I was new to the academy and my colleagues were the same men who had been my professors and still treated me as if I were a student. Even later and at another institution, as the person in charge of the doctoral program, I have had to be fierce in advocating for increased budgets for student programs and for sustaining budgetary commitments at a time of crises, crises that seem to come in cycles. What I learned early on was to be prepared and, as had been the case when I was a student, to be overprepared whenever I went in to see a higher-up with any kind of request or report. The dismally funded university that I worked at along the border gained tremendous clout as the state of Texas faced a lawsuit filed by the Mexican American Legal Defense Fund (MALDEF) in the mid-1980s. The suit was not "won" by MALDEF, but the benefits to the school where I was teaching and to others in south Texas taught me that, indeed, it matters little if you win the battle; what matters is that you win the war. The creation of a new campus for Laredo, however fraught with political undertones, provided an essential growth spurt that has not stopped. The lessons continue as I have moved into another system and have continued to militate within the academy on behalf of students. At the start of this century a crisis looms as fewer graduate students of color enroll, per capita, in graduate school. In my field of English, the decline is frightening. Just when the demographics are changing and the Latino population in the country is growing, the number of Latino graduate students in English is declining.

Along with the battles against a system that, due to its Western orientation and cultural history, is antagonistic to those of us who come with a different system, there are the battles that we must wage against our own: those who, blinded by the hatred and anger, cannot see beyond the immediate and are often self-destructive. Our ultimate goal is not to erase or abolish the tenets of Western civilization, whose unwilling children we are, but to reshape them to be more truly representative of reality, a reality that includes African and indigenous knowledges on an equal footing with the privileged Western civilization model. That is another lesson my beloved borderlands world has taught me: there is never *one* way of doing things, of thinking about things, or more importantly, of being. As Anzaldúa points out in *Borderlands/La Frontera*, those who hold that—because we speak in various languages—border residents are somehow limited do not recognize how limiting it is to have only one linguistic code to think with (76–81). My cross-cultural experience is not limited because I reside along an international border. Rather, I have been afforded opportunities beyond the limited ones those in the interior experience. For instance, as a child I learned to translate two monetary systems, two measuring systems—the U.S. and metric—and several worlds that often collided: the *tejano*, the *mejicano*, and the *anglo*. This uniquely borderlands phenomenon, at one time generally limited to the geographical space where I grew up, has now, at the beginning of the twenty-first century spread to wherever greater Mexico, to use Américo Paredes's term, happens to be, in Idaho, Utah, Chicago, New York, indeed in every state including Alaska and Hawaii (xiv).

And there are other places where I feel I belong that are not as intimately bound to geography. Libraries and bookstores are such sites of empowerment for me. I feel at home with books. It has been in books that I have found solace and where I have felt most at home when I have been away from home. In Nebraska, I immersed myself in books during my graduate studies; doing research in the archives in Spain, I would lose myself for hours. One time during a long trip to Colorado, I walked into the university library in Boulder and felt an excitement and an anticipation that was akin to feelings one gets when driving into a familiar and beloved space. It is the feeling I get driving south as I near Laredo or as I deplane at the airport. The feeling of being home. But it isn't just the presence of books that is comforting: books themselves, especially novels, offer me a place to feel at home. And I revisit some books that I love, rereading them over and over and feeling at home in the world the author has created.

While some creative writers bemoan that they must teach and write scholarly papers as part of their academic appointments, I don't see teaching and scholarly writing as mutually exclusive and relish the interrelatedness of these three aspects of my work: creative writing, scholarship, and teaching. Even this quirky site-specific pleasure I can trace back to that girlhood in Laredo where the small public library offered a myriad of experiences. My favorite book in third grade was *Eloise*, the story of a little girl who lives in a hotel in downtown New York. I suppose it was her independence that I yearned for as well as a world that was so different from mine. But I also yearned to inhabit the worlds found in other books, books that I read in Spanish and that offered alternative dreams. Yes, books and the spaces that hold them have been sites of empowerment for me.

I love to read and to talk about what I read; I often tell students that that is why I am a professor and not a lawyer. Writing and reading are my home, and the academic life is a life of writing and reading and talking about what one writes and reads. The cultural geography of this terrain is both comforting and threatening, as is that of my geographical homeland. The terrain of the academy, including the professional organizations, can be difficult to inhabit. Because of my myriad interests and areas of work, I belong to a number of these organizations and, aside from the tremendous expense such affiliations require, they demand and expect a level of participation that can be a drain on precious energy. The Modern Language Association, the National Association of Chicana and Chicano Studies, the American Folklore Society, the American Studies Association, the Latin American Studies Association, the National Women's Studies Association, Mujeres Activas en Letras y Cambio Social, and others, all provide their members opportunities for sharing and being with others of like mind, both in the literature they publish and in the membership gatherings. Yet I have found that even in these enclaves of professional unity, there can be dissent and discord. However, they provide a "safe space" where we can speak a common language and engage in discussions with like-minded colleagues. It is my reaction to these enclaves that provides a place where I can be who I am, where I can survive as an academic and as a scholar. It is what allows me to feel at home. My "homeland" is in my heart; I am destined to be in the borderlands, to be in worlds whose multivalenced ethos nurtures and inspires me.

Bibliography

Anzaldúa, Gloria. *Borderlands/La Frontera: The New Mestiza*. 2nd edition. San Francisco: Aunt Lute, 1999.

———. "Let Us Be the Healing of the Wound." *One Wound for Another: Chicana/os Latina/os in Cyberspace*. Ed. Clara Lomas and Claire Joysmith. Mexico City: Universidad Autónoma de Mexico, 2005.

Longoria, Arturo. *Adios to the Brushland*. College Station: Texas A&M P, 1997.

Lorde, Audre. "The Master's Tools Will Never Dismantle the Master's House," *Sister Outsider: Essays and Speeches*. Trumansburg, NY: Crossing, 1984.

Paredes, Américo. *A Texas-Mexican Cancionero: Folksongs of the Lower Border*. Austin: U of Texas P, 1995.

Pérez, Emma. "Irigaray's Female Symbolic in the Making of Chicana Lesbian Sitios y Lenguas (Sites and Discourses)." *Living Chicana Theory*. Ed. Carla Trujillo. Berkeley: Third Woman, 1998.

17

Bones of Summer

Mary Clearman Blew

Landscape. What one can see in a single view. Drive west toward Seattle at seventy or eighty miles an hour on Interstate 90 and landscape will be a rolling gray blur of sagebrush through the insulation of the car window, the dammed and degraded Columbia River a brief glimpse of silver, a few raw towns bypassed, and then two double-lane highways unfurling upward through inky fringes of evergreens that hide the giant patches where timber is being harvested on the Cascade Range. Never mind the timber. From the warmth of the car, what is visible through a veil of rain on the windshield is the endless interstate and the busy, increasing traffic that nips in and out as double lanes become triple lanes for the descent down the west side of the Cascades—triple lanes and access lanes and underpasses and loops and whorls buzzing with traffic, past towns with names that used to have meanings, Snoqualmie, Issaquah, only a blur, until finally there's the skyline of Bellevue on the east shore of Lake Washington, great glass and steel towers completely surrounded by residential developments and featureless strips and malls and parking garages and apartment complexes beyond complexes beyond complexes, all looped and overlooped by freeways meeting freeways, freeways passing over and under freeways, serpentine and circumferencing freeways.

Landscape. The single view. Pull over the automobile in one of those trouble lanes, step outside that upholstered cocoon with the string quartet emanating from the speakers and the smell of coffee from the vacuum cup and landscape becomes a stench of heated tires and exhaust and a cacophony of hurtling, shrieking metal, tons of metal, seven or eight lanes of shrieking, speeding metal like a crazed herd bent only on speed, speed. What is their destination, what is contained in those single human heads so briefly visible through the flash of glass, who knows? Learning whether there is purpose in what looks like chaos is not the task at hand. The task at hand is learning whether there is a way through the labyrinth of freeways on foot. Whether it is possible to walk along what looked from the automobile like a low-lying streak of silver, what now turns out to be a line of buckled and dented metal rails fixed to short posts, whether it is possible to walk here without being struck from behind by one of those crazed, speeding hunks of metal and turned into a sodden pulp. Surely there is a way. Coyotes and raccoons, survivors to the last, find a way along forgotten creek beds and ravines, sneak through brush and Scotch broom, dart openly when they must. But is there a human way, if a life depends upon it, to cross the freeway on foot and reach one of those apartment complexes, clearly visible on the other side of the seven or eight lanes of hurtling metal?

In one of those anonymous apartment complexes within a labyrinth of freeways in Bellevue, there lived, during the winter of 1969, a young woman who lay awake at night and listened to the roar of traffic that ebbed around three in the morning but never completely died away. She had spent the past five years in a graduate literature program in Missouri, but, now that she had successfully defended her dissertation, she had nothing to do and nowhere to go. She had expected to find a college or university teaching job after she finished her dissertation, but there were no jobs, or at least none that she could find in Seattle or its sprawling suburbs. During the days, after her husband had left for the junior high school where he taught and while her children were in school, she obsessively cleaned the apartment and tried to read or sew, and at night she lay awake listening to the buzz of the freeways and wondered where her life had gone wrong.

In later years she wondered why she hadn't done more to help herself. It was true that she was trapped without transportation behind the loops and whorls of the buzzing freeways, but it was also true that a shuttle bus traveled daily from one of the Bellevue motels to downtown Seattle, and surely she could have learned the schedule and found a way on foot through the freeways to the motel. Another woman would have made the effort, enjoyed the city, wandered along the piers in the heady salt breezes off Elliot Bay, browsed in the shops, bought a few exotic vegetables or spices in the open air market. But she didn't. The city wasn't what she wanted; she wanted a job. Without a job she had nothing to do, nothing that mattered, and still she felt exhausted, dragged down by some strange buzzing force that she didn't understand, weighted by the effort of getting through another day of small tasks.

Everyone who knew her was baffled by her unhappiness. Here she was, living in a comfortable apartment with a faithful, hardworking husband and two beautiful children. If she thought she had to have a job, she could find one right there in Bellevue. Secretarial jobs, clerking jobs—did she think she was too good for a secretarial job? What gave her that idea? It was 1969, after all, and the women's magazines were filled with dire warnings for women who tried to pursue careers—she was being self-centered, selfish—and our young woman didn't disagree. She was willing to accept whatever label anyone pasted on her, but she wasn't willing to accept the dead end she'd found herself in. Why were there no college or university teaching jobs in English, when there had always been jobs, when she had been told there always would be jobs? Was it some flaw in herself, some inadequacy she had never forced herself to face?

(It was 1969. There was no MLA Job Listing, there were no articles about the sudden surplus of young PhDs in the humanities, hundreds of young PhDs in the humanities, hundreds more being churned out by the graduate schools in the next year and the next, and hardly any jobs. It would take some time before the young PhDs would realize they were all in the same boat. In 1969 our young woman supposed that she was the only one who couldn't find a job, and her sense of failure ate away at her.)

What are we to make of this young woman, looking back at her after so many years? That she was naive—well, to say the least! Tiresomely naive and tiresomely self-absorbed, as though she had no idea how narrow her view of the world was, how scant her experience. She did possess a kind of dumb determination. Endurance was probably her strongest point. She hung on for the long haul, yes she did.

She and her husband had married in a seethe of teenage lust to the lyrics of popular music and almost immediately were disappointed to discover that they were married to each other and not to their ideas of each other. But they were making the best of it. There were the children, after all. Also, they both came from families where marriage was forever. Also, they were both were afraid of what life might do to them without the other as a prop. So they made the best of it. They did collect grievances like troll's gold, however, counting coins of resentment in secret and letting them pile up.

But back to the story. What became of the young woman? Did she sit in that Bellevue apartment, weeping and spinning her troll's gold out of flammable straw until her mind blurred into the inexorable buzz of freeway traffic? Was she finally crushed into some semblance of a teacher's wife by the weight of all that pavement? Lost within those miles of curving triple and quadruple lanes and loops and interstices, the roaring overpasses and echoing underpasses and the dizzy busy cloverleafs, as tangled and snarled and knotted as though they had become not just the labyrinth, but the very thread of Ariadne, spun into a concrete monster?

No. She didn't. What she did was pore over the classifieds in the *Seattle Times* as the winter passed and the summer dragged into July, until one day she came upon an advertisement for what seemed to her like the last job in the world. An assistant professor of English was wanted at Northern Montana College in Havre, Montana. *Call Dr. George Craig, Chairman*, the ad read, and listed a phone number.

She dialed. Listened to a faraway ring.

"Northern Montana College," said a throaty voice, suddenly, from six hundred miles away.

Apparently she was connected with the college switchboard.

"Dr. George Craig, please?"

"I don't think he's in the building. Wait a minute—I think I just saw him walk by."

The young woman could hear running footsteps and the voice calling, "Dr. Craig! Dr. Craig! You've got a phone call!" She was trying to visualize what kind of college she had reached, when the phone was picked up again and a man said, hesitantly, "Hello?"

"My name is Mary Clearman," she began, "and I saw your ad in the *Seattle Times*—"

"You have your doctorate?" he interrupted.

"Well, yes, I defended last December." She was going to continue, to explain her teaching experience, the subject of her dissertation (*Aspects of Juvenal in Ben Jonson's Comical Satires*), the journals where she had submitted articles, the letters of recommendation that she could have sent to him, but Dr. Craig gave her no time.

"Would you like to come for an interview?"

"Well—*yes*," she said, after a startled instant.

"You do have your doctorate."

"Yes."

"We'll send you an airline ticket."

Landscape. What one can see in a single view. It's only her second time in flight, and twisting in her cramped seat to look down at the miniaturized interstate threading its way through the Cascade Range, she marvels at the way her perspective has been so abruptly altered. From the lofty altitude of thirty thousand feet she can see the square patches of managed timber reduced to a quilt in varying green and also the untouched and hollowed peaks that once belched and rumbled fire and lava in a forgotten eon but now hold lakes like tiny mirrors that reflect even tinier clouds and passing shadows until they, too, are lost from her view. The mountains roll back, the gray prairie stretches to the Rockies and the prairie beyond the Rockies that she never expected to be returning to. The flight from Seattle has taken less than two hours.

On the airport tarmac in Great Falls, Montana, the wind hits her in the face and rips off her false eyelashes, which she snatches out of thin gritty air as they fly by, to the momentary astonishment of the passenger walking behind her. Inside the terminal she darts into the women's room to repair her face and sees—what? A face she's never had confidence in, hence the ridiculous false eyelashes and the hair stiffened by spray, and now she must take this inadequate face to meet the impatient Dr. George Craig, whose abrupt invitation for an interview she and her husband had puzzled over.

She squares her shoulders and forces herself to walk out of the shelter of the women's room and into the dusty white light where a few rows of cracked plastic seats and a vending machine are the only amenities in this country terminal, and a handful of passengers are still waiting for their luggage, and a short man with a graying crewcut has approached a very fat young woman in flip-flops and a faded sundress:

"Are you Dr. Clearman?"

The flip-flop woman shakes her head, suspicion crossing her face as though he's made an indecent suggestion, and turns her back, and now there's nothing for our young woman but to get a grip, step up, and admit, "I'm Dr. Clearman."

He turns, stares at her. In her high heels she's a head taller than he is. Forever after she wonders if he would rather she had been the flip-flop woman.

It takes about two hours to drive down from the airport at Great Falls, through town, and north on Highway 87 to Havre (population something less than ten thousand), which lies along the Milk River, thirty miles short of the Canadian border. Rainfall up here on the high prairie is likely to average about eleven inches a year, and the hot wind is constant, burning off what moisture there is and draining the color out of the landscape. Newcomers, expecting the glamorous Montana of the mountains to the south and west, are likely to be stunned, then appalled, at the endless shades of gray. Sagebrush on low hills and cutbanks, shadows of clouds, emptiness between earth and sky. *People really live out here?*

Yes, but not very many. Montana, with over 145,000 square miles making it the fourth-largest state in the United States, has a population of about 800,000, of which fewer than 100,000 live along that 250–mile northern stretch between Glasgow and Shelby known as the Highline, where James J. Hill built his railroad during the heyday of the homestead movement in 1910 and hoped to transform the desert into a cornucopia of 360–acre family farms. Rain will follow the plow, he promised the homesteaders, but of course it didn't, and the farms failed during the depression and drought of the 1920s. In the years since then, dryland farming techniques and hybrid seeds have turned the prairie into a cornucopia of wheat, but not in the way Hill imagined. Today the farms are vast, and one man with monster machinery representing a capital investment of hundreds of thousands of dollars can cultivate and harvest the acreage once tilled by twenty men. As the population grows sparser, it grows grayer. The young leave to find work, while the old watch satellite television and drive miles on paved single-lane highways to do their shopping. They worry about the weather and curse the federal government, but when some well-meaning researcher suggests, *Why not turn this prairie back into grazing land for buffalo and antelope? Who lives out here, anyway?* they answer in a thin but sturdy chorus: *We do!*

But we're trying to cover too much local history here, and also we're getting ahead of our story. In late July of 1969, the impervious clouds float high above their shadows, the sun beats down, and hawks keep watch from the crossbars of power poles for anything that moves. It may be hard for many to imagine moving out there, slowed to the pace of a pulse through the heat and the wheat, but the young woman doesn't have to imagine. She knows the scent of sun-baked seeds and the pungency of sagebrush, the scratch of wheatheads on her arms and legs; she knows how sweat feels when it trickles through her hair and how barbed wire sounds when it sings in the wind. The sun weighs down upon her, drags her toward the drowsy earth where the stones and bones are buried. She'll be buried here if she isn't careful. She knows something about a kind of isolation that is different from what she knew in Bellevue: the isolation of distance and weather and the isolation of minds.

Yes, she knows a little of what she's getting into as the car with the State of Montana license plates driven by Dr. George Craig creeps north through ripening wheat fields riven by sage-choked coulees. There's nothing out there but the hawks and the power lines and the white mile markers. Occasionally there's a deserted homestead shack, occasionally there's an occupied farmstead within its dusty and windblown shelterbelt. Nothing else but the same clouds she so recently flew over.

Dr. George Craig knows this highway well, but he keeps glancing at the withdrawn woman beside him, trying to gauge her reactions. The truth is, news of the PhD glut hasn't reached northern Montana yet. Dr. George Craig needs to hire an assistant professor with a doctorate if his college is going to keep its accreditation; he needs to hire a PhD so badly that he'd probably not commit murder for one, but just short of that. Is there any possibility at all that this strange young woman from Seattle in her dark green linen dress and her elaborate coiffure and her eyelashes would come to this place to live?

At last he ventures, "Is this your first visit to Montana?"

"Oh, no," she says, "I was born and raised here," and to her astonishment, he lets out his breath in relief.

So you know what you're getting into.

As they near Havre, George Craig turns off State 87 onto the old highway, which angles past the wheat fields to meet the welcome green of a few willows and box elder trees and the windswept roofs of houses with small watered lawns. The young woman is trying to mesh what she sees with the only other time she visited Havre, with her father when she was in her teens and they were chasing an auctioneer who had stolen a milk cow. Also the story her grandmother used to tell, about driving up to Havre from the homestead with a team and wagon to meet the train from the East and camping overnight on the prairie on the way up and the way back. What a growing-up she's had, if George Craig only knew. He'll never know, if it's up to her. Not that she's ashamed of her background, exactly, but it seems too complicated to explain, on the one hand, and irrelevant on the other. She's a scholar, after all. She's spent years learning Latin and reading the classics, so what do stolen milk cows have to do with her?

She'll live long enough to consider the answer to that question, to understand that her scholarship grew from her fear of suffocation, of being buried alive under that blinding sun. Also, to her surprise, she'll live to see Montana transformed from nowhere to somewhere glamorous (though never the Highline; it will never be glamorous, not the shortgrass prairie up here on the northern brow of the world where the wind blows constantly, and the sun beats down, and the temperature rises to +110° in the summer and drops to -45° in the winter). But the glamorization of Montana and the West lies far in the future. For now, George Craig has driven past the streets of modest houses where the wind has bowed the trees and scoured paint off siding, and he has stopped on a bluff overlooking the Milk River with the town of Havre curled around it. Perched on the brow of the bluff, interrupting endless dusty blue sky, are the few brick buildings of Northern Montana College.

He parks in front of one of the buildings. Two long brick wings support a squat tower that will hold the next eighteen years of her life.

"This is Cowan Hall."

Place is where we imagine ourselves to be. Juvenal's Rome of the second century, for example. *Who but the wealthy get sleep in Rome?* The mobs, the noise, the surging crowds, the dense mass of people—why did the Montana girl ever choose to walk those dangerous streets in the footsteps of the old satirist? Or the equally congested streets of Ben Jonson's seventeenth-century London— what was she looking for? Yes, it's true, in part, that she was fleeing the silence of the high plains; it's true, in part, that she was trying to reinvent herself in a milieu as far removed as she could find from the place she was born or from what she was intended to be. Years later her gorge still rises when she thinks about the dearth of expectations for her, the easy way the ranch girl's dreams were dismissed. *Let her teach in the rural schools until she marries, then let her be a good wife. What? Being a country teacher, being a wife isn't good enough for her? Who does she think she is?*

But to settle for the suffocation theory is to overlook a single truth about the woman the Montana girl was becoming: she loved her scholarship. Loved it. Loved her painstaking translations from the Latin, loved the careful juxtaposition of texts, loved the language, loved the complex tracery of ideas and images that the old satirist passed on from Rome to London. Most of all she loved the timelessness of absorbing herself in her work, the out-of-body experience of dissolving library walls and fading street sounds, the sensation of one mind touching another over centuries through words. Was she perhaps a bit naive in her love, as she was naive in so many other ways? Unaware of how ridiculous she looked, with the dust of carrels and seldom-opened texts filtering down on her stiff-sprayed hair, her make-up? Yes, call her naive, call her ridiculous, but still admit that single truth: she loved her work.

And if she returns? That first moment on the steps of Cowan Hall, she has a dim inkling of the battles she will have to fight if she returns, but how fierce the battles, how stiff the price she'll pay, she cannot possibly imagine. Who could imagine an assistant professorship costing her scholarship? Or her marriage? Who could have imagined Northern Montana College?

It's as though a tribe of gypsies camped here one night and decided to start a college, remarked one of her colleagues, years later, but it wasn't gypsies: it was sodbusters who founded Northern in the 1930s, in the depths of a depression that sent every starved and windblown community scrambling for whatever public institutions might provide a payroll. A college, why not? Havre was two hundred miles over bad roads from the state college in Bozeman, nearly three hundred miles from the university in Missoula, distances that in those days of chugging Model Ts were far greater than they are today, and the young men and women of the Highline needed access to higher education that was closer to home. So a board was appointed, and a president hired, and classes were begun in church basements and whatever rooms the public schools could spare. The president offered a two-year curriculum of Latin and Greek, taught by himself. He hired a young man to teach chemistry, told him to build his own lab, and, by the way, to organize and coach a basketball team, which the young man did. The idea was that the graduates of the two-year curriculum would then transfer to the University of Minnesota (and many of them did). Everyone was so poor that some of the older faculty remembered lending money to their students so they could stay in school.

Eventually, enrollment grew to a whopping five or six hundred students, and money was found to construct a couple of buildings from bricks salvaged from an abandoned military fort. After World War II, a new president arrived with his own ideas for Northern Montana College, which were to junk the Latin and Greek and add vocational programs in everything from automotive transmissions to flight instruction to cosmetology to teacher education. To accommodate teacher certification, the curriculum stretched to four years. By 1969, enrollment had grown to its all-time high of nearly 1400 students. The vocational-minded president had departed, leaving behind his practical programs and part of an airplane, and a power struggle had replaced him in the president's office with an ex-professor of education. The idea now was to strengthen the four-year academic programs for accreditation, hence the need to hire assistant professors with PhDs.

Our young woman, mercifully unaware of all this history, walks into Cowan Hall for the first time and hears her heels ring on the floors in the still white light that floods through the tiers of single-pane windows. Most of the faculty and staff are gone for the summer, George Craig explains, as he introduces her to a small dark gnome of a woman, who pokes her head from around her switchboard in a closet near the stairs. She turns out to be the possessor of the throaty voice. One of the English professors who is around is a Stephen Liu, who teaches Shakespeare and writes poetry (and will write more poetry, once he moves to the University of Nevada, Reno, and isn't teaching quite so much freshman composition). There are five or six others in the English department, and they all teach freshman composition courses and the literature courses leading to the BS degree in teacher education and to a tiny BA degree in English.

What can be accomplished in this place, wonders the young woman, whose idea of a college is the University of Missouri at Columbia. What can be imagined here, what will the future hold?

The future: she will often feel as though she has exchanged the myth of Ariadne and the labyrinth for the myth of Sisyphus. As teacher education programs shrink and vocational programs flourish and the job market continues to worsen, she and other liberal arts faculty will find themselves in a No-Exit bastion of curriculum quarrels, campus politics, budget cuts, crises of all kinds. But no! They'll insist they're not rolling a rock uphill. They're fighting for their programs, for the liberal arts, in the face of ridicule from the other side of the campus: *What some people think this college is all about! Where do they get the idea that college is about ideas, when everyone knows it's about job skills?*

While she herself—because the nearest university library is three hundred miles away and it's the 1970s, with no internet, only a clunky interlibrary loan system that may or may not produce Xeroxed articles after a six-weeks' wait—without quite knowing that she's doing it, will stop trying to keep current with her scholarship. Instead, she'll pick up the threads of fiction that she spun as an undergraduate. She'll write short stories about the isolated ranches and the silent people who live and struggle against weather and change and bankruptcy; she'll bare the bones of her people and the bones of the people they displaced.

Confrontation: that's the word. She won't let them bury her alive. If her fiction seems light years distant in theme and tone from *Aspects of Juvenal in Ben Jonson's Comical Satires*, who better than the old satirist and the university-trained stepson of a London bricklayer to be looking over her shoulder?

But now it's late July of 1969, and George Craig shows her around the campus and the town, takes her to dinner with his wife, then drops her off at the Havre Hotel, where she can hear the coupling and uncoupling of boxcars while she thinks about the opportunity she's being offered and the risks that, as yet, are shadows on the margins of her thoughts. Although she knows that what can be seen in a single view is not all there is, she won't venture into those shadows, won't ask herself what will become of her marriage or whether she can survive the reassembling of the pieces of herself.

In the morning, George Craig will drive her back to the airport in Great Falls and tell her that they can offer her $11,000 for ten months. He'll ask her what she thinks.

She says that she's got to talk it over with her husband.

Yes, of course, he agrees, but his face falls. He thinks she's going to turn down the offer.

She already knows she will accept.

18
Singing, Speaking, and Seeing a World

Janice M. Gould

I come from a people on my mother's side, the Konkow Maidu, a California Indian tribe, whose stories of creation and of the land are rooted in time immemorial. My mother was born in 1912, and in her generation the children did not learn to speak "Indian," or so my mother believed. Mom recalled her mother and grandmother speaking Konkow together and could remember a song her grandma taught her when they went to gather materials for making baskets. While the music and poetry that gave shape to our indigenous ancestral world must have been part of my mother's earliest childhood, that influence was cut short. Her mother passed away when my mother was four years old.

With the end of her mother's life, Mama's cultural landscape changed. It was already a rich blend of cultures—French and Konkow from her mother, Irish and Konkow from her father. She remembered her mother's *pommes de terre,* fried in lard or bacon grease, and *café au lait* with evaporated milk. She recalled her father's fiddle playing, her brothers clogging to the tunes. She could recollect the old-time hymns they would sing: "Rock of Ages," "He Walks with Me," and "Shall We Gather at the River." When her mother died, the family did gather at the river, in what my mom considered a Konkow ceremonial. Each person wore a wreath of flowers. They waded into the river and sank down, letting the river lift the wreath and carry it downstream, past the eddying pools and great boulders, through cascades of white water, with their prayers.

If my mother had understood Konkow and if the stories had been told to her, she would have heard a tribal narrative about how the earth was made and how people came to live on it. In one version of this legend, Earthmaker, long ago, enlisted the aid of Turtle. He asked Turtle to dive beneath the dark swirl of waters upon which Earthmaker had been floating and bring something back. With the bit of mud that Turtle carried to him in his beak or beneath his nails, Earthmaker, with the help (and hindrance) of Coyote, created the Konkow world—breathing, speaking, and singing it into existence. [1]

In that landscape—upon that land—my people dwelt for at least a thousand years. It is said that people never had to venture far from their homes, for all was provided: game for hunting, fish, birds, plants, and other human beings with whom to gather for happy celebrations or for mourning. Then, in a very short time in the mid-nineteenth century, the people were wiped out by disease, starvation, and murder. Everything they knew as "home" was confiscated or stolen, and many of those who survived were removed by military order from the towns and villages where they lived. The children were sent to boarding schools run by the government, where they were supposed to learn English and forget their native languages and customs. They were expected to assimilate into American culture and society.

I reach back past my mother's memory to that of my grandma and great-grandma, as far back as I can. What is there? A place so rich and a landscape so varied it takes your breath away: huge flocks of migrating birds and runs of king and other salmon all the way down the coast of San Buena Ventura and up the Sacramento River to the American, Yuba, and Feather rivers. Enormous oak trees, massive forests of old-growth timber. Flowers, butterflies, clouds, the wind. Indian people of diverse backgrounds, with over one hundred languages being chanted, spoken, and sung. The beauty of our land, the red soil of our earth.

Laguna poet and scholar Paula Gunn Allen writes in her essay on the poetry of American Indian women, "We are the dead and the witnesses to death of hundreds of thousands of our people, of the water, the air, the animals and forests and grassy lands that sustained them and us not so very long ago" (*Sacred* 155). Even today in the part of the Sacramento Valley the Konkow people occupied, many species of birds, including flycatchers, orioles, shrikes, herons, magpies, snow geese, red-tailed hawks, and many more, nest in the wildlife refuges or touch down there on migratory journeys. The numbers must pale, however, against what the Native inhabitants of the land witnessed. Indeed, the Feather River and Plumas County were named for the many feathers or *plumas*, as the Spanish explorers noted, that could be found there.

Allen goes on to say, "The impact of genocide in the minds of American Indian poets and writers cannot be exaggerated. It is a pervasive feature of the consciousness of every American Indian in the United States...." (156). Trauma of this kind is not easily spoken about, and there is a deep guardedness in many Indian people, a discomfort in bringing up painful memories, a desire to keep tragedy and suffering to oneself. Nevertheless, as Allen points out, American Indian women poets have not only served a crucial role in bringing into speech the wide sense of loss and destruction but have also forged a language in which to celebrate the continuance of life and traditions, even those changed by time and circumstances.

I never knew my Konkow grandparents. I grew up, instead, with a sense of their absence in my mother's world. I became a scholar to learn about the traditions my mom could not tell me, in part because of her reticence and because there were things she had not learned and did not know. I studied American Indian literature, history, and anthropology to understand what happened to the Konkow and other Native people and to my mother and her family. I learned how to do research in order to find answers to questions I couldn't ask my mom, either because I could not imagine those questions or because I feared my mom's answers. My mother and I allowed silences to grow around us, constructing barriers to knowing one another fully and to revealing ourselves, both of us mixed-bloods. We were familiar with keeping secrets and living in different cultural arenas.

I became a poet in order to start talking about my life—my experience as a lesbian, a mixed-blood, a woman with an inner landscape of mountains and stars, sunrises and setting moons, pastures in fog and rain, bright noontides. I became a poet to speak of the places I've passed through and the cities where I grew up. I also became a poet to describe a landscape of loneliness and fury, sadness and loss, and moments of happiness in loving and being loved.

I was in my late twenties when I walked into a little book shop on Shattuck Avenue, near Francisco Street in Berkeley to scout through the shelves of books looking for poetry. I was searching for something I could fall in love with, some clear vision of the natural world. I wanted some language that spoke from the heart of things, carefully and respectfully, like the poetry I was reading by Gary Snyder, William Stafford, Maxine Kumin, and Kenneth Rexroth. I found such a book that day, but it was not poetry. What I picked up was a thin book with gray paper covers published by the University of California in 1964, titled *Maidu Grammar*, by William F. Shipley.

How excited I was to find this volume! I had no idea that such a book had been written; I wasn't even sure that speakers of Maidu were still around. I didn't realize that Konkow and Maidu were two separate, though related, languages.[2] I knew, at that point in my life, only that no one in our family spoke this language. I believed it had passed away with my grandparents. When my mom sang her basketry song to me, I listened attentively, but despite years of training as a musician I could never learn to reproduce the quarter tones of that music. I think we both assumed that all our Konkow speakers had died with my grandmother's generation.[3]

A few years later as a student at UC Berkeley, I was to learn that the Department of Linguistics produced a number of grammars from various California Indian tribes. In the linguistics library, one could find collections of stories and grammars from all over the world, many of them transcribed in IPA (International Phonetic Alphabet) and translated into English. Finding Shipley's work on Maidu helped lead me into the study of linguistics and later to declare it as my major as an undergraduate. I wanted to know how to read his book. Sections headed with words like "Morphemics" and "Morphotactics" seemed indecipherable, and I was not confident that I would ever understand the elegant and austere language of that grammar. Yet what hooked me was not only the puzzle of how one might speak Maidu but that Shipley's primary informant, Maym Gallagher, was a relative of mine.

A somewhat distant relative. Maym Benner had married my half-uncle, Lee Gallagher. My mother and aunts remembered Maym—they called her Maymie—but could not recollect ever hearing her speak Maidu. "Of course, it's possible," they said. My mom had stopped living in the Feather River canyon after their mother, Helen (Gallagher) Beatty, passed away in 1917. That was when my mother, Vivian, was adopted by the Lane sisters, Beatrice, Henrietta, and Clara, who took her from her home in the Feather

River canyon and brought her to live in Berkeley. My two surviving aunts, Lillian and Grace, my mother's older sisters, followed my mom to the Bay Area to work and to go to school, while their brothers stayed in the canyon and got jobs as cowboys and loggers. The three girls eventually found it difficult to stay in touch with their other siblings and their father.

But our connection with the Feather River canyon was not severed with my mom's adoption. Mom returned to her birthplace, Belden, in Plumas County, various times when she was growing up. She returned as an adult to bury her father, Harry Beatty, who died of tuberculosis in the 1930s. My mother took my two sisters and me to the canyon when we were children, and we visited there throughout our adolescence and into young adulthood because my Aunt Lillian, who married my uncle, Ivan Brockett, had returned to the canyon to live. We stayed with Ivan and Lillian many times during summers, or we camped nearby, until they moved down to the Sacramento Valley, near Gridley. Even then, we continued to go up to the canyon, to camp and swim, to explore the country, and to hike up Yellow Creek where my grandfather had staked a claim in a little mine that, in his lifetime, produced only enough gold to buy staples.

Although she couldn't teach us our ancestral language or stories, my mother wanted us to know the country where she was born. This "motherland" rooted us in an indigenous landscape—the steep, narrow canyon, the live oak and dogwood, the cedar and spruce coated in dust, the bright heat of summer and the sparkle of light on water, the drying lichens on granite, the whir of cicadas. Unlike others from that area, my mom's family avoided being rounded up for the 1857 or 1863 removals to the Nome Lackee and Round Valley reservations.[4] Many Konkow people who were marched to these reservations managed to return to the Mother Lode country. Some of these were enrolled at the Berry Creek or Mooretown Rancherias, small acreages in the foothills set aside for Indians. My older sister, who studied our family's genealogy, tells me that our family names, Beatty and Orcier, are not on those enrollment lists. Nor is the name of my great-great-grandfather, Dr. Charley, who was said to be a medicine man.[5] He lived at Berry Creek, in the hills east of Oroville, and so would have been a likely candidate for removal. Our connection to the land was not through a reservation or rancheria, but through my mom's and aunts' memories of their family's homestead, though a legal property claim was never discovered in the state archives.

The first time we went to the canyon, I was eight years old. It was raining when we came to Belden, a one-street village situated across the Feather River from the highway. We didn't go into the town but pulled over after we crossed Yellow Creek, which tumbles down a box canyon and empties from the north into the river. The little Belden graveyard is on a hill above the highway. My mother found the trail, and we kids ran ahead to where part of her family is buried. The graves were untended, and there were no headstones, only markers with typed inscriptions faded by weather and time. Mama tried to remember exactly where her dad and certain brothers and sisters were buried.

The graveyard frightened me a little. It seemed so old, so abandoned by the living. The graves were covered with leaves and wet grass, and the concrete around the plots looked ancient and pocked. Mom said her grandmother and mother were buried on the homestead behind their house, no longer standing, about a mile farther along the road. Someone else owned that property now. We didn't visit. The day was cold and dismal, and we soon got back in the car and headed down the canyon. As we passed the old homestead land at Little Indian Creek, Mama told us about the ghosts that haunted their house, how those spirits would laugh and talk in a language the family could not understand. It would sound as if people were setting the table; they could hear dishes rattling and the voices of children laughing, playing with a hoop.[6] She said that no one felt scared of these phantoms because they all seemed to be having a good time. I didn't fully trust the jollity of my mother's explanation. I felt scared, and I wondered where all the other Indians were buried. Where were their graves? Where were their spirits now?

These are questions I carry with me, even as an adult. When I came to know the "magical realism" in Native American poetry and fiction by authors such as Joy Harjo, Luci Tapahonso, and Louise Erdrich, I felt a deeper understanding of, and familiarity with, the unusual and uncanny aspects of my mother's recollections. But Native writing encompasses more than a literary device: my mother's memory was more than a means to render a colorful past. Deep in the sediment of indigenous poems and stories is the disturbing idea that the dead are with us, not far down the trail, not as buried as we think. The removal and relocation of Native Americans has gone on for a long time, and in many communities even the graves and bones have been displaced by non-natives. As cultural theorist Angelika Bammer says, "What is displaced—dispersed, deferred, repressed, pushed aside—is, significantly, still there: *Dis*placed but not *re*placed, it remains a source of trouble, the shifting ground of signification that makes meanings tremble" (xiii).

When Hopi/Miwok poet Wendy Rose unearths a dead woman's voice in "I Expected My Skin and My Blood to Ripen," this vocalization disrupts the self-assured master narrative of the country. Speaking of the desecration of bodies after the Wounded Knee massacre, the woman tells of the theft and sale of the clothing that she, her child, and the other murdered people wore. Or in Louise Erdrich's *Tracks*, the uneasy Pillager clan lies beneath the forested land that, through fraud and chicanery, is sold off to a timber company. The Pillagers' power retreats, but it doesn't die. Again and again, Native writers ask us to look at what's being done to this land and to Native people. They listen to the hauntings, and they ask us to think ahead, to think with our hearts, to be thankful, and to forgo selfishness.

As I write this, I hold a full-time, nontenured position in a small liberal arts college in Oregon's Willamette Valley. Willamette University is a pleasant place to teach in the state capital. I like my colleagues and enjoy the students. I was hired by the English department to chair a three-year position in creative writing, so I teach a course in poetry titled Imaginative Writing and a course in Native American literature. Though a small group of Native American students attend Willamette, I believe I am the only American Indian faculty member on campus.

A few miles from the university stands Chemawa Indian Boarding School. Like the university, it was founded in the 1800s by a Methodist mission, headed by a man named Jason Lee. The original site of the school seems to have been Forest Grove, a town perhaps thirty or forty miles northwest of Salem. The school was the second off-reservation Indian Boarding School in the nation run and supported by the federal government. It opened in 1880.[7] Like Carlisle Indian School in Pennsylvania, the government placed a military man in charge of the institution. The Indian students who attended the school were children born to Oregon tribes, and the school also admitted Native students from California, Washington, and Alaska. At one point, there was a Navajo contingent of students from Arizona or New Mexico.

I often think about Chemawa and other Indian schools from time to time as I drive to work and back home along the I-5 corridor. From the highway you can see the old red and white water tank; it still stands on the school grounds with the word "Chemawa" printed on it. The Southern Pacific railroad runs right alongside the institution, a reminder that many schools were placed near tracks; some students were sent by train to the schools. When they were children, my aunts and uncles took the train to attend and board at Greenville Indian School in California. Many Indian people I've met here in Oregon have older relatives who were educated at Chemawa. The school is still in operation, and it continues to board Indian students from across the country. Unlike the earlier Chemawa, today's school houses children who have not been able to succeed in school elsewhere, due to emotional and psychological problems. I understand that for visitors to enter or leave the facility requires a certain clearance from the authorities at the school.

I remember seeing the door to the jailhouse at Chemawa. It was on display in the state library a few years ago. Most Indian schools had a disciplinarian, often an Indian man. Children who misbehaved or who ran away from the school were subject to punishment. The most incorrigible runaways—and these could be as young as five or six years old—were put into a jailroom or stockade (Adams, *Education* 224). Chemawa's heavy oak prison door was scratched and pocked. Children had carved symbols and signs into the door—zigzags, circles, and a deeply incised star. Today, holding cells house children who get in trouble. A recent scandal at Chemawa, however, where a young Indian woman died from alcohol poisoning while being locked down and then neglected, has made the government suspend the practice of incarcerating students—for the time being.

Every class in Native American literature I teach, I tell about the boarding schools and the nation's drive to assimilate Indian into Euramerican culture. Most of my students have never heard of the Indian boarding school system or many other aspects of federal policy regarding American Indians. It typically comes as a shock to most students to learn about the removals of children from their homes and families, including kidnappings; the kind of schooling they received; the enormous amount of labor they had to perform; the Christianizing of the students; the illnesses that spread through the schools; the punishments of the children for speaking their own languages; the deaths they faced; and the loss, loneliness, and longing they endured.

We look at the "before and after" photographs of Indian children commissioned by Carlisle's superintendent, Richard Henry Pratt. The first set of photos was taken just after the children arrived at the school in their sometimes traditional, sometimes ragged clothing. The second set of photos, taken some weeks or months after the children were at school, shows groups of students cleaned and tidied up in their school uniforms, which for boys was a military-style tunic and pants and for girls a long Victorian dress. The boys' hair was cropped close, and the girls' was up off their necks. The photographs were meant to convince private funders, members of Congress, and the President that their continued support would literally transform young Indians, bringing them out of a state of "savagery" and into "civilization." The photos made a visual argument for that transformation: the change from "uncouth" and "uncultured" heathens or pagans to almost-citizens could be best and most readily achieved through the off-reservation boarding school.

In my Native American literature class, we read various works that deal with the schools. Indian education is a frequent motif brought up by Native authors, and though stories abound in Indian communities about the schools, no larger work of fiction yet deals exclusively with the Indian school. Nevertheless, a poem like "Indian Boarding School: The Runaways," by Louise Erdrich,[8] is certainly better understood once my students have an idea about why Indian school kids tried to escape from these institutions. Erdrich, like many other Native American writers, includes the problems of schooling throughout her novels. For example, in *Tracks*, the child Lulu has been sent away to boarding school (probably Flandreau) by her mother, Fleur, because after the theft of her land, Fleur has no means to take care of her daughter. Lulu angrily misinterprets Fleur's gesture as abandonment. Upon Lulu's return to the reservation as a young woman, the old man, Nanapush, tries to impress upon Lulu what Fleur was up against and why she had sent her away. This is one of the significant burdens of his narration throughout the novel.

During the 1890s, Carlisle's Richard Henry Pratt realized that if children could be "inoculated" against their home cultures and families once they returned to the reservation, it would save the school a lot of trouble reassimilating the children to Euramerican school culture once they returned to the institution in the fall; or, especially if they had graduated, it would prevent children from being tempted to succumb to tribal ways of thinking and behaving. Reformers called this "going back to the blanket" (Adams, *Education* 291) To that end, a little propaganda book titled *Stiya: A Carlisle Indian Girl at Home*, was published and distributed to students to take home with them. One of the interesting things about this book is that while it appears to be written by one of the Indian girls, named "Embe," it was in fact written by one of Pratt's teachers at Carlisle, Mariana Burgess (M.B.).[9]

In one of my lectures about Indian boarding schools, I like to read aloud the opening vignette of this story, when the train that has carried Stiya home deposits her at the Laguna Pueblo depot. As the story, appropriately titled "Disappointment," begins, Stiya is anxious to see her parents, though reluctant to return to the reservation. Here is Stiya's experience of seeing her mother and father after many years away, according to Burgess:

> *Was I as glad to see them as I thought I would be?*
> *I must confess that instead I was shocked and surprised at the sight that met my eyes.*
> *"My father? My mother?" cried I desperately within.*
> *"No, never!" I thought, and I actually turned my back upon them.*
> *I had forgotten that home Indians had such grimy faces.*
> *I had forgotten that my mother's hair always looked as though it had never seen a comb.*
> *I had forgotten that she wore such a short, queer-looking black bag for a dress, fastened over one shoulder only, and such buckskin wrappings for shoes and leggings.*
> *"My mother?" I cried, this time aloud.*
> *I could not help it, and at the same time I rushed frantically into the arms of my school-mother, who had taken me home, and I remembered then as I never did before how kind she had always been to us. I threw my arms around her neck and cried bitterly, and begged of her to let me get on the train again. (2–3)*

In this passage, it seems clear that Stiya's "shock" is engendered by feelings of revulsion upon seeing her mother and father. The Pueblo girl's mother is particularly marked for condemnation because of her "queer-looking" clothing that is somehow also immodest. The necessary and absolute undoing of the warm and beloved relationship between Indian parents and their children is the message. In *Stiya*, it cannot be repaired until the parents adopt the Indian child's vision of how Indian life now ought to be.

The purpose of education for Indians, as David Wallace Adams points out, was to inculcate them with an assimilationist creed and to persuade them that the loss of their tribally held land and, indeed, of the whole continent, was both "inevitable and entirely justified" ("Fundamental" 19). On "Franchise Day" in 1890, students at Carlisle School stood at attention, listening to a poem (perhaps also penned by Mariana Burgess) that praised the Dawes Act and spelled out how, in compensation for the loss of their lands, Native children now had education and the promise of citizenship. The last stanza reads

> But welcome the ruin, if now by our losses,
> We gain thousand fold in a better estate.
> A man may be chief in the empire of reason.
> Education, not land, makes a citizen great.[10]

Learning to accept, approve, and possibly even love our own disenfranchisement from our ancestral land seems to me one of the cruelest aspects of American assimilation policies. Often, as I drive to work through the beautiful farmland in the Willamette Valley, I consider what this land once was and who lived here—in Salem, the Kalapuya people. Though the majority of my students come from Oregon, most of them don't know the name of the tribe who inhabited a large part of the valley; they know nothing about how the people lived, nothing about the language they spoke or where their villages were located. It is not entirely my students' fault. They acknowledge in my class, usually with embarrassment or consternation, that they were not taught much, if anything, about Indian history in their high school history classes. They did not know to ask for this history, to demand it. They did not learn to question what the "other side" of the story of this nation—this land and its landscape, this land and its myriad inhabitants, human and nonhuman—could be.

It may be that the United Statesian is permanently lost from this land. He or she bears no story within about the sacred origins of *this* place, or if he or she does, it is typically a story removed from the long line of tellers who, steeped in the power of language, spoke or sang the world into being. Throughout what is now called the Americas, indigenous people gave shape to their human being and becoming by understanding the nature of relationship with the land. By coming to terms with that relationship, they found a language to express knowledge of the sacred. Linda Hogan tells us that in Native American oral tradition, "words function as part of the poetic processes of creation, transformation, and restoration" ("Who" 169). Native people and land were, and are, inextricably bound in a dynamic, sacred, and ever-sustained kinship; language and story are the umbilicus that tied all of this "American" creation to the earth.

For Native people, the land is much more than a landscape. As Leslie Marmon Silko reminds us,

> *So long as the human consciousness remains within the hills, canyons, cliffs, and the plants, clouds, and sky, the term landscape, as it has entered the English language, is misleading. "A portion of territory the eye can comprehend in a single view" does not correctly describe the relationship between the human being and his or her surroundings. This assumes the viewer is somehow outside or separate from the territory she or he surveys. Viewers are as much a part of the landscape as the boulders they stand on.* (27)

Much of Native American literature written today could help us deal with the rift, the breach that is engendered by the poor relationship between humans and what, to the Indian way of thinking, is still our mother. In a novel like *Tracks*, we are shown that physical illness—smallpox, tuberculosis—was not the only thing that devastated Indians. The corrupting influence of greed, which is a sickness of soul, an obsession brought about by shame, envy, and the desperation born from these powerful and sticky emotions, is what ultimately harms the Chippewa families with whom Erdrich is concerned. Greed splinters the clans and kinships formed to ensure survival and resist disappearance. Greed is the relentlessly "mean spirit," as Linda Hogan envisions it in her novel of the same title, that has often driven United Statesians to trick, deceive, cajole, coerce, and destroy whatever stands in the way of the nation's "progress" and "prosperity."

We speak, in this country, of having respect for diversity. Many believe that the bad old days of racist hatred and discrimination are behind us in our new-found valuing of multiculturalism. Yet we go on wasting and discarding Native people by disrespecting their traditions, undermining their tribal sovereignty, giving lip service to what we can learn from them, but really learning nothing. For we have not understood their examples, and we have not advanced spiritually. We have not healed the separation between us and this beautiful land. Is this restoration and healing possible? Anything is possible when the power of consciousness is behind it, when the power of language heals rather than destroys, when caring for this land, our beloved mother earth, takes precedence.

Notes

1. In another version of the creation story, Earthmaker and Coyote are floating in the water that is everywhere when they come across a meadowlark's nest. Earthmaker stretches and pulls the nest until it becomes the earth. The version I cite is from Roland Dixon, an anthropologist who recorded the story probably from Konkow informants living at Chico. See Dobkins. See also Shipley, *The Maidu Indian Myths and Stories of Hanc'ibyjim.*
2. Konkow has the variant spellings Concow and Konkau. It is one of three Maiduan languages, the others being Mountain Maidu and Nisenan. One etymology for Konkow is "koyomkawi" which, according to Russell Ultan, means "meadowland" (2). The Konkow and Maidu people, not surprisingly, often chose meadows for homesites. Before Lake Almanor was created, the vast acres of land there were called Big Meadows, and many villages stood at that site. Anthropologist Francis Riddell writes that other dialects of Konkow were spoken "along the lower reaches of the Feather River Canyon up to about Richbar, in the surrounding hills, and in the adjacent parts of the Sacramento Valley" (370). My mother's families were from Yankee Hill, in the foothills above those "lower reaches," and Belden, on the Feather River, perhaps ten miles west of Richbar.
3. Linguist Russell Ultan wrote in 1967, "At the present time, there are an estimated fifty or so individuals living in the same general area who have some knowledge of the language [Konkow]. They are for the most part over sixty years old and the degree of fluency varies considerably from remembering a few words or phrases to the ability to use the language freely in conversation. To my

knowledge, however, Konkow has not actually served as a primary means of communication for some time" (1). I was told by an acquaintance that my uncle, Ernest Beatty, had a large repertoire of gambling songs; I suppose many of these were in Konkow or Mountain Maidu. When I told my mother and my Aunt Lillian of this, they both expressed surprise. Then one of them commented, "Well, the boys probably learned things we [girls] didn't."

4. See Jewell, 38–46, and Hill, pages 39–42.
5. According to Jewell, a much-remembered medicine man, Dr. Charlie, lived in a now deserted Indian community on Dogwood Creek, which may have been near Berry Creek (148).
6. The hoop game, writes Jeannine Gendar, "was immensely popular through much of North America. Except for the northwestern part of the state, it was played in all of California." Gendar quotes Thomas Mayfield, a miner's son who lived among the Yokuts, referring to the hoop game: "Here was always an excited, shouting, yelling, laughing group, generally intent upon their game and as happy as it is possible for human beings to be" (31).
7. For a list of schools and their opening dates see Adams, *Education for Extinction*, 57.
8. Published in Erdrich's first collection, *Jacklight*.
9. For more about Stiya, see my essay "Telling Stories to the Seventh Generation" in *Reading Native American Women*.
10. Quoted in Adams, "Fundamental Considerations," 20.

Bibliography

Adams, David Wallace. *Education for Extinction: American Indians and the Boarding School Experience, 1875–1928*. Lawrence: U of Kansas P, 1995.

———. "Fundamental Considerations: The Deep Meaning of Native American Schooling, 1880–1900." *Harvard Educational Review* 58 (1988): 1–28.

Allen, Paula Gunn. *The Sacred Hoop: Recovering the Feminine in American Indian Traditions*. Boston: Beacon, 1986.

———, ed. *Studies in American Indian Literature: Critical Essays and Course Designs*. New York: MLA, 1983.

Bammer, Angelika, ed. *Displacements: Cultural Identities in Question*. Bloomington: Indiana UP, 1994.

Burgess, Mariana. *Stiya: A Carlisle Indian Girl at Home*. Cambridge: Riverside, 1891.

Dobkins, Rebecca, Frank R. LaPena, and Carey T. Caldwell. *Memory and Imagination: The Legacy of Maidu Indian Artist Frank Day*. Oakland: Oakland Museum, 1997.

Erdrich, Louise. *Jacklight*. New York: Holt, 1984.

———. *Tracks*. New York: Holt, 1988.

Gendar, Jeannine. *Grass Games and Moon Races: California Indian Games and Toys*. Berkeley: Heyday, 1995.

Gould, Janice. "Telling Stories to the Seventh Generation: Resisting the Assimilationist Narrative of Stiya." Hernandez-Avila 9–20.
Heizer, Robert F., ed. *Handbook of North American Indians: California*. Vol. 8. Washington: Smithsonian, 1978.
Hernandez-Avila, Ines, ed. *Reading Native American Women: Critical/Creative Representations*. Walnut Creek, CA: Altamira, 2003.
Hill, Dorothy. *The Indians of Chico Rancheria*. Sacramento: California Dept. of Parks and Recreation, 1978.
Hogan, Linda. *Mean Spirit*. New York: Atheneum, 1990.
———. "Who Puts Together." Allen, *Studies* 169–77.
Jewell, Donald P. *Indians of the Feather River: Tales and Legends of Concow Maidu of California*. Menlo Park: Ballena, 1987.
Riddell, Francis A. "Maidu and Konkow." Heizer 370–86.
Rose, Wendy. *Bone Dance: New and Selected Poems, 1965–1993*. Tucson: U of Arizona P, 1994.
Shipley, William F. *Maidu Grammar*. Berkeley: University of Californa, 1964.
———, ed. and trans. *The Maidu Indian Myths and Stories of Hanc'ibyjim*. Berkeley: Heyday, 1991.
Silko, Leslie. *Yellow Woman and a Beauty of the Spirit: Essays on Native American Life Today*. New York: Simon, 1996.
Ultan, Russell. "Konkow Grammar." Diss. U of California, 1967.

19

Making Places Work
Felt Sense, Identity, and Teaching

Jeffrey M. Buchanan

In late winter over spring break, I rearrange my office yet again. This is at least the third time I have done so since I arrived at Youngstown State University not quite two years ago. To rearrange, I have to pick up the piles of papers from the floor, I have to sort the stuff to keep from the stuff to throw away, and I have to make more files and actually file stuff away. I have to move bookcases that are now almost full of books. But I am willing; the space just isn't working as well as I want it to work. I am uncomfortable in the most immediate landscape of my academic life.

It is certainly true that the spaces in which we live and work shape us, and it is also true that we shape the spaces in which we live and work. Conventionally, once spaces are endowed with meaning, they become places. The term "space" is most often used by geographers to reference the space between things; the space of my office is the area between its four walls. "Place," on the other hand, has to do with agency. Places do not rest between walls; they are made. Place is space human agents have acted on and made meaningful. Place, though, Kevin Hetherington notes, is derived from an act of placing, is an effect of a labor of division, of ordering and arranging, of bringing in and keeping out (184, 187). Places are relational; they make knowable a space in relation to any other.

As I imagine a new layout for my office, I bear certain things in mind. I have no window through which to look out of the building. The door and the small threshold window parallel to it offer the only visual access beyond the enclosed office space. I want to work aligned toward the door, then, so I can glance out into the hallway and visually escape my confinement whenever I feel the need. But I want my computer screen partially hidden from anyone walking by or stopping in; I don't want any visitor to be able to see what I'm working on at first glance. For I am uncertain about the activities that I perform when I am in my office. Do I spend my time in this place as other academics do? Am I doing what an assistant professor is supposed to be doing? I don't want my computer screen to potentially reveal my ignorance.

My office space, a place central to my working life, is one of the landscapes through which I move daily. What I get accomplished in my office is partly determined by the landscape of that office. And landscapes, I am quickly proving, are never static. Don Mitchell writes that "'Landscape' is best seen as both *a work* (it is the product of human labor and thus encapsulates the dreams, desires, and all the injustices of the people and social systems that make it) and as something that *does work* (it acts as a social agent in the further development of a place)" (94, Mitchell's emphasis). As I rearrange my office, I wonder, What kind of work can I make here? What kind of work won't I be able to do here? Youngstown is a scarred and storied place, an urban landscape, marked by cracked asphalt and pocked pavement, symbolic, I think, of uncertainty, failure, loss. What kind of place can I make here? And how will this place place me?

In 1802, when two brothers found iron in the side of a hill, Youngstown's future was certain. Iron mixed with limestone and then fired by wood and coal equaled steel. John Young, the land speculator who imagined Young's Town as a stopover, supplying goods to farmers moving west, had, it turned out, laid out a city "on the flat lands of the north bank of the Mahoning River" (Skardon 1).

Seventy-five miles east to Pittsburgh. Seventy-five miles west to Cleveland. Young's Town became the center of Steel Valley. Connected by river and canal, the valley lived on water, and water lived as Youngstown lived. Like the valley's human resources, water was invited into the mills to work (Turner). Young's Town's most desired space, the Mahoning River floodplain, was divided up among U.S. Steel, Republic Steel, and Youngstown Sheet and Tube and was filled by stores of materials, columns of smokestack, rail line next to rail line.

As rail lines and waterways carried the products of Youngstown's labor out, the abundance of work created both the actuality and promise of opportunity and wealth. On the one hand, Youngstowners desired cultural institutions and an infrastructure to represent their success and make their city great; they started an opera house, a theater, and a symphony, built an art museum and a library, and placed churches in among houses in every neighborhood (Skardon 15, 19). They made their city a work, a product to be admired. Yet the promise of and need for work required workers. About 1900, water brought an entirely new wave of immigrants; this labor was raw: "foreign," rural, Central European, Catholic, Orthodox, Jewish, non-English-speaking, and lacking in knowledge of democratic government (Skardon 6). On the other hand, then, Youngstowners needed the cultural institutions and infrastructure to assimilate its new arrivals, to do work, to ensure the growth and wealth of their city. As the city expanded geographically and open space became the place of neighborhood, a system of parks was carved out, reserving space for recreation and leisure amid the growing demand of and for work. A YMCA, too, was organized, although its primary purpose was educational—education for assimilation. The YMCA quickly established a reading room full of the most outstanding periodicals of the era and offered public lectures, literary and debating societies, concerts, and night classes (Skardon 27–28, 30–31). These classes gave birth to Youngstown State University.

YSU's first students (although it was known as Youngstown College then) came after working shifts in the mills or in the rail yards. Expectations on both sides of the educational transaction were practically driven; classes would help the "foreign" integrate in ways that would insure competent job performance at the mills, so they were designed to teach non-native speakers English and mill-related subjects like mechanical drawing, applied mechanics, algebra, and accounting (Skardon 23, 31–36). There were even special lectures given on the making of iron and steel. Natural and human resources made Youngstown a steel town, and it remains a steel town even now that the railways, waterways, and, more recently, highways have carried the products and the promises of work elsewhere.

The student in my office asks, since I have now evaluated a few of the products of his labor, if I can tell him how he measures up, against other students in our class and against other students I teach at the university, if his writing shows promise—of passing the course and of perhaps something more. This student is enrolled in my section of English 2601, Intermediate Writing for Teachers, a class required for students who want to gain admission to our College of Education and be teachers but required of only those who have averaged below a 3.0 GPA in our introductory composition sequence. I teach two classes of student at Youngstown State University: the relatively inexperienced student (and inexperienced writer) in introductory composition and the upper-division student in English education. I place students in English 2601 in the first category, even though they are no longer inexperienced college students, because they come from a wide variety of academic disciplines and exercise disparate ways of making knowledge as a result and because they still struggle to write effectively and successfully. Because their performance in their previous writing classes has caused them to have to take this extra developmental (or remedial) course, they have little confidence in their ability to perform as writers, little excitement about confronting the challenges writing presents, and little understanding of how successful writing and successful writers work. The other class of student, the future English teachers, has already come to see themselves as writers.

The student in my office wants to know how he compares to this other class of student, to the student preparing to take charge of his or her own classroom. In general, the problems dogging these two kinds of student, these two kinds of writers, are different. The work I do with composition students is directed more at sentences and paragraphs, with issues like organization and learning to write in both narrative and analytical modes; the work I do with teacher candidates is directed more at content-specific ideas and forms. Those who have matriculated to upper-division status, the future English teachers, are practiced users of academic convention; those who enroll in English 2601 are struggling users of it.

To make these differences evident, the student in my office would have to see me work, see my work, and see his peers' work, but he is not asking to see. As I sit and read essays from composition students—as I sit and work on the products of their labor—and then write back, I refer to a rubric I have previously drawn up to articulate the features of good essay writing and measure whether a student paper meets my criteria, then describe the differences between the standard and the student's performance as part of a response that also provides thoughts about how to minimize those differences. To do that work, that kind of reading and writing, of comparing and contrasting, of receiving and imagining, I draw on a felt sense, a way of knowing that acknowledges feeling and affect but that is also informed in this context by critical reflection on previous experiences with texts—both archived and lived. For my work is to attempt to read what a student writer is trying to do, what a composition does and does not do, and to write a response that encourages revision, a way of seeing and doing again that belongs to the student and not to me, the teacher. This kind of work, which I characterize as a process of attempting in my previous sentence, is uncertain at best, significantly a question of feel. Because one does not approach a student paper knowing already what one will do with it; one responds as one reads, choosing how to express that response, how to suspend or drop, how to lay gently or aggressively cut comments, questions, critique. It is, in many ways, like this moment in my office, when I decide what to say back and how—when, to communicate with this student, I choose words and dispositions through which to deliver them.

The response I give this student I lay gently before him; I wish to be honest about the shortcomings of his writing but also encouraging and appreciative of his interest and willingness to work. His ideas are mature and weighty, I tell him, due, most likely, to the fact that he's a few years older than most of his peers; his sentences and paragraphs do not yet match. (Back and forth I go, from strength to weakness to potential strength). But there is no doubt of his interest in writing and his willingness to work; his attention to his own writing and his curiosity about others' writing suggest that he will improve. Because the act of writing, he says, intrigues and attracts him: he feels its potential power and imagines he might exercise it some day more strategically, perhaps expertly. Can I, he is asking, corroborate these feelings, based on what I know of writing and on what I have seen from others? He asks, in this moment, for no formal comparison of his writing to others', knowing, in this moment, that I have no immediate access to other students' papers, no evidence to support any one claim I might make. I give him what he asks for: an impression, a kind of knowing based on sense and feel; no grand claim—a small thing, really, that might potentially mean everything.[1]

Fifty years ago, I imagine this student writer would not have even looked for a place within the university. Not because he couldn't make one for himself but because one was guaranteed for him elsewhere. Grand work, working with steel. Good pay. Good benefits. The work was large, performed at high volume on vast amounts of land, and demanding—marked by sweat, dirt, and heat.

The work he must look for now is small; he intends to work with children. He has changed his major, he says, to elementary education because he has had rewarding experiences interacting with children. They respond well to him, and he is able to teach them. The relationships he will build with his future students will be simple but intricate, as human relationships often are. They are like the relationships he is building now to words and the sentences he writes on the page. As a writer, he is learning to find satisfaction in small things; we both take pleasure in his pointing out a spot in his paper where I had read "progression" to mean a general sense of improvement and development when he had meant a more literal movement from one place to the next, evidence of one reader misreading. Teaching is most often not grand work; it is more like one reader misreading.

In fact, teaching and writing are similar activities; both require the imagining of potentials—potential sentences and potential practices—and the choosing of one over another. The choice is made after considering the potential effects of all and the context—audience and purpose or students and school culture—in which they will be exercised. This work, too, I think, owes much to a felt sense, a way of thinking and acting informed by intellectual resourcefulness and experience, guided by instinct and attention to readable signs. The work of negotiating the complexity of the writing and teaching situation and of coming to a "principled judgment" draws heavily on the affective life of the writer and teacher.[2] We make decisions from the gut, but the gut is the landscape on which our most fundamental theoretical and philosophical positions on reading, writing, knowing, and teaching are grounded; it is the space in which our beliefs and values are placed. Our identity, then, where we come from and how we have learned, is tied inextricably to place and necessarily affects our work—and vice versa.

In Youngstown, everyone honors work, but work no longer makes an individual honorable. In the old days, I'm told, a YSU student asleep in class would have remained undisturbed because of the respect working a long shift in the mill garnered. A sleeping student today would be waked. Not because the instructor wouldn't have sympathy for the student's work schedule but because whatever his job, it could never be as noble as working steel. The absence of steel mills now dominates our landscape; Youngstown is governed by loss and used-to-be's, and the role of Youngstown State University has changed from offering services to support the local economy to conceiving initiatives to drive it. The student, in this landscape, doesn't step into a place ready-made, for the ready-made places have left with the mills; he or she must make a place on his or her own.

Most of my students today come from the suburbs. All work while going to school. Most come from working-class families, and many are first generation college students. YSU is looking to expand its enrollment, to draw students with different backgrounds from greater distances, and to build more housing in which they might live, but, right now, it remains a regionally focused, community-centered university, serving students who work and commute to campus.

I chose to work in Youngstown because this landscape is familiar to me. I feel comfortable here. I grew up in Detroit, in a working-class neighborhood in a blue-collar city. I taught high school English in its public schools. I am interested in the problems particular to urban education; I am occupied intellectually by ideas like absence, lack, and loss. I know struggle. I tread comfortably in this place; in it I fit.

I grew up in a working-class city neighborhood that was given a kind of elegance by gothic-arched elms lining the street. They were big trees, stretched across, gently touching each other from opposite sides of the street. And they were diseased trees, all coming down one summer when the city tree trimmers rolled through, felling, cutting, chipping, and stumping. My father was a tree trimmer, who literally played a part in changing the neighborhood. But we kids, too, sensed the significance of the moment and wanted in. We took part as much as kids could take part—by watching, following, absorbing, marking the moment by taking our place in it. Or, as kids, perhaps we were just fascinated by trucks and chainsaws and the noises they made, fascinated enough to chase on bikes after them, up and down block after block.

It's the first moment of change that I recognize taking place. A landscape gripped by absence, evidence of our own lack. One couldn't help staring at the piles of sawdust mounded in holes where the trunks of trees used to stand. The maple and ash trees planted in place were an unequal exchange. What was lost would never come back.

Right after the elm trees came down, our bicycles began disappearing, but there was no mystery in their absence. We watched groups of black teenagers riding down the streets of our neighborhood, our white neighborhood, riding double, looking for bikes. We watched them as we were taught—because we all knew that once the blacks started moving in, crime would increase, and the neighborhood would be lost. Or maybe it was that crime would increase, and then the blacks would start moving in, and the neighborhood would be lost. In any case, we feared the replacement of race in our neighborhood.

Because neighborhoods are not static: they are constantly changing. And whites were moving out of ours before any black person or family moved within blocks because they were afraid a black person or family would move within blocks. We knew that our neighborhood would eventually become a predominantly black neighborhood or an integrated one. White families were moving out, not in. The question was how many would stay. What part would we play in placing our neighborhood's future and our own?

We were so occupied staring at the signs—the dying trees, the bike-stealing teens—that the signs misled us. One kid gave a bike away to a white kid who claimed to be his brother's friend. But we had only one version of what a bike thief would look like.

One afternoon, some kid saw a bike taken, saw a group of black teens riding away with one of our bikes. Somehow word got out to an older brother who worked just a few blocks away at a muffler shop. A number of guys from the muffler shop jumped in a van and chased the stolen bike down. They drove up alongside the fleeing kids, slid open the side door, and shot them—with fire extinguishers. They reclaimed the bike and apparently the neighborhood, too, for the thefts stopped. We believed we had stopped time as well.

And maybe we had, for I remember nothing being made of the first black family actually moving on our block. Maybe we had grown up; maybe the folks who would have made a fuss had moved out. I don't know. I do know, though, something about dealing with issues of race because I experienced them. I know something of white fear and white flight. I know something of the history of urban, transitional neighborhoods. I know something about integration and segregation. And I know about these things, I want to claim, because I know something, too, about trees.

Believe it or not, in the midst of work on this very essay, I rearranged my office space at home. My wife and I have now been in our house one year, and most of the furniture for my home office is new. A reclining chair arrived just before Christmas, a new desk just after. Once I painted, I began moving things in slowly. I placed two tall but skinny bookshelves, then the desk, and finally the chair. Yesterday, I arranged the desk so that it now sits just below the window. As I write, I can look slightly off to the left of the computer screen into our backyard. I want to claim already that this placement is more generative, but I guess it is too early to tell. The recliner is in a better place now, too, although it is clear I need a table and reading lamp to sit on either side of it. I also need to have a few pictures framed for the walls.

Just out the window, I look at our unkempt grass and a surprisingly large number of mature trees. In our yard, there are ten that I can see from my desk and four more just beyond the boundary of our fence. One, though, is dead and will have to come down. Fortunately, it is the smallest tree, and I will take it down myself. I took an even smaller one down last fall.

Already this spring, I have been up on my extension ladder with a chainsaw, trimming the trees in our front yard. A ladder and a chainsaw, I imagine, are not early purchases for most homeowners, yet they were among the first things I bought. And later today, I will go outside and split wood with a maul, wood collected from a neighbor who had a few trees removed. My father is a laborer, a tree trimmer, a retired city forestry worker who eventually worked his way up to foreman, and I learned to work by working with and for him. When he worked for the city, he left the house early, came home around four o'clock, then went back out to work for himself for a couple of hours. He even worked Saturdays, except when it grew too cold outside. When I was old enough to hold a rake and shovel, I went to work with him. It was this extra labor, I imagine, that paid for my education. With that education, I essentially closed the door on working the way my father worked. As a PhD, I will not be a laborer; I will not labor as my father labored.

Those who do labor as my father did refer to themselves sometimes as tree artisans, tree surgeons, or even branch managers, yet I wouldn't equate tree work with art, surgery, or managing. In some ways the work is mysterious, hard to accurately name, difficult to explain. Or perhaps that's just the way my father approached it.

When my father climbed a tree, I stayed on the ground. Tying off a branch, he'd want to know only if I was ready. If I said yes, he'd start cutting. If I said no, he'd tell me to grab the rope. There were no instructions as to what to do with the rope, no intellectual interrogation of the situation. And I don't think he could articulate much about what he was up to. He could show you how he tied the knot (and he knew what kind of knot he tied) and explain why he cut it from the top, the bottom, or from the right or left side. But he wouldn't explain it using formulas or numbers. He'd say, "cut it here," and he'd represent the angle with his hand. Or he'd say, "do it like this" and again draw it with his finger. He didn't stop working to talk, explain, or instruct.

In fact, his sometimes "bull in the china shop" mentality produced mistakes, bad breaks, or accidents, which then interrupted the work required for a particular job. A problem had to be responded to; if a limb "hung up," one had to pause to figure out how to get it down. My father often cursed his tools for failing to operate at his pace. A pole saw that was dull made him spend more time, cutting each branch. And his first response to any problem was always to exert more physical force; if a limb stuck, he didn't look to improve the angle of the saw, he put more pressure on its cutting blade. There seemed a rhythm to his work, and it was felt, sensed, achieved by doing.

With the other end of the rope, then, I might hold the branch suspended in the air after it was cut, I might take it quickly to the ground, or I might do some combination of the two. It depended. My father didn't discuss (and didn't care to discuss) what to do with a limb before it was cut; he expected me, however, to do something with it once it was. And once it was cut, I knew clearly that I wasn't supposed to allow it to smash a gutter, break a window, crush our equipment, knock my father out of the tree, or land on a car—this would be an incredible interruption. If the limb swung, I might drop it quickly to a roof or, if it swung away from the house, I was to drop it quickly so that it couldn't swing back through a window. Often, I was just to suspend it so that it could be steadied and dropped straight down slowly. It was always a question of feel.

Dropping a tree was equally a test of felt sense. When the landing area is restricted, a tree trimmer doesn't measure angles or the length of the tree or the space between the neighbor's tree and the porch. He looks around. Then looks at his tree. He makes a notch to encourage the tree to fall in that direction, then he walks around to the other side of the tree and begins cutting. My father felled trees that weren't too large this way. Sometimes, he'd tie a rope to it, give me the other end, and tell me to pull as he was cutting. Then the rope, too, served as a guide for the falling tree's path. Still, we never measured or paced distance off; we just eyed it and did it. I'm not saying this method is foolproof. My father has destroyed gutters, broken patio stones, even broken a coworker's arm, but it's the way he does it—and it's the way I learned.

When I was an undergraduate, I worked every summer gardening. I planted trees and shrubs, dug out large new flowerbeds, shoveled wheelbarrows full of mulch. I used a spade, a pickaxe, and a wheelbarrow. It was a job made available because, thanks to my father, I already owned such skills. In the summers of my college years, I took great pleasure in returning to a more physical kind of work, work that took me to a space away from reading books and writing papers and back to a place of memory, a place that reconnected me to my father's work.

Like Carolyn Kay Steedman, who writes about her own ability to clean and keep house, an ability learned from her mother's manual labor, I, too, take great pride in my ability to survive by my hands: I can rake, shovel, haul, and prune. I wonder what sons with fathers who aren't tree trimmers do to mark the arrival of spring. The son of a tree trimmer, who values his father's work, trims his own trees and splits wood to burn this winter in his fireplace. For the son of a tree trimmer lives among trees and makes sure the house he buys has a fireplace. These are material things placed within this life's landscape, placed to call back a childhood prominently marked by trees.

In her essay "I Stand Here Writing," an essay whose title invokes Tillie Olson's story, "I Stand Here Ironing," a story about a woman constrainedly placed by the circumstances of her life, Nancy Sommers retells a joke told by a student in an essay about the nature of the learning process. The joke involves a drunk, a canary, a gin and tonic, and a question: Do lemons whistle? The question is asked by the drunk, and when told no, he replies, "Then I'm afraid I just squeezed your canary into my gin and tonic." Sommers's student explains that the joke relies on "a connection made between two things . . . which have absolutely nothing in common except for their yellowness" (426). And its value is that it forces dissolution of the things that require us to see a lemon and a canary as distinct. Sommers's student writes, "This knocking down of barriers between ideas is parallel to the process that occurs in all learning. The barriers that we set . . . suddenly crumble; the boundaries . . . are extended to include other modes of thought" (427). The joke makes us seek a logical way of relating two things we are not used to relating, and, in the process, we learn. We learn about the constructed nature of our positions and practices and about connecting the various and disparate source material that informs our own lives and work, and we learn how the various landscapes through which we have moved have placed us within the geography of our own lives.

I work now in Youngstown, at Youngstown State University, but I didn't learn to work here. Yet I can connect what I have learned about work, about a physical but felt kind of labor, to how I work now in academia. At times, relying on felt sense is effective and satisfying, creating rhythm and pace; at times it is not, causing disruption and mistakes. But when I remember the struggle to place myself here, when I reflect on how the places where I have been influence the shape I try to give to the spaces I inhabit now, I see potential for the work I might do in the classroom. For "to expose the locations and the mechanisms" of placing, of what makes us who we are, allows us "to question their formation, systematically, in a reflexive way," to revise them (to both see again and see differently), and to imagine alternatives (Salvatori and Kameen 106).

As students and teachers, we can't control all the forces at work in the spaces of our lives, nor do we always accurately identify them. Dutch Elm disease, the loss of the steel industry, grand narratives of race and class cannot be counteracted by a signal individual, but one can learn to recognize and to respond to their presence. When we teach, we stand in and out of positions that have come before us, that can and should be read, as Salvatori and Kameen argue, "as reinscriptions of discourses and traditions that circulate so pervasively among us as to seem both natural and inevitable" (108–9). Salvatori and Kameen identify two teaching positions that function oppositionally; they name them "critical theory" and "creative writing." The first represents teaching as "eminently theoretical" and "unconcerned with practice"; the second represents teaching as "essentially instinctive" and "fundamentally unteachable" (106). The position I am characterizing here, which I name "felt sense," is meant to bridge the two, although it may seem to be aligned with "creative writing."

To be sure, a representation of teaching that makes a place for feeling and affect, instinct and intuition, conjures up notions of the innately gifted sage performing magic. How, indeed, does one teach intuition? Yet one can, I think, teach students how to use intuition, feeling, and disposition and teach them what informs, shapes, and composes a felt sense. This calls for critical reflection, a rereading of our histories as students and learners through and against theory. To work in this way is to act as a teacher or as a writer might act, in a classroom or on a page—within a space that is bounded—and it emphasizes perhaps the most taken-for-granted activity practiced by teachers and students: reading. As English teachers, we read literary texts (and, as planners, we read them with an eye toward how we might use them in our classrooms), student texts, the texts of our classrooms, the behavior and actions of our students; we read ourselves, the physical space of the classroom, and the institutional contexts in which we work. Much of this kind of reading is hard to characterize and describe, and I doubt that it is ever taught in teacher preparation programs, although it should be. Further, as we move in English studies from the study of literature to the study of texts and as we, consequently, give student texts a larger place in our classrooms (and reading a larger place in our work activities), we are learning to respond to and teach student writers differently. Because we have come to see reading and writing as interconnected activities, we are helping our students develop as writers by helping them develop as readers. To teach students to read their own writing critically and to learn to read one's own work as a writer is to make use of felt sense—to feel when one needs a transition to connect disparate ideas, for example, or to sense when an appropriate conclusion is to call back an image from a paper's opening—a sense that relies on a memory of other experiences with texts and a willingness to reread. To work in this way is to work within the boundaries of the page and of the classroom; it is to place ourselves within a landscape of competing forces, forces that give it shape but that we also shape to place ourselves.

To view teaching as a complicated set of theories and practices constructed by theorists and practitioners, an activity that is social, shared, collaborative, and corroborative, one that has a history—and not necessarily a unified one—of assumptions, expectations, positions, methods, behaviors, and roles is to more accurately represent the nature of its work (Salvatori and Kameen). Teachers, too, have complicated histories. Reflexivity, the active intellectual engagement of the contact between these histories, must be part of the work and study of teaching, the work a teacher performs and the work a teacher teaches teacher candidates to perform. To teach habits of reflection does not require one to be overly articulate; in fact, this kind of work is often best demonstrated not through extended intellectual interrogation but through attention to pace and disruption, by drawing an angle with one's hand, by saying simply, "Grab the rope." This is work that is never perfectly performed, often creating discontent and revealing prejudice; it is often counterinstinctual and resisted. But it is because conventionally accepted and unquestioned versions of teacher work feel so comfortable and comforting. These feelings, however, are neither natural nor innate. They are learned in the spaces and through the practices that place us in the roles we exercise while at work (Salvatori and Kameen). What matters, finally, is not what way of knowing or working one exercises, only that one traces how that version of teaching or writing or studenting has come to find its place in the practices of our performing selves and working lives.

The very first time I walk into my newly rearranged office, I hesitate. I don't immediately recognize the place. That moment leaves like a shiver, and I settle in. I like what I've made. I've met my criteria. I'm aligned toward the door. I can see into the hallway. Anyone entering can only half see my computer screen. I imagine getting used to this; I imagine being comfortable here for a long time.

But I know, too, I'm all too willing to rearrange again. A friend once complimented me on being such a willing reviser when I write. And I am. I'll happily cut lots of text and replace and rearrange almost endlessly. I can see that part of myself in my search for placing the stuff in my office just right. Or is the rearranging of my office more about placing myself right? The office is part of me; I'm a part of the office. I'm still figuring out who I can be in this place. And I'm betting now that I won't ever quite figure it out; I'll change again—perhaps as early as next summer.[3]

Notes

1. I am continually surprised by the frequency with which my students, in accounts of how they have come to want to be teachers, make reference to the significance of a comment from one of their previous teachers. A comment such as "You'd make a good teacher one day" can shape the trajectory of their future lives.

2. For an illustration of the complex negotiation involved in teaching, see Ruth Vinz's *Composing a Teaching Life*, 115–21. I take the term "principled judgment" from this section of Vinz's text as well. Earlier, Vinz also discusses the importance of the relationship between who we are and what and how we teach.
3. I wish to thank Rona Kaufman for her help with the revising of this essay.

Bibliography

Hetherington, Kevin. "In Place of Geometry: The Materiality of Place." *Ideas of Difference: Social Spaces and the Labor of Division*. Ed. Kevin Hetherington and Rolland Munro. Oxford, UK: Blackwell, 1997. 183–99.

Linkon, Sherry, and Bill Mullen. "Gender, Race, and Place: Teaching Working-Class Students in Youngstown." *Radical Teacher* 46 (Spring 1995): 27–46.

Linkon, Sherry Lee, and John Russo. *Steeltown USA: Work and Memory in Youngstown*. Lawrence: UP of Kansas, 2002.

Mitchell, Don. *Cultural Geography: A Critical Introduction*. Malden, MA: Blackwell,. 2000.

Salvatori, Mariolina, and Paul Kameen. "The Teaching of Teaching: Theoretical Reflections." *Reader* 33/34. (Spring/Fall 1995): 103–24.

Skardon, Alvin W. *Steel Valley University: The Origin of Youngstown State*. Youngstown: Youngstown State U, 1983.

Sommers, Nancy. "I Stand Here Writing." *College English* 55:4 (April 1993): 420–28.

Steedman, Carolyn Kay. "Exiles." *Ways of Reading: An Anthology for Writers*. 5th ed. Ed. David Bartholomae and Anthony Petrosky. Boston: Bedford, 1999. 643–71.

Turner, Leanne. "Youngstown." *Mahoning River Watershed Project*. Sept. 2001. Ohio Board of Regents, YSU Public Service Institute, U.S. EPA, and Ohio EPA. 2 Mar. < http://www.ysu.edu/mahoning_river/youngstown.htm>.

Vinz, Ruth. *Composing a Teaching Life*. Portsmouth: Boynton, 1996.

VI
Coda

20

Running in Place

The Personal at Work, in Motion, on Campus, and in the Neighborhood

Rona Kaufman

All events and experiences are local, somewhere. And all human enhancements of events and experiences—all the arts—are regional in the sense that they derive from immediate relation to felt life.
It is this immediacy that distinguishes art. And paradoxically the more local the feeling in art, the more all people can share it; for that vivid encounter with the stuff of the world is our common ground.
Artists, knowing this mutual enrichment that extends everywhere, can act, and praise, and criticize, as insiders—the means of art is the life of all people. And that life grows and improves by being shared. Hence, it is good to welcome any region you live in or come to think of, for that is where life happens to be, right where you are.

William Stafford, "On Being Local"

I begin my run at the first seam in the sidewalk, the moment I turn left from the walkway that links the apartment building to the street. I have a block and a quarter of flat ground before I start to go uphill—a gentle uphill, at first, a leisurely grade that levels out for a few steps before it turns sharp. The hill eases some for a block, but it is still an incline, and this one feels more cruel than leisurely: I have survived the hard part but still have work to do. And then it levels out before I get a nice downhill—the downhill that inevitably complements, before or after, an uphill. Round the corner, through the parking lot of the gas station where I fill my car's small tank roughly every ten days but where I always note the fluctuations in gas prices. Uphill again and past the antique store whose owners move their furniture out daily—without complaint and without conversation, to each other or to me, as we compete, as least for a moment, for sidewalk. Still uphill and past the Youth for Christ, past the Tacoma Little Theater with a (mercifully) new mural on its outside wall, past the urban gardeners, past the local tavern, past the home-based "Hubby's Helper." And finally to the block that tells me I've run one mile and am about to be rewarded for it with a lovely downhill, a downhill that will just about take me to the place I'm allowed to stop and be done with the run. I rarely do turn there—three long blocks of level ground, past Rust Mansion, a right turn down a steep and partially bricked road that I still, two years later, have trouble navigating—but doing so takes me to twenty minutes. Enough to count.

That I am an academic who runs is no big deal, no big news. Many academics I know—Scott Slovic and Lee Torda explicitly in this collection alone—make running an ordinary part of their weeks, even doing so in extraordinary ways: I can name off the top of my head five friends, five academic women, who have run marathons. It's not a surprise that people who make a living off their minds need outlets for their bodies. Yet it's with some discomfort—and usually with qualification—that I say I'm a runner. Not because I haven't clocked enough miles. I have. I have been running, with a few significant breaks, since May 1997. But because I don't look like a runner. I weigh a lot. I weigh more than most of you. I don't fit the bill.

I begin my Advanced Composition for Teachers course with Linda Brodkey's autoethnography, "Writing on the Bias." Brodkey writes in beautiful, precise, pointed details about growing up a white, working-class girl in the Midwest, about watching her mother sew and learning how to dance, and about wrestling with the rules, institutionally and self-imposed, of writing. Brodkey concludes, as a middle-class academic who has studied how writing has been institutionalized, that "writing is seated in desires as complicated as those that give rise to dancing and sewing, where the rules of play are also subject to the contingencies of performance" (51).

I then ask my students to write their own autoethnographies, focusing on literacy. This isn't a surprising move for a specialist in composition and rhetoric. Many writing teachers start with the personal essay, not necessarily because it's easier than other forms but because the personal essay can help some students develop their own questions, understand how experience positions them as learners, and see the stakes involved in their learning. The words *can* and *some* in the previous sentence are important, because not all students write easily about their own lives—and some students don't want to write about their lives at all.[1] I don't start all classes with personal narratives—although in all at some point I incorporate written reflection, whether it be autobiography, personal essay, memoir, or autoethnography. But in this class for future teachers, I intentionally pull as many writing stories out of students as possible, in working out an understanding of literacy, which starts for me and with me as *how reading and writing have been defined at different times, by whom, for whom, and to what effects*. And knowing that teachers often fall back, for better or for worse, on the ways that they were taught, I want to put as many firsthand accounts of teaching on the table, publicly—available for critique and revision—as soon as possible.

We also start with "Writing on the Bias" because that is the essay my teacher started with. It wasn't the first class I'd had in composition theory or pedagogy, but it's the first one that helped me read my experiences of literacy through an academic lens. It's from that professor, Kathryn Flannery, that I draw my definition of literacy. And it's by her that I was introduced to the concept of praxis—the intersection of theory and practice. An intersection, perhaps, at which to locate the personal.

I rarely turn down the cobblestone hill and end my run at twenty minutes. When I do, it's usually because my time has run out—the demands of the day allowing only twenty minutes of exercise—rather than because my legs have given out. I run four different routes: the bare minimum, the short, the medium, and the long. All are defined by minutes. The short run is in the thirties; the medium in the forties; and the long in the fifties. (I've run sixty minutes—not in the sixties, but sixty—a few times, but not often enough to count it in my repertoire.) All of the routes are the same for the first eighteen minutes or so: they all start up that gradated hill on a leafy street, move through a small commercial district, and are rewarded with a lovely downhill at about the mile mark. A colleague who runs—a marathoner and kind of neighbor—knows the basics of my route and tells me it's a shame that it starts with a hill. But I don't mind. Or rather, I know that it's my best option. I live in Tacoma, Washington, a place that's lined by two mountain chains: the Olympics, to the northwest, and the Cascades, to the southeast. Tacoma isn't all hill, but the hills are a reality, a part of a regular day. Any way I turn when I leave my apartment building will very soon take me to an uphill, some steeper than others. And perhaps there's something in my Jewish soul—a hard-earned tradition of mistrusting anything that comes too easily and feels too good—that likes to have the uphill first. An opening six minutes of downhill would leave me terrified of what was to come.

And having grown up 2,500 miles from here—in Pittsburgh, in the Alleghenies—the hills are my best reminder of my geographic home.

It's at the intersection of I Street and Anderson—about minute twenty-two—where I have to make my first critical decision: will this be a short run or something bigger? At this intersection, my legs are easily persuaded that they are tired, and a stretched-out, gentle uphill has just started again. I can turn, head back toward the leafy street, run on the closed-to-traffic bridge that crosses the gulch and keeps the street safe and quiet. Or I can stick with I Street until it becomes 21st, keeping me with traffic and more visibility than I like, but making me, perhaps paradoxically, stronger and smaller. I find the next few minutes of running difficult almost always, but experience tells me that the line between closing down and opening up is at thirty minutes. If this were a video game, thirty minutes would buy me another life, another stab at victory; after thirty minutes of running, experience tells me, my body tells me, it's just a matter of being willing to continue.

I don't think I've ever regretted persevering. Running gives me a huge boost, both in terms of strength and in terms of self-esteem: I am unrelentingly proud of every minute I run. Plus, this is how I get to know my neighborhood; this is how I learn my new landscape. Still, I'm not an outdoorsy person. I'm far more comfortable inside than I am out. I come by this honestly: my parents grew up in city neighborhoods in Pittsburgh, in working-class families, the children of immigrants, children who lost their fathers at three and fifteen. Although three of my four grandparents came from rural places—farms in Ireland and Russia—I don't know that my parents spent a lot of time outdoors, at least not removed from technology and machinery and human construction. I'm not sure that they had much leisure to. But they both expertly know their way around Pittsburgh, a city that, because of its mountains and rivers, doesn't grid easily, a city that is notoriously difficult to navigate. They know where they're going far better than I do.

For a long time, I thought *place* was somewhere else—outside, in the West, by a lake or in the mountains, certainly not made by people. I thought place belonged to the people who could name the things that they saw—name plants and trees and know how to read them, know all the ways that an evergreen tells us about its life. I don't now claim place—attend to place—because I live in the Pacific Northwest, because I take out-of-town visitors hiking in Mount Rainier National Park, because I crane my neck every day in hopes of a glimpse of the mountain, but rather because I have moved far from other places I have called home. I claim and attend to place in order to find my bearings. To find myself here. And there.

When you run slowly, as I do, right now running a twelve-minute mile, you have time to see a lot. I see a lot that gets me angry: neighbors who set their sprinklers to water the sidewalk, cars that pull into crosswalks, unraveled condoms left in pedestrian and spectacular spots of my route. But I also see a lot that makes me glad to be here. A neighbor grows the most beautiful and fragrant roses between two slabs of concrete; I know that she benefits from the roses, but there's something about the position of the roses, flanked as they are by sidewalk and road, that makes me read her gardening as an act of generosity, a gift to those who pass. A man plays guitar, seems to be learning guitar, as his daughter rollerskates on the bridge over the gulch. And then there are the trees. Spring comes earlier here than any place I've ever lived before. Dogwoods and cherries—names I whisper in awe and uncertainty. What I do know is that for about three months, these trees fill up with tiny pinkish-white blooms, and initially it takes a forceful wind to shake them down. The fuller the trees become, though, the less coaxing it takes for them to shower me with blossoms. They blanket the sidewalk, cushion my steps. For these stretches, my run feels like the equivalent of walking down the Academy Awards' red carpet. The blossoms give the world, and me in it, a kind of grace.

When I have visitors, we inevitably go for a walk, so strong is the pull of beauty in this immediate place. I take them to my favorite nook, a cluster of bricked streets lined tightly with houses and also with uninterrupted views of Commencement Bay. I point out both the water and the unraveled condom. Almost everyone gets annoyed or embarrassed, says something like, "Geez, Rona." But the bay and the discarded condom both make up the space, and both seem strange to find on an ordinary walk around one's neighborhood. Why not say so?

Candace Spigelman argues that, despite some "inroads" by established scholars, "personal writing remains untrustworthy or 'sentimental'" (63). In part, it's a matter of genre. Memoir, autobiography, personal narrative, autoethnography—all rely on and call attention to the subjectivity of the writer and knower in some way, but they make different claims, or different degrees of claims, about the nature of scholarship. Ruth Behar writes, "No one objects to autobiography, as such, as a genre in its own right. What bothers critics is the insertion of personal stories into what we have been taught to think of as the analysis of impersonal social facts" (12). Writing about the conventions of scholarship in the humanities, David Bleich and Deborah H. Holdstein note that self-reference and self-reflection are mostly confined to life-writing genres: "One may include reference to scholarly work in life-writing, but one cannot include life-writing in scholarly work" (2).

Yet personal writing in the academy does have a deep history, one that runs across disciplines.[2] Cathy N. Davidson writes that "scholarship always has some personal stake, even when unstated" (1069)—and many scholars make their stakes known through different forms of personal writing. Advocates (and practitioners) of the personal argue that the nature of knowledge—knowledge that isn't universal or general—requires an understanding of who makes the knowledge. As Lorraine Code argues, if much of our understanding of knowledge is based on a formula like "S knows that p . . ." shouldn't we "pay as much attention to the nature and situation—the location—of S as [we] commonly pay to the content p" (20)? Through reflexive inquiry, scholars work to acknowledge—and work to understand—the forestructures they bring into their projects, trying to discern what assumptions and experiences they bring into a text, interaction, or experience that make them able, even likely, to see some things but not others, to hear some things but not others, to draw some conclusions but not others. Feminist scholars especially look at the tradition of scholarship, a tradition that has excluded those outside the dominant culture, to consider ways of knowing that have been previously overlooked and undervalued (Harding; Lather; Belenky, et al; Alcoff). Others consider the issues of risk and reciprocity, especially with those who have informants; they ask, *If I'm willing to risk my informants' bodies, my informants' stories, must I be willing to risk my own as well?* and in doing so, make the relationship between researcher and subject one of identification rather than distance. Others argue that the personal is central to praxis, that one must attend to the particularities of one's experience to develop a theory of practice and a practice of theory (Delpit). Still other scholars believe in the personal because of the nature of language—the impossibility of objective interpretation, the social negotiation involved in producing and consuming text, the social construction of form (LeFevre).

Critics (and practitioners) of the personal argue, on the other hand, that the personal lacks rigor, that it cannot be challenged, that it renders response difficult, maybe even impossible. Victor Villanueva, author of a critical autobiography, *Bootstraps*, writes of a colleague bumping into him in the library and saying, "I didn't think your kind of writing required the library" (50). Others argue that scholars who write personally are navel-gazers who, so fascinated with themselves, cannot turn their attention to another. Others argue that the personal merely reorders, rather than eradicates, privilege: some stories still can't be told, even if they're authentic stories (Gere, Miller). Those who go ahead and *tell* those stories risk making their readers uncomfortable to the point of paralysis. Some scholars worry that the researcher's story will obscure or eclipse her subject's, while other scholars complain about the pressure of involuntary disclosure, the pressure for researchers to write of their own lives when they'd rather focus on their subjects'. Ellen Cushman suggests, "While the ethics of representation have admirable goals, the incessant focus on the personal as political has led scholars to ask invasive and troublesome questions about a researcher's background and identity, resulting in flat, or worse, narcissistic disclosure about the researcher's positionality" (44–45). And others point to the difficulty of writing the personal well. In writing about the importance of writing vulnerably, of letting oneself be affected publicly by knowledge, Ruth Behar notes that the stakes are high: "a boring self-revelation, one that fails to move the reader, is more than embarrassing; it is humiliating." She continues, "Efforts at self-revelation flop not because the personal voice has been used, but because it has been poorly used, leaving unscrutinized the connection, intellectual and emotional, between the observer and the observed" (13–14).

Renato Rosaldo's "Grief and a Headhunter's Rage" is a useful text in which to demonstrate both possibilities and limitations of the personal in scholarship. "Grief and a Headhunter's Rage" is the introduction to *Culture and Truth: The Remaking of Social Analysis*, a study of the Ilongot people and their practice of headhunting. Rosaldo writes that the Ilongot explain their practice of headhunting simply: an older man will say "that rage, born of grief, impels him to kill his fellow human beings." Rosaldo cannot make him elaborate; the relationship between grief and headhunting is "self-evident." "Either you understand it or you don't," Rosaldo writes. "And, in fact, for the longest time I simply did not" (1–2). This admission of not understanding is profound, because Rosaldo has spent thirty months living with the Ilongots, studying and writing about their culture and their "most salient cultural practice" of headhunting. And yet Rosaldo dismisses, to himself at least, their brief explanations as "too simple, thin, opaque, implausible, stereotypical, or otherwise unsatisfying" (3). Likely associating grief with sadness, he writes, "Certainly no personal experience allowed me to imagine the powerful rage Ilongots claimed to find in bereavement" (3).

It's not until fourteen years later—"repositioned" (3)—that Rosaldo understands the Ilongots' explanation. He has suffered the unexpected loss of his wife, anthropologist Michelle Rosaldo, who fell off a cliff while conducting fieldwork. The anger that Rosaldo feels at his wife's death "overlap[s]" with—but is not the same as, Rosaldo is clear to point out—the Ilongots' anger at their families' deaths: he is careful not to "reckless[ly] attribut[e] . . . one's own categories and experiences to members of another culture" (10). Yet, he argues, "My use of the personal serves as a vehicle for making the quality and intensity of the rage in Ilongot grief more readily accessible to readers than certain more detached modes of composition" (11). His personal experience—an intimacy with grief and loss—has certainly made Ilongot grief more accessible to him; his layering of experience, in turn, can make his work more accessible to us.

"Grief and a Headhunter's Rage" shows—for me, in powerful ways—how the personal can make possible important ways of knowing often left out of traditional scholarship. As Rosaldo tells us, thick description, a methodology (most often associated with

Clifford Geertz) that relies on keen observation and relentless description, can go only so far, because the Ilongot headhunter *won't* elaborate. Rosaldo asks, "Do people always in fact describe most thickly what matters most to them?" (2) and answers *no*. The ethnographer needs to listen for the "cultural force of emotion" rather than elaboration, and Rosaldo can recognize—hail—the force in others because he experiences it himself. Personal experience here opens up a way of knowing that traditional study did not.

At the same time, "Grief and a Headhunter's Rage" points perhaps to a limitation of the personal: if one has not experienced a profound and sudden loss, can one not understand the culture of the Ilongot? One would understand *differently*, but Rosaldo makes no claims about a superiority of knowledge. The language of one of Rosaldo's final conclusions is significant: "Such terms as *objectivity, neutrality,* and *impartiality* refer to subject positions once endowed with great institutional authority, but they are arguably neither more nor less valid than those of more engaged, yet equally perceptive, knowledgeable social actors" (21). Positionality, sociality, and engagement are not more valid than objectivity and impartiality, but they aren't less, either. I know of no personal writing, in fact, that claims that personal history is more real, more true, than traditionally received, more "objective" histories. Brodkey writes of autoethnography, "Such texts do not attempt to replace one version of history with another, but try instead to make an official history accountable to differences among people that communitarian narratives typically ignore" (28). As Kathryn Flannery puts it in this volume about growing up in Levittown, "I cannot say that having grown up in Levittown gives me greater access to some 'truth' about the place, but rather the experience of having been made the subject of scholarly attention adds a certain kind of personal edge to my academic work. . . . [L]earning as an adult that scholars and social critics had held such families as my own under their academic lens was sufficiently alienating to incline me to seek out alternative forms of intellectual work."

The intertwining of personal experience with knowledge claims, however, continues to make many scholars uncomfortable. Richard Miller argues that much of the response to the personal in scholarship depends upon *taste*. He draws on Bourdieu's work in *Distinction: A Social Critique of the Judgement of Taste* to argue that a person's tastes are very much *embodied*, natural, despite education and social class. He quotes Bourdieu, arguing that "tastes are perhaps first and foremost distastes, disgust provoked by horror or visceral intolerance ('sick-making') of the tastes of others." Bourdieu explains, "The most intolerable thing for those who regard themselves as the possessors of legitimate culture is the sacrilegious reuniting of tastes which taste dictates shall be separated" (qtd. in Miller 271). Bourdieu's work, Miller argues, helps us to understand why some of us recoil at one kind of academic work (the personal, for example) and embrace another. Miller asks us to move from the *ideal* (how one is supposed to feel) to the *real* (how one actually feels), and he asks us to consider the ways embodied taste plays out in both production and consumption. He wants us to consider "the profound sense of discomfort that can be produced when, in an academic setting, the request is made that one see or hear the actions, events, or details of another's life as warranting sustained attention" (276).

In making his argument, Miller tells lots of stories, stories about people at risk: his father's second suicide attempt; a speaker at a conference giving a reading of the television show, *Rescue 911*; Foucault's longing for his dead teacher, Jean Hippolyte; students in his graduate seminar outing themselves, to different reactions, as gay or Christian; Toni Morrison's Pecola longing for "the bluest eye." Miller is making an argument about "really useful knowledge," about "writing that matters" (278). This isn't just a matter of words, Miller argues; it involves more than the academic tendency to reduce all surfaces to signs. Eventually, we have to deal with a body.

One summer in Ann Arbor, where I lived for six years as a graduate student, I started running at dusk. I had been running for two years at that point, and I switched from being a morning runner to an evening runner because I was having trouble waking early enough to beat the heat. Midwestern summers are hard on my body, the air thick and warm. I feel heavy in it. Heavier. I was an experienced enough runner at that point to know that running when it was too warm proved costly—immediately, since I would feel tired and sluggish all day, and with effects, since I would dread future runs in the heat. So I switched to evening, trying to time my run so that it ended just as the sun set, hoping to grab as much cool air as possible and still be safe, a woman alone, out and about, on the Old West Side. I kept a journal of nightrunning that summer, and in it I recorded beautiful gifts of the neighborhood at night: an outdoor dinner party serenaded by two violinists, low-hanging clouds lined parallel with the horizon, a perfectly round moon. And maybe because of these gifts, I kept running longer and longer, making it to a record, at the time, of fifty minutes. Of course, running longer meant running in the dark, because I consistently failed to time the end of my run with sunset. I didn't think much of this, so strong did I feel in my body, until one night my legs had found such joy in rhythm that I kept running, kept running out of the neighborhood, into the lit street of town, until a car, a sedan, passed and a man yelled out the window, "Keep running, fat bitch!" Then I stopped.

At home, I told a friend about the comment thrown at me from the passing car, but I edited it. I said that he yelled, "Keep running, bitch"—the "fat" too painful, too violent, to say out loud. I did run a few more evenings that summer. It was the end of August at that point, and I wanted to make it to Labor Day, to have a full, a complete, summer of nightrunning. And I was being stubborn, too, trying to claim my ground, not wanting a bully to scare me out of it. But I was skittish afterward: every human voice made me jump, and I would work my way closer to home, circling my block like a wounded bird. After Labor Day, when the semester started, I returned to running in the morning, and I learned that safety isn't just an issue for the dark. Like when the yippy dog put his teeth on my ankles. Like when a woman put her hands on me—put her hand on my back and grabbed my forearm—and then laughed and said, "That'll teach you to run with a Walkman," as she passed.

No one's laid a hand on me running in Tacoma, but my body still garners more attention than I'd like. I tend to think of myself as invisible when I run, but I'm often called out of my inner world—placed by people who are surprised to find me here. I'm talking about something different here than the acknowledgement—breath-efficient *hey*s and chirpier *good mornings*—that runners give to other runners. And it's different from the exchanges I have with the people I feel most in community with: the straight-backed man in the 1980s windbreaker and umbrella, no matter what the weather, who looked at me skeptically my first year but now gives me warm-smiled *hello*s; the old, old runner, hunched at a 45-degree angle, who disappeared for a while but returned with a cane and now walks; the woman in her early forties, maybe, with a big, yellow dog, who told me once, after an absence, "We hadn't seen you for a while. We were worried." These are people whose absences I notice, too, and worry about—people I'm as aware of as the first seam in the sidewalk, the downhill after the first mile, the intersection at which I must decide how long to run.

I'm talking, instead, about people who feel the need to encourage me, to keep me in motion. Mostly the comments come from people of color and women, people I would mark in some way as outsiders, like me. An old woman, white and white-haired, sits on the balcony of her ground-floor apartment, heaping ashtray beside her, and regularly gives me the power fist, tells me to keep it up. A tall African American man with legs that come up to my head, rigid posture, and the most at-ease stride I've ever seen passes me and says something like, "Good for you. Keep going." There's the white Youth-for-Christ woman, who has stopped me three times—the third time this morning, I kid you not; once stopped her car to stop me—to tell me I'm an inspiration, that she's been watching me, that I've lost a lot of weight, that my face is bright and happy, that she has started running again after having a baby. There's the Latino who stopped me to ask me if I would go running with his girlfriend, a beautiful, "thick" woman who wants to exercise but is too self-conscious. He does shift work or else he would go with her, but would I consider? (How she is too self-conscious to run by herself but not too self-conscious to run with a stranger is more thinking than I want to do in the first mile of my run.) And then there's my African American mail carrier, who gives me regular *you go, girl*s and asks, "How far you running these days?" He talks to me no matter where he sees me on our overlapping routes and now talks to me even when I'm not running, even when I'm in my school clothes.

But lately white men—young men—have started saying things, too. A goateed man on a bike says, "Good for you," as we pass in an intersection. A man with a hyper dog tells me with no hint of flirtation or salaciousness, "Looking good." And just the other day I saw a skinny, balding man in his mid- to late twenties with long shorts and shoes that didn't appear to be made for running—he looked like a punk, like someone who should be loitering on a sidewalk. But he was running, though he stopped right before I passed him just after the bridge, at the summit of a hill. He yelled, "Hey! You're making me look bad!" I decided to give what I usually get. I yelled back, "Keep it up! Keep it up!" I meant it sarcastically. But he said, "Okay," as though it were a new idea, and he took off. He ran, from what I could see, at least eight straight blocks before I ended my run and went home.

In this public commentary—some of which I've come to enjoy, some of which I have always despised (and likely always will)—I see the associations that people make among appearance and health and fitness, among weight and stamina and commitment, between weight and the need for encouragement, between weight and privacy. Running, my body becomes public—to be read like a text—and I feel my performance, if not my surfaces, are often misread.

So it is fitting, then, that my academic projects are often about what I think has been misread or overlooked—student writing, book clubs, women's recipes. I revel in their surfaces, grateful that they've left traces of their insides. And I work to stop wishing away the visibility of my body in public space. This semester, I made food the theme of my Writing 101 class—food because it's a broad theme through which to bring in interdisciplinary readings and assign writings in multiple genres—despite a fear of exposure. Of course, it has the potential to be a tender subject for some of the students in the class, mostly the women: food and bodies can make for a tense intersection. And last semester I ran the Lute Loop, a 5K through the paths of our campus, with the students in my senior writing seminar, so strong was the spirit of community in the class. Of course, I did ask the photographer from the student newspaper—fortunately for me, also one of my students—not to take my picture. But I am learning. I'm learning. I'm learning to let my body be a site of learning.

Linda Brodkey writes that the self in a social world is "dynamic" and "elusive" and needs to be understood in motion: "To know that a man is white and middle class or a woman black and middle class is to know too little and to believe too much about them. Social identities are the serious, impish, ridiculous, generous, wary, contradictory singular selves constructed and reconstructed in ludic, painful, hostile, prosaic relations of sociality" (28). I want to argue that place be considered an active participant in that social world, not just a container, a receptacle, for action, but an actor itself that pushes and pulls and shapes. Place often appears in forms of life-writing, whether it's the scholarship in life-writing or the life-writing in scholarship. But scholars often use place as a metaphor, as a point of social location—place stands in for ethnicity, or class, or religion—rather than speak to the particularities of landscapes themselves as a shaping force. Place collapses into *placeholder*, a stand-in for something else, to be chronically displaced and replaced and displaced more. Place can become as disembodied as a written text, even though, I would argue, places and texts are bodies first. When Scott Russell Sanders calls for "a richer vocabulary of place," we must include a knowledge of bodies, an understanding of landscapes as bodies and bodies as landscapes (18). Place and body are closer than we thought: they're the same.

The thing about a running route is that you never actually get anywhere. You might swing out wider, go a block or two farther to add time or distance. You might go down a path or an alley to see where it takes you, to see something that you don't usually see. But the whole point is to return to where you started. When I run, this is my consuming desire: to return to where I've started, to make it home, and to have earned it. To see how long and how good my body can feel to be in motion—to act—and then to make it home, strong.

One of the main ways that I know the world is through my body; it's not the only way, of course, but it is a primary way. And, for better or for worse, one of the main ways that the world knows me is through my body. That I often feel misread not only tells me something about the nature of knowledge, about the primacy of surfaces, but also makes me put myself out in the world more to try to change what those surfaces mean, even if I do so with awkward, hesitant steps. So that if people do talk to me while I'm running, instead of assuming that I'm barely there, they might say something like my German-accented neighbor, likely in his sixties, as he mended his fence: "I wish I could go with you." Or the blond with headphones, walking fast, whose body appeared younger than her face: "I wish I could do that." I am remembering that the word *praxis* comes from the Greek for *action*. In praxis, it isn't that theory determines practice or that practice governs theory; theory and practice have no distinct hierarchical relationship, one way or the other. The relationship is symbiotic. Theory and practice dance and grapple and perform and are actualized in a way that is profoundly social, embodied, and placed.

Notes

1. See Patricia Sullivan's "Composing Culture: A Place for the Personal" for an example of a student who resists mandatory personal writing.
2. See Diane P. Freedman and Olivia Frey's excellent anthology, *Autobiographical Writing across the Disciplines: A Reader*.

Bibliography

Alcoff, Linda Martin. "The Problem of Speaking for Others." *Who Can Speak? Authority and Critical Identity*. Ed. Judith Roof and Robyn Wiegman. Urbana: U of Illinois P, 1995.

Behar, Ruth. *The Vulnerable Observer: Anthropology That Breaks Your Heart*. Boston: Beacon, 1996.

Belenky, Mary Field, Blythe McVicker Clinchy, Nancy Rule Goldberger, and Jill Mattuck Tarule. *Women's Ways of Knowing: The Development of Self, Voice, and Mind*. New York: Basic, 1986.

Bleich, David, and Deborah H. Holdstein. "Recognizing the Human in the Humanities." *Personal Effects: The Social Character of Scholarly Writing*. Ed. Deborah H. Holdstein and David Bleich. Logan: Utah State UP, 2001.

Brodkey, Linda. *Writing Permitted in Designated Areas Only*. Minneapolis: U of Minnesota P, 1996.

Code, Lorraine. "Taking Subjectivity into Account." *Feminist Epistemologies*. Ed. Linda Alcoff and Elizabeth Potter. New York: Routledge, 1993.

Cushman, Ellen. "The Butterfly Fix(at)ion." *The Politics of the Personal: Storying Our Lives against the Grain*. Symposium collective in *College English* 64.1 (September 2001): 44–46.

Davidson, Cathy. "Critical Fictions." *PMLA* 111.5 (October 1996): 1069–71.

Delpit, Lisa. *Other People's Children*. New York: New, 1996.

Freedman, Diane P., and Olivia Frey, eds. *Autobiographical Writing across the Disciplines: A Reader*. Durham: Duke UP, 2003.

Gere, Anne Ruggles. "Articles of Faith." *The Politics of the Personal: Storying Our Lives against the Grain*. Symposium collective in *College English* 64.1 (September 2001): 46–47.

Harding, Sandra. "Who Knows? Identities and Feminist Epistemology." *(En)Gendering Knowledge: Feminists in Academe*. Ed. Joan Hartman and Ellen Messer-Davidow Knoxville: U of Tennessee P, 1991. 100–115.

Lather, Patti. *Getting Smart: Feminist Research and Pedagogy with/in the Postmodern*. New York: Routledge, 1991.

LeFevre, Karen Burke. *Invention as a Social Act*. Carbondale: Southern Illinois UP, 1987.

Miller, Richard. "The Nervous System." *College English* 58.3 (March 1996): 265–86.

Rosaldo, Renato. "Grief and a Headhunter's Rage." *Culture and Truth: The Remaking of Social Analysis*. Boston: Beacon, 1989. 1–21.

Sanders, Scott Russell. *Writing from the Center*. Bloomington: Indiana UP, 1997.

Spigelman, Candace. "Argument and Evidence in the Case of the Personal." *College English* 64.1 (September 2001): 63–87.

Stafford, William. "On Being Local." *Northwest Review* 13.3 (1973): 92.

Sullivan, Patricia A. "Composing Culture: A Place for the Personal." *College English* 66.1 (September 2003): 41–54.

Villanueva, Victor. *Bootstraps: From an American Academic of Color.* Urbana: National C ouncil of Teachers of English, 1993.

———. "The Personal." *The Politics of the Personal: Storying Our Lives against the Grain.* Symposium collective in *College English* 64.1 (September 2001): 50–52.

Contributors

Charles Bergman teaches English at Pacific Lutheran University. He has published three books on wild animals and environmental issues, as well as more than eighty essays and articles. His third book, *Red Delta*, won several awards. Most recently he has written on hunting in America for *American Literary History*, and his essay on hunting in the Renaissance will appear in the forthcoming series, *The Cultural History of Animals*. In 2006–2007, he will be a Fulbright senior scholar at Universidad San Francisco de Quito in Ecuador, where he will study the development of an ecological consciousness in Latin American literature.

Mary Clearman Blew is the author of several memoirs, collections of essays, and short fiction collections. Her most recent book, *Writing Her Own Life: Imogene Welch, Rural Schoolteacher*, appeared in 2004. She teaches creative writing at the University of Idaho.

Jayne Brim Box is an aquatic ecologist, who lives and works in Alice Springs, Australia.

Jeffrey M. Buchanan grew up in Detroit and taught high school English in its public schools. He is currently working as assistant professor of English and teacher education at Youngstown State University, teaching classes primarily in English education and composition. He has published essays in *Reader* and *ISLE*.

Norma Elia Cantú currently serves as professor of English at the University of Texas at San Antonio. She received her PhD from the University of Nebraska–Lincoln. She is the editor of a book series, Rio Grande/Rio Bravo: Borderlands Culture and Tradition, at Texas A&M University Press. Author of the award-winning

Canícula: Snapshots of a Girlhood en la Frontera and coeditor of *Chicana Traditions: Continuity and Change*, she is currently working on a novel tentatively titled *Champú, or Hair Matters*. She is also working on a manuscript on the Matachines de la Santa Cruz, a religious dance drama from Laredo, Texas.

Katherine Fischer chairs the Language and Literature Department and is English professor at Clarke College in Dubuque, Iowa, as well as a writer and newspaper columnist. Her book, *Dreaming the Mississippi* (U of Missouri P, 2006), chronicles life on today's river. When not on campus, Kate can usually be found crick-stomping through the backwaters of the Mississippi.

Kathryn T. Flannery is professor of English and women's studies at the University of Pittsburgh, where she serves as director of the Women's Studies Program. She is the author of *Feminist Literacies, 1968–1975* (U of Illinois P, 2004) and *The Emperor's New Clothes: Literature, Literacy, and the Ideology of Style* (U of Pittsburgh, 1991), as well as articles on performance pedagogy, feminist polemic, and the teaching of writing.

Diana Garcia is associate professor and director of the Creative Writing and Social Action Program at California State University–Monterey Bay. Her collection of poetry, *When Living Was a Labor Camp*, received the 2001 American Book Award.

Janice M. Gould's tribal affiliation is Konkow. She was raised in Berkeley, California, and attended the University of California at Berkeley, receiving her BA in linguistics and her MA in English before moving to Albuquerque to attend the University of New Mexico, where she completed her doctoral work. Janice's poetry has been awarded grants from the National Endowment for the Arts and from the Astraea Foundation, and she has published three collections of poems, *Beneath My Heart* (Firebrand), *Earthquake Weather* (U of Arizona P), and *Alphabet* (May Day), an artbook/chapbook. Janice coedited with Dean Rader *Speak to Me Words: Essays on American Indian Poetry* (U of Arizona P), the first volume of its kind to look exclusively at Native American poetry.

Seán W. Henne teaches education and English courses at West Shore Community College in Michigan's lower peninsula. He is very interested in Michigan-based writing and is in the planning stages of developing an experiential program for undergraduates based around that topic.

Rona Kaufman is assistant professor of English at Pacific Lutheran University in Tacoma, Washington, where she teaches composition, rhetoric, and creative nonfiction, directs the writing center, and is director of writing for the First-Year Experience Program. She has written about reading, writing, and the grammars of difficulty, and her work has appeared in *JAC* and *ISLE*. She is starting a new project on the literacy and cultural work of recipes.

Deborah A. Miranda is a mixed-blood woman of Esselen, Chumash, French, and Jewish ancestry. She is enrolled with the Ohlone/Costanoan Esselen Nation of California. Deborah received her PhD in English from the University of Washington in 2001. Her first book of poetry, *Indian Cartography* (Greenfield Review 1999), won the Diane Decorah First Book Award from the Native Writer's Circle of the Americas; her second collection is titled *The Zen of La Llorona* (Salt Press 2005). Deborah's other projects include a manuscript titled *"In My Subversive Country": Searching for American Indian Women's Love Poetry and Erotics* and a poetry collection in progress titled *The Uses of Anger and Other Praise Poems*, as well as a collaborative project, *The Light from Carissa Plains*, that incorporates her grandfather's oral history of post-Mission Indian life in California from 1902 to 1988. Currently, Deborah is assistant professor of English at Washington and Lee University, where she teaches creative writing (poetry), composition, women's literatures, and Native American literatures.

Kathleen Dean Moore is professor of philosophy and University Writer Laureate at Oregon State University, where she directs the Spring Creek Project for Ideas, Nature, and the Written Word. She is the author of *The Pine Island Paradox*, *Riverwalking*, and other books.

Erin E. Moore, a graduate of the College of Environmental Design at the University of California, Berkeley, is visiting assistant professor in the School of Architecture at the University of Arizona.

Robert Michael Pyle is an independent scholar, writer, and biologist, dwelling along a tributary of the Lower Columbia River in southwest Washington state. His fourteen books include *Wintergreen, Where Bigfoot Walks, Chasing Monarchs, Walking the High Ridge, Sky Time in Gray's River,* and *Nabokov's Butterflies.* Pyle's column, "The Tangled Bank," appears in each issue of *Orion* magazine. His writing has received the John Burroughs Medal, a Guggenheim Fellowship, and other awards. Robert has taught place-centered writing in many settings, including Utah State University, Evergreen State College, and the Aga Khan Humanities Project in Tajikistan. Recently he served as Kittredge Distinguished Visiting Writer at the University of Montana.

Jennifer Sinor is associate professor of English at Utah State University. A former military brat, she is currently writing a memoir titled *Autobiography of Loss* that reflects on a childhood spent in service. Her book *The Extraordinary Work of Ordinary Writing* recovers the diary of her great-great-great aunt Annie Ray, a homesteader on the Dakota prairie. Jennifer teaches creative nonfiction and women's life writing at Utah State.

Scott Slovic is professor of literature and environment and head of the graduate program in literature and environment at the University of Nevada, Reno. He has been studying environmental literature and ecocriticism for the past twenty years, and his many publications in the field include such books as *Seeking Awareness in American Nature Writing: Henry Thoreau, Edward Abbey, Annie Dillard, Wendell Berry, Barry Lopez* (1992), *Getting Over the Color Green: Contemporary Environmental Literature of the Southwest* (2001), and *What's Nature Worth? Narrative Expressions of Environmental Values* (2004). He served as founding president of the Association for the Study of Literature and Environment from 1992 to 1995, and since 1995 he has edited the journal *Interdisciplinary Studies in Literature and Environment.* He has been a Fulbright scholar in Germany, Japan, and China.

Poet and writer Michael Sowder lives in Cache Valley, Idaho, and teaches across the Utah border at Utah State University. His poetry collection, *The Empty Boat,* won the 2004 T. S. Eliot Prize (Truman State UP, 2004) and was nominated for a Pulitzer Prize. His chapbook, *A Calendar of Crows,* won the 2001 New

Michigan Press Award, and his critical study, *Whitman's Ecstatic Union, Conversion and Ideology in* Leaves of Grass, was published by Routledge in 2005.

Lee Torda is currently on leave from her position as assistant professor in the English department at Bridgewater State College, where she coordinated the first-year writing program. While on leave, she is serving as the director of undergraduate research for the college. She has published and presented on the theoretical and classroom connections between reading and writing processes.

Charles Waugh is assistant professor of English at Utah State University, where he teaches courses in creative writing and American studies. He has recently returned from a year at the Vietnam National University, Hanoi, where he taught a literary, cultural, and environmental history of the U.S. and delivered the first lectures on ecocriticism in Vietnam. He is the fiction editor of *Isotope: A Journal of Literary Science and Nature Writing*, and his fiction and nonfiction have appeared in the *Wisconsin Review*, *Knock*, *Studies in American Fiction*, *Interdisciplinary Studies in Literature and Environment*, and *Proteus*.

Mitsuye Yamada's most recent publication, *Camp Notes and Other Writings*, is a newly combined edition of her first two books (Rutgers UP, 1998). Her writings heavily focus on her bicultural heritage, women and humanrights issues. She is presently adjunct associate professor in Asian American studies at the University of California–Irvine. She is a former member of the board of directors of Amnesty International USA and presently an active member of the Committee on International Development of AIUSA, which funds and promotes development of humanrights work in Third World countries. She is a founder and director of Multicultural Women Writers. She is a member of Interfaith Prisoners of Conscience (IPOC), an organization that works to free political prisoners in the United States.